The Futures of the Present: New Directions in (American) Literature

Edited by
Danuta Fjellestad and David Watson

Routledge
Taylor & Francis Group

LONDON AND NEW YORK

First published 2017
by Routledge
2 Park Square, Milton Park, Abingdon, Oxon, OX14 4RN, UK

and by Routledge
711 Third Avenue, New York, NY 10017, USA

Routledge is an imprint of the Taylor & Francis Group, an informa business

British Library Cataloguing in Publication Data
A catalogue record for this book is available from the British Library

ISBN 13: 978-1-138-68515-4

Typeset in Times New Roman
by RefineCatch Limited, Bungay, Suffolk

Publisher's Note
The publisher accepts responsibility for any inconsistencies that may have
arisen during the conversion of this book from journal articles to book chapters,
namely the possible inclusion of journal terminology.

Disclaimer
Every effort has been made to contact copyright holders for their permission to
reprint material in this book. The publishers would be grateful to hear from any
copyright holder who is not here acknowledged and will undertake to rectify
any errors or omissions in future editions of this book.

Contents

Citation Information

The chapters in this book were originally published in *Studia Neophilologica*, volume 87, issue S1 (2015). When citing this material, please use the original page numbering for each article, as follows:

Introduction
The Futures of American Literature
Danuta Fjellestad & David Watson
Studia Neophilologica, volume 87, issue S1 (2015) pp. 1–7

Chapter 1
Minds, Messages, and the Moral Imagination in the Media of Fiction:
Inanimate Alice *between Cognitive and Rhetorical Paradigms*
John David Zuern
Studia Neophilologica, volume 87, issue S1 (2015) pp. 8–28

Chapter 2
"Take that you intellectuals!" and "kaPOW!": Adam Thirlwell and the Metamodernist Future of Style
Alison Gibbons
Studia Neophilologica, volume 87, issue S1 (2015) pp. 29–43

Chapter 3
The Paradoxes of "Unnatural" Mimesis in Gordon Sheppard's HA!
Danuta Fjellestad
Studia Neophilologica, volume 87, issue S1 (2015) pp. 44–54

Chapter 4
Utopia, Sort of: A Case Study in Metamodernism
Timotheus Vermeulen & Robin van den Akker
Studia Neophilologica, volume 87, issue S1 (2015) pp. 55–67

Chapter 5
Don DeLillo's Point Omega, *the Anthropocene, and the Scales of Literature*
Pieter Vermeulen
Studia Neophilologica, volume 87, issue S1 (2015) pp. 68–81

Chapter 6

The Space of Genre in the New Green Novel
Caren Irr
Studia Neophilologica, volume 87, issue S1 (2015) pp. 82–96

Chapter 7

A Sociological Imagination
Susan Hegeman
Studia Neophilologica, volume 87, issue S1 (2015) pp. 97–103

Chapter 8

The Role of Place in the Post-Apocalypse: Contrasting The Road *and* World War Z
Petter Skult
Studia Neophilologica, volume 87, issue S1 (2015) pp. 104–115

Chapter 9

Walking as a Metaphor for Narrativity
Marina Ludwigs
Studia Neophilologica, volume 87, issue S1 (2015) pp. 116–128

For any permission-related enquiries please visit:
http://www.tandfonline.com/page/help/permissions

Notes on Contributors

Danuta Fjellestad is Professor of English at Uppsala University, Sweden. She is primarily interested in the experimental American novel of the twentieth and twenty-first centuries.

Alison Gibbons is Senior Lecturer in Stylistics, English Language, and Literature at De Montfort University, Leicester, UK. Her research is positioned at the interface of language, literature, and culture.

Susan Hegeman is Professor of English at the University of Florida, USA. Her research fields include American studies and cultural studies; she teaches on these subjects as well as American Indian literature.

Caren Irr is Professor in the Department of English at Brandeis University, MA, USA. Her fields of research include US literature and culture since 1900, critical theory, and film and media studies.

Marina Ludwigs is Senior Lecturer in the Department of English at Stockholm University, Sweden.

Petter Skult is currently writing a doctoral dissertation on post-apocalyptic science fiction, with a focus on the novels of Paul Auster, Cormac McCarthy, and Margaret Atwood. He is based at Åbo Akademi, Finland.

Robin van den Akker is Lecturer in Continental Philosophy and Cultural Studies at Erasmus University Rotterdam, The Netherlands. He writes on contemporary aesthetics and culture, and the digitization of everyday life.

Pieter Vermeulen is a Postdoctoral Researcher at the Centre for Irish Studies, KU Leuven, Belgium. He specializes in novel theory, critical theory, and contemporary Anglophone literature.

Timotheus Vermeulen is Assistant Professor in Cultural Studies at Radboud University Nijmegen, The Netherlands. He researches contemporary aesthetics, art, film, and television

David Watson is Associate Professor of English at Uppsala University, Sweden. He works on contemporary and nineteenth-century American fiction.

John David Zuern is Associate Professor in the Department of English at the University of Hawai'i at Mānoa, USA. His research focuses on literary criticism and theory, fiction, life writing, and electronic literature.

The Futures of American Literature

DANUTA FJELLESTAD & DAVID WATSON

In October 2008 American literature was catapulted into the international media limelight with the news that it was deemed to be unworthy of the prestige of the Nobel Prize by nobody lesser than the (now former) permanent secretary of the Swedish Academy, Horace Engdahl. According to Engdahl, American writers were simply not up to Nobel standards: they were insular and ignorant, and they failed to participate in the big dialogues of literature. The response was fast, furious, and predictable: American literary critics and journalists hurled thunderous accusations at the Nobel committee. Michael Dirda, a Pulitzer Prize–winning book critic at the *Washington Post*, denounced Engdahl as holding "an insular attitude towards a very diverse country"; David Remnick, another Pulitzer Prize author and editor for literature at the *New Yorker*, pointed out that that the Swedish Academy itself has been guilty of conspicuous ignorance over a very long period: "You would think that the permanent secretary of an academy that pretends to wisdom but has historically overlooked Proust, Joyce and Nabokov, to name just a few non-Nobelists, would spare us the categorical lectures." Harold Augenbraum, Executive Director of the National Book Award organization, offered to send Engdahl a list, claiming that such comments made him think "that Mr. Engdahl has read little of American literature outside the mainstream and has a very narrow view of what constitutes literature in this age."[1]

The essays in this volume are penned by scholars who, unlike Horace Engdahl, are indisputably well read in American literature and who see it in the context of global literary trends. Less interested in identifying a single genus of American literature worthy of a Nobel Prize than curious about the future of literature, the writers address questions such as: What can we say about twenty-first-century American fiction? What are its dominant themes, stylistic characteristics, or aesthetics? What does it share with the novel outside of the United States? What are the new voices shaping its form? In short, what is the current state and the future of American literature after the "century of the American novel"?

The urgency of these and similar questions is inevitably prompted by the sense of the passing of postmodernism and the "death" of related poststructuralist theories. Titles such as "What was postmodernism?" (McHale 2007) and *The mourning after: Attending the wake of postmodernism* (Brooks & Toth 2007) attest to the passing away of the classificatory scheme that for decades has provided a framework wherewith to make sense of new literature, even if only to gauge its distance from a postmodernist aesthetic. This sense of an ending of a literary paradigm can be linked to a concern about the rapidly shrinking interest in (poststructuralist) theory since the late 1990s. Frantically, numerous critics were debating reading and thinking in the post-theory age (cf. Docherty 1996;

---

[1] These and similar comments were widely reported in media; see for instance Simpson 2008.

1

Cunningham 2002; Eagleton 2003). Less a concern for authors and publics than critics, this loss of the cognitive map provided by postmodern theory also meant the loss of a critical language whereby to recognize and talk about the new or, at least, the contemporary. This sense of loss, however, promptly gave way to intense forging of new frameworks for critical thought within which to make sense of literature.

But if postmodernism began losing its efficacy as a description of the contemporary by the turn of the century, then where are we now? At first glance the situation is much more complex than when Dale Peck, writing a decade ago, singled out two literary strains "in vogue," which he named "recherché postmodernism and recidivist realism," both of which, in his opinion, "suck" (220).[2] It would not be an exaggeration to say that we have entered a taxonomic wilderness in which there is very little agreement as to how to name the contemporary period, much less how to approach the notion of the contemporary itself. Perhaps a provisional account would indicate that three general approaches towards contemporary literature have emerged, though the boundaries between them are certainly porous: (a) viewing contemporary literature as broadly continuing well-established traditions; (b) periodizing the contemporary as a distinct epoch like postmodernism but breaking with one or more of postmodernism's distinguishing features; (c) attending to the contemporaneity of recent literature, how it relates to the world we live in and is shaped by its institutions.

From one perspective, a perhaps underappreciated effect of the weakening of the grip of postmodernism on accounts of contemporary fiction is that it brought into view postmodernism's others – realism and writing marked as ethnic. Aided and abetted by the cultural wars and multiculturalism of the 1990s, postmodernism's waning revealed how a focus on postmodern experimentation occluded throughout the so-called postmodern decades the continuation of a realist tradition adept at adapting to the times and the emergence of different ethnic literary traditions (see Hungerford 2008: 410–415). In the new century, accounts of contemporary fiction not only had to reckon with the loss of the familiar coordinates provided by the postmodern framework but also with the continuation of these traditions. Consequently, Christian Moraru (2011) zigzags between works by Don DeLillo, Suki Kim, Jumpha Lahiri, Azar Nafisi, and John Updike in his account of how a cosmopolitan and relational imaginary is supplanting postmodernism. In a reading of the ambivalently post-racial aesthetic of Colson Whitehead's novels, Ramón Saldívar (2011: 14) both identifies the emergence of a new literary genre, speculative realism, and claims, furthermore, that

> by returning to the real in its heterogeneous forms, we notice that realism acquires a different quality than literary history has assigned it over the last forty years. Instead of conceiving of a timeline that takes us from naive realism to plodding social realism, to triumphant modernism and demystified parodic postmodernism, something else results: When placed within a horizon that includes naturalism and realism, social realism, surrealism, magical realism, and perhaps speculative realism, Realism emerges as the substratum of narrative that has never been superseded entirely within the history of narrative forms. The aesthetic and political implications of this revision of literary history are immense and yet to be fully explored.

Indeed, a broad survey of contemporary fiction reveals not only that realism has not been superseded, but also that writing linked to particular forms of identity

---

[2]Peck's "recidivist realism" resonates with what James Wood (2004) calls "hysterical realism" and with Zadie Smith's (2008) much more positive term "lyrical realism."

continues to proliferate. Authors such as Jonathan Franzen, Marillyne Robinson, Edward P. Jones, Ha Jin, and Louise Erdrich may be difficult to group together; nevertheless taken together they attest to the importance of realism and cultural pluralism to contemporary fiction.

Nonetheless, it would be a hard argument to make that contemporary fiction has completely forsaken experimentation. The weird worlds of Blake Butler, Brian Evenson, Ben Marcus, and George Suanders, the experimental minimalism of Lydia Davis and Jenny Offill, and the formal experiments of writers such as Mark Z. Danielewski suggest a lingering desire for formal innovation in recent literature. Concomitantly, contemporary criticism has continued to attempt to frame the contemporary as a period distinct from what preceded it. Sharing the "-modern" as a common reference point, terms such as "cosmodernism" (Moraru 2011), "digimodernism" (Kirby 2009), the "exomodern" (McGurl 2011), and "post-postmodernism" (Nealon 2012) orient themselves towards past cultural and literary formation to signal their rupture with them, consecrating the contemporary thereby as incommensurable with what came before. Inviting us to read the "modern" as *now*, the contemporary, these terms work by adding to this empty placeholder what they take to be its distinguishing feature. For Moraru, the contemporary needs to be thought in terms of the cosmopolitan networks and transnational cultural formations. McGurl, on the other hand, identifies the contemporary with an increased awareness of the longer temporalities that connect us to periods outside of and external to modernity. Kirby, in turn, invites us to imagine contemporary culture as an effect of digital technologies, while Nealon identifies the contemporary with the intensification of postmodernism and the multiplication of its effects. It is perhaps possible to suggest that these critics share an almost modernist desire for periodization, for a cultural and literary history marked by ruptures rather than continuities.

These large-scale attempts at defining the contemporary are complemented by more circumscribed attempts at linking contemporary literature to the world we inhabit. Concerned centrally neither with continuities with past formations nor with periodizing ruptures, this third approach to the contemporary might best be described as singling out the contemporaneity of literature, what Terry Smith describes in relation to fine art as the sense of its timeliness, that it is an "art of that which actually *is* in the world, of what it is to *be* in the world, and of that which is to come" (2006: 692). From this perspective, contemporary literature is simply the literature that is produced now, and it gives evidence of its contemporaneity by connecting itself to one or another aspect of contemporary existence.

Central to this approach is identifying what aspect of the contemporary to highlight: 9/11, the war on terror, financial crises, migrant movements, environmental concerns, new media, digital cultures, transformations in how we think of the family, sexuality, ourselves as human beings, animal life. The list is endless, and the results diverse. Timothy Aubry (2011) ascribes a therapeutic function to contemporary fiction, in particular works by David Foster Wallace, Khaled Hosseini, and Anita Shreve. Richard Gray (2011) takes 9/11 as the pivotal event shaping contemporary American literature, including the work of writers such as Don DeLillo, Claire Messud, Ken Kalfus, and Jonathan Safran Foer. In her reading of Richard Powers, Leslie Marmon Silko, and Marge Piercy, among others, Heather Houser (2014) shows how contemporary fiction is concerned with diagnosing what she terms "ecosickness." Ranging across a corpus of one hundred twenty-five recent American novels, Caren Irr (2013) identifies a resurgent political fiction concerned with geopolitical issues. Relatedly, new or refurbished genres are identified with a predictable regularity: speculative realism (Colson Whitehead and Junot Díaz), cli-fi (Peter Matthiessen, Lydia Millet, Nathaniel Rich), the credit crunch novel (Paul Auster, Peter Mountford, Joshua Farris, Jess Walters), the world-systems novel (Dave Eggers, Moshin Hamid), the neuronovel (Richard Powers, E.L. Doctorow, Rivka Galchen, Jonathan Lethem), hysterical realism (David Foster Wallace, Denis Johnson, Jeffrey Eugenides, Michael Chabon) – the list is as extensive as that of the various foci critics have selected to exemplify the contemporaneity of recent American fiction. Nearly all of these genres, unsurprisingly, ultimately name a literary response to a social factor.

A similar approach informs Peter Boxall's ambitious *Twenty-first-century fiction: A critical introduction*, in which he frames contemporary literature as a belated response to the representational crises instantiated by postmodernity's rearrangement of space and time. For Boxall, diverse authors like Eggers, Cormac McCarthy, Roberto Bolaño, William Gibson, Don DeLillo, and Chimamanda Ngozi Adichie respond to ruptures in how we think of time and the body, and how technological, political, and aesthetic forms relate to the material environment. Boxall firmly situates contemporary fiction within its political, cultural, and material contexts, nominating, unsurprisingly, the post-apocalyptic environmental novel as the genre with the strongest claim on the future.

But recent criticism also approaches the contemporaneity of recent fiction from a different angle than its relation to contemporary crises by paying attention to the institutionality of this fiction. That is as much to say that growing attention is given to the institutions and sites where literature is produced, shaped, and disseminated. MFA programs (McGurl 2009), New York publishing (Harbach 2014), even McSweeney's (Hungerford 2012) have all received attention as contemporary sites where literature is produced and shaped in particular ways. By drawing attention to how these sites molded literary production, critics clarify how the nature of recent fiction is contingent on the history and characteristics of non-literary institutions, thereby enabling a different way of mapping the contemporary. It may be possible to suggest, additionally, that what is emerging today is amongst other things a sociological approach to literature. Attentive to the various institutions modulating literary production – MFAs, publishers, but also challenges to print, and digital transformations – this approach is intent on positioning literature as one contingent institution among many others in the world.

Irrespective of the angle of vision or emphasis, all the essays in the volume take for granted that American literature does have a future, even if it is impossible to ignore the all-too-frequently voiced anxieties about the death of literature, of the novel, and of the print book. While this is not the place to rehearse such anxieties, it cannot be denied that the essays have been written in the shadow of an explosion of what is collectively referred to as "new media," an explosion that is rapidly changing the ecosystem of literary genres and forms as well as the production, reception, and circulation of books. These changes elicit both panic and euphoria, both moods spread through attention-grabbing titles such as "The end of books" (Coover 1992), *The Gutenberg elegies: The fate of reading in an electronic age* (Birkerts 2006), or *Print is dead* (Gomez 2008).[3]

The rise of new media, at least, proved less calamitous than some have imagined. At this point in time there seems to be a growing chorus of voices

---

[3]In 1998, *The New York Times* used the rubric "The last book" to report on the project at the Media Laboratory at MIT called "The last book." In Sweden in 2001, one of the pioneers of the sociology of literature studies, Johan Svedjedal, published a collection of essays entitled *Den sista boken* (Eng.: *The last book*, 2001).

asking "to put an end to the digital utopias and print eulogies" (Piper 2012: xi) and to realize that the future entails a coexistence of print and electronic texts (Darnton 2009; Piper 2012) and that "print and electronic textuality deeply interpenetrate one another" (Hayles 2008: 160). This coexistence is not necessarily without tensions; the strategies of remediation, appropriation, and "poaching" characterize the contact zones between the two. Nevertheless, in literature, these strategies, as N. Katherine Hayles (2002; 2005) has indefatigably argued, may be seen as various ways of asserting the robustness of print. Strikingly, the mammoth *Cambridge history of the American novel* (2011) ends with Robert Coover's upbeat "A history of the future of narrative," in which he identifies the advent of the computer and the World Wide Web as groundbreaking for new literary formations; the future belongs to electronic texts, he predicts, even if "codex-style bound books with paper pages will no doubt continue to be published for a time" (1177). "Whatever the future may be," asserts Robert Darnton, "it will be digital" (2009: xv). Acknowledging "nothing is riskier than predictions," Hayles goes even further and proclaims "digital literature will be a significant component of the twenty-first century canon" (2008: 159).

One of the digital texts that have already entered the canon is *Inanimate Alice* by Kate Pullinger and Chris Joseph (2005 onward). This web-based multimedia novel is the subject of investigation by John David Zuern in "Minds, messages, and the moral imagination in the media of fiction: *Inanimate Alice* between cognitive and rhetorical paradigms" in this volume. His insightful reading of the third of the novel's ten episodes, "Russia," shows how this electronic text activates the moral imagination of its readers/viewers/users by employing the affordances of digital media. Zuern balances his focus on the specificity of this born-digital text with an interest in the ethical agency of all literature; taken as a whole, the essay constitutes an important contribution to recent narratological theories about "reading minds."

Like Zuern, Alison Gibbons too takes up the question of contemporary literature's engagement with ethics, but she does so via a close stylistic analysis of Adam Thirlwell's *Kapow!* (2012), a multimodal novella which takes advantage of the affordances of paper. In Gibbons's reading, *Kapow!* offers a metamodernist vision of the present and future of literature: its role is to insist that readers think critically and defiantly about their own place and complicity in the intimately interconnected world events. In "The paradoxes of 'unnatural' mimesis in Gordon Sheppard's *HA!*" Danuta Fjellestad also focuses on recent experiments with the format of the book and the consequences of such post-postmodern experimentation for narratological approaches to literature, and for our understanding of the category of the unnatural.

Timotheus Vermeulen and Robin van den Akker also target contemporary experimental art to forward an argument about a paradigm shift from postmodernism to metamodernism in their essay "Utopia, sort of: A case study in metamodernism." They discuss David Thorpe's collages, Ragnar Kjartansson's performances, and Paula Doepfner's installations for their oscillations between decay and transcendence, the permanent and the transitory, melancholy and hope, enthusiasm and despair, seeing these oscillations as driven by an attempt to re-imagine utopia. Thorpe, Kjartansson, and Doepfner are only three of many contemporary artists whose work signals that a utopian turn is part and parcel of the shift from postmodernism to metamodernism.

Turning towards a more canonical author, Don DeLillo, Pieter Vermeulen offers in "Don DeLillo's *Point omega*, the anthropocene, and the scales of literature" a theoretically rich account of the text that might very well be resistant to utopian imaginaries. In Vermeulen's reading, DeLillo's novel localizes contemporary debates about cultural transnationalism and cosmopolitanism within an expanded spatial and temporal frame that ultimately opens up into an engagement with a nonhuman otherness – the vast stretches of geological time in which the human hardly figures. Drawing on the theories associated with the contemporary nonhuman turn, including object-oriented ontology, Vermeulen poses the pressing question of whether the form of the novel is indeed capable of reckoning with the nonhuman world we inhabit.

Caren Irr likewise views the contemporary novel as inextricably linked to the world. Her "The space of genre in the new green novel" offers a synoptic account of the emergence of a group of novels dedicated to environmental problems and its complex relation to its predecessor. As Irr suggests, the new green novel functions in the mode of critique, targeting approaches to environmental problems grounded in liberal individualism in particular. At the same time, she identifies a strain in this genre that seeks to identify the potential for an alternative, collective response to environmental degradation. Susan Hegeman, in "A sociological imagination," is similarly interested in alternative social movements. Tracing the history of the "sociological imagination" through half a century, she argues that social movements, especially in the wake of the financial disaster of 2008, are the preeminent sites for the emergence of artistic and intellectual movements, movements which then can imagine the future of the present beyond the apparent closures of neoliberalism.

Finally, two essays in this book turn away from explicitly addressing developments in contemporary literature, asking instead what this literature means for the traditional topoi of literary analysis. Petter Skult, in his "The role of place in the post-apocalypse: Contrasting *The road* and *World War Z*" illustrates how contemporary post-apocalyptic narratives such as the ones by Max Brooks and Cormac McCarthy force a reconsideration of how we make sense of place and space in literary texts. In "Walking as a metaphor for narrativity," Marina Ludwigs's investigation of Joshua Ferris' enigmatic *The unnamed* uncovers what walking – an involuntary activity in the novel – reveals about narrative desire and narrativity itself. Like Skult, she makes clear how contemporary texts force us to return to the classical categories of literary interpretation and rethink them for the still-new century.

The reader of this introduction will have doubtlessly noticed that we have audaciously – perhaps even brazenly – skipped what Caroline F. Levander (2013: 2) calls "the thorniest question of all," that is, the question of what counts as "American literature" or whether it makes sense at all to retain this designation in an increasingly global culture. An eyebrow or two may have been raised at the inclusion of an article on *Kapow!*, written by a *British* writer, in this special issue. We hasten to assure the reader that we have no intention to annex Adam Thirwell's book to American literature or to expand this category even further; instead, this article (as well as references to other non-American novels and authors) serves as evidence that trends in literature exceed national boundaries. This has always been the case. But we want to hold on to the concept of American literature and, to cite Sinclair Lewis's sentiment expressed in his December 1930 Nobel lecture, we have "every hope and every eager belief" for the future of American literature. Making no claim to comprehensiveness, this volume takes up the issue of the future of American literature in full awareness that whatever this future holds, it is unlikely to be what we expect.

REFERENCES

Aubry, Timoth. 2011. *Reading as therapy: What contemporary fiction does for middle-class Americans*. Iowa City: University of Iowa Press.
Birkerts, Sven. 2006. *The Gutenberg elegies: The fate of reading in an electronic age*. London: Macmillan.

Boxall, Peter. 2013. *Twenty-first-century fiction: A critical introduction*. Cambridge, MA: Cambridge University Press.

Brooks, Neil Edward & Josh Toth (eds.). 2007. *The mourning after: Attending the wake of postmodernism*. Amsterdam: Rodopi.

Coover, Robert. 1992. The end of books. *New York Times Book Review* 21(6), 23–25.

Coover, Robert. 2011. A history of the future of narrative. In Leonard Cassuto, Clare Virginia Eby, & Benjamin Reiss (eds.), *The Cambridge history of the American novel*, 1168–1181. Cambridge: Cambridge University Press.

Cunningham, Valentine. 2002. *Reading after theory*. Oxford: Blackwell.

Darnton, Robert. 2009. *The case for books: Past, present, and future*. New York: Public Affairs.

Docherty, Thomas. 1996. *After theory*. Edinburgh: Edinburgh University Press.

Eagleton, Terry. 2003. *After theory*. London: Penguin.

Gomez, Jeff. 2008. *Print is dead: Books in our digital age*. New York: Macmillan. .

Gray, Richard. 2011.*After the fall: American literature since 9/11*. Malden, MA: John Wiley & Sons.Harbach, Chad. (ed.). 2014. *MFA vs. NYC: The two cultures of American fiction*. London: Palgrave Macmillan

Hayles, N. Katherine. 2002. *Writing machines*. Cambridge, MA: MIT Press.

Hayles, N. Katherine. 2005. *My mother was a computer: Digital subjects and literary texts*. Chicago: University of Chicago Press.

Hayles, N. Katherine. 2008. *Electronic literature: New horizons for the literary*. South Bend, IN: University of Notre Dame Press, 2008.

Houser, Heather. 2014. *Ecosickness in contemporary US fiction: Environment and affect*. New York: Columbia University Press.

Hungerford, Amy. 2008. On the period formerly known as contemporary. *American Literary History* 20(1–2), 410–419.

Hungerford, Amy. 2012. McSweeney's and the school of life. *Contemporary Literature* 53(4), 646–680.

Irr, Caren. 2013. *Toward the geopolitical novel: US fiction in the twenty-first century*. New York: Columbia University Press.

Kirby, Alan. 2009. *Digimodernism: How new technologies dismantle the postmodern and reconfigure our culture*. London: Continuum.

Kirsch, Adam. 2008. Nobel gas. *Slate*, 9 October. http://www.slate.com/articles/arts/culturebox/2008/10/nobel_gas.html. (last accessed on 5 February 2015)

Levander, Caroline F. 2013. *Where is American literature*. Hoboken, NJ: Wiley Blackwell.

Lewis, Sinclair. 1930. The American fear of literature. 12 December. Speech. http://www.nobelprize.org/nobel_prizes/literature/laureates/1930/lewis-lecture.html (last accessed on 16 January 2015).

McGurl, Mark. 2009. *The program era*. Cambridge, MA: Harvard University Press.

McGurl, Mark. 2011. The new cultural geology. *Twentieth Century Literature* 57(3–4), 380–390.

McHale, Brian. 2007. What was postmodernism? *Electronic Book Review*, 20. http://www.electronicbookreview.com/thread/fictionspresent/tense (last accessed on 19 October 2014).

Moraru, Christian. 2011. *Cosmodernism: American narrative, late globalization, and the new cultural imaginary*. Ann Arbor: University of Michigan Press.

Nealon, Jeffrey. 2012. *Post-postmodernism: Or, the cultural logic of just-in-time capitalism*. Stanford, CA: Stanford University Press.

Peck, Dale. 2004. *Hatchet jobs: Writings on contemporary fiction*. New York: New Press.

Piper, Andrew. 2012. *Book was there: Reading in electronic times*. Chicago: University of Chicago Press.

Pullinger, Kate & Chris Joseph. 2005 (continuing). *Inanimate Alice*. http://www.inanimatealice.com/ (last accessed 2 January 2015).

Saldívar, Ramón. 2011. Historical fantasy, speculative realism, and postrace aesthetics in contemporary American fiction. *American Literary History* 23(3), 574–599.

Simpson, Aislin. 2008. Nobel literature prize judge: American authors "insular and ignorant". *Daily Telegraph* online, 2 October. http://www.telegraph.co.uk/news/worldnews/northamerica/usa/3120602/Nobel-literature-prize-judge-American-authors-insular-and-ignorant.html. (last accessed on 7 February 2015)

Smith, Terry. 2006. Contemporary art and contemporaneity. *Critical Inquiry* 32(4), 681–707.

Smith, Zadie. 2008. Two paths for the novel. *New York Review of Books*. 20 November.

Svedjedal, Johan. 2001. *Den sista boken*. Stockholm: Wahlström och Widstrand.

Wood, James. 2004. Hysterical realism. In James Wood, *The irresponsible self: On laughter and the novel*, 178–194. New York: Picador.

Minds, Messages, and the Moral Imagination in the Media of Fiction: *Inanimate Alice* between Cognitive and Rhetorical Paradigms

JOHN DAVID ZUERN

1. Introduction

For scholars and teachers of literature in the United States, disturbing trends within the American education system are instilling a new urgency into old critical debates about the value of fiction, poetry, drama, and other forms of creative writing for the intellectual and moral development of their audiences. At American public universities, and at many private schools across the country as well, institutional support for the humanities has been shrinking over the past several decades as increasingly scarce resources are routed toward disciplines that appear to have more immediate economic and social benefits. Seeking justifications for downsizing and eliminating programs focusing on literature, culture, and the arts, upper-level university administrators turn to the results of assessment protocols that typically apply the same criteria to research and teaching in all disciplines, putting the humanities at a disadvantage in comparison with the more "productive" social and natural sciences.[1] Although the study of literature may appear to have a more secure position in American primary and secondary public schools, where it remains a key component of the language-arts curriculum, the same narrow pragmatism and the emphasis on quantifiable outcomes are reflected in a new set of curriculum recommendations, the Common Core State Standards, which were introduced in 2010 and have been adopted by public school systems in an overwhelming majority of the states.[2] The Common Core prescribes an approach to literary analysis that relies heavily on a text-immanent orientation to literary analysis reminiscent of the American New Criticism, encourages the absorption and measurably "correct" application of critical terminology, and privileges "informational" non-fiction over novels, short stories, poems, and dramas. Critics allege that a pedagogy founded on Common Core recommendations reduces the encounter with intellectually, emotionally, and ethically challenging texts to one among many learning routines designed to prepare students for the tightly circumscribed demands of state-mandated standardized testing rather than for the complex challenges of social life.[3]

---

[1] Among the many recent commentaries on this dire situation are Bok (2013), Delbanco (2012), and Jay (2014).
[2] The full title is "The Common Core State Standards for English Language Arts & Literacy in History/Social Studies, Science, and Technical Subjects." The document can be downloaded at the Common Core State Standards Initiative web site.
[3] Tim Murphy's (2014) article in *Mother Jones* provides an accessible overview of the history and controversy over the Common Core in the context of the ideologically polarized political climate of the United States during the period of its implementation.

One especially trenchant and theoretically sophisticated critique of the Common Core has recently emerged within the field of narrative studies, framed by Peter Rabinowitz and Corinne Bancroft's essay "Euclid at the Core: Recentering Literary Education," which serves as the anchor text for a 2014 issue of the journal *Style* devoted to a forum discussion of the Common Core's language-arts recommendations. In "Euclid at the Core," Rabinowitz and Bancroft propose an alternative pedagogy grounded in a model of the relationship between works of literature and their readers that elegantly combines components from both rhetorically oriented and cognitively oriented approaches to the study of narrative, bringing together – though not necessarily harmonizing – two positions in a critical dialogue that has been animating scholarship in narrative studies since the "cognitive turn" of the 1990s. Given their focus on the Common Core, Rabinowitz and Bancroft's arguments are most immediately relevant to language-arts teachers in primary and secondary schools, but they have broad implications for teachers of literature at all levels and, moreover, for all critics and theorists of narrative forms.

While I fully concur with Rabinowitz and Bancroft's critique of the Common Core, my principal aim in this essay is to point out what I see as a limitation – and potentially a risk – in Rabinowitz and Bancroft's privileging of the cognitive paradigm to promote "mind-reading as the central principle" (2014: 19) of an effective literary pedagogy. I am particularly concerned with the ramifications of associating, as they do, the *ethical* agency of fiction so closely to the reader's imaginative capacity to access and evaluate the mental functioning of characters and authors. I am also interested in widening the scope of Rabinowitz and Bancroft's proposal, which focuses predominantly on literature in print, to encompass fictions in digital formats, including computer games, which are now the primary medium in which many Americans are engaging with stories, and which are increasingly finding their way into the curricula of American schools. Rather than call into question the undoubtedly powerful effects of literary mind-reading, I want to show how the rhetorical configuration of some fictional texts, especially (but by no means exclusively) those employing the affordances of digital media, can activate the moral imagination – appealing to readers, calling them to account, and obligating them – in ways that cannot be readily subsumed under the model of mind-reading. For that reason, the potentially salutary effects of these rhetorical structures might escape the notice of theorists and teachers who, when accounting for a reader's moral engagements with a text, privilege the role of *minds* over the ethical impact of the text's specific function as a *message*, a message that at times presents itself not only as an invitation but also as a demand, a summons, or a plea.

My investment in identifying an ethical agency in fiction that does not rely on a reader's telepathic relationships with characters or authors has been prompted by the specific institutional pressures under which I work as a teacher of literature at an American university. In what follows, after an overview of Rabinowitz and Bancroft's proposal, I offer a brief description of those formative pressures and explain why they have led me to prioritize the rhetorical aspects of fictional texts, in particular their specific strategies for appealing to the reader's moral imagination, over the texts' explicit or implicit representations of mental functioning whenever fiction is recruited in the service of an ethics-education agenda – as it has been in most of the literature classes I have been teaching for more than a decade. I sketch a theoretical rationale for this prioritization by way of a comparison of David Herman's cognitively oriented concept of "joint attentional frames" (or "scenes") with Richard Walsh's rhetorically oriented concept of "interpellation," indicating why I find Walsh's formulation better able to isolate the kind of ethical experience I am seeking to identify, one that remains relatively autonomous from whatever mind-reading, identification, or empathy the narrative might also solicit. To provide an example of a work of fiction that in my view provides such an experience, I analyze an episode in Kate Pullinger and Chris Joseph's web-based electronic novel *Inanimate Alice*, a text that allows me to extend the discussion Rabinowitz and Bancroft inaugurate in "Euclid at the Core" to fictions in digital formats. Returning to "Euclid at the Core," my conclusion reiterates the value of separating at least one component of fiction's ethical agency from its invitation to read characters' and authors' minds, especially in light of the moral quandaries confronting students poised to begin their professional lives in the present-day political and cultural climate of the United States.

2. Mind-reading at the core

As I note above, Rabinowitz and Bancroft's proposal draws theoretical resources from both the rhetorical and cognitive paradigms for the study of narrative. In place of the Common Core's under-theorized, reductive program for textual analysis, they "propose starting instead from the rhetorical relationship between author and reader mediated by a text, recognizing that this relationship is both socially conditioned and rule governed" (2014: 8). This aspect of their approach upholds the tenets of a critical paradigm elaborated by theorists like James Phelan (1996; 2005; 2007; Herman et al. 2012), Richard Walsh (2007), and Rabinowitz himself, recently in partnership with Phelan (Herman et al. 2012), which emphasizes the rhetorical function of the fictional narrative as a constructed, mediated *message*, "somebody telling somebody else on a particular occasion for some purpose that something happened" (Phelan 1996: 219). At the same time, when Rabinowitz and Bancroft assert that "part of the essential design of a literary text is the *expectation* that the reader or viewer will engage in the act of mind-reading" (2014: 11), they invoke the work of theorists like David Herman (2004; 2013; Herman et al. 2012) Patrick Colm Hogan (2003; 2011), Alan Palmer (2004), and Lisa Zunshine (2006; 2008), who have enlisted what cognitive scientists and philosophers of language call Theory of Mind—our built-in capacity to recognize that other people have thoughts and feelings that resemble our own—to establish a critical paradigm emphasizing the role of the *minds* of characters, readers, and authors in the experience of fiction.

Referring in particular to Zunshine's (2006) conviction that the pleasures and benefits of reading fiction lie in its unique capacity to exercise readers' theory of mind,[4] Rabinowitz and Bancroft conjoin rhetorical and cognitive orientation in the compelling metaphor of an invitation: "As a speech act, literature is fundamentally an invitation, specifically an invitation, *designed for us*, to read the mind of the author" (12). The virtue of this formulation, from a pedagogical

---

[4]Zunshine offers a succinct explanation of benefits of fiction's "sociocognitive complexity" in her response to "Euclid at the Core" in the *Style* forum (2014, see especially 89–90). Zunshine's objection to the Common Core's marginalization of fiction is one of the most incisive in the issue: "The decision to teach elementary and secondary students more literary nonfiction and less fiction will affect the future of higher education as severely as drastic budget cuts, yet more insidiously" (91).

standpoint, is that in principle the text remains a discrete object of analysis (as a crafted message, the components of which can be identified and described) while at the same time readers are encouraged to enter active intellectual and emotional relationships with it (as an opportunity to read minds). On the whole, this model of fictional discourse as a dynamic invitation is far more amenable to a rich, stimulating, and rigorous pedagogy than the static conception of the literary text promulgated in the Common Core standards.

Rabinowitz and Bancroft also seek to demonstrate how their approach fosters students' engagement with the ethical dimensions of literature, and it is on this point that I take some exception to their otherwise inspiring vision. They rightly fault the Common Core model for skirting difficult ethical issues; in their view, "recognizing the ethical issues characters and authors raise either intentionally or not is essential to choosing which texts to include in the curriculum — and, even more, how to talk about them" (25). They steer clear of the assumption that fiction achieves ethical, "pro-social" effects by promoting the reader's empathy with characters, heeding in particular Suzanne Keen's critique of that position (2007), but insofar as their conception of fiction's ethical effects remains contained within their model of reading as "mind-reading," it seems to presuppose the same fluid boundary between real readers and fictional entities that underwrites the fiction-promotes-empathy argument.

In this regard, I concur with Brian Richardson's response to "Euclid at the Core" in the *Style* forum. In keeping with his advocacy in *Unnatural Voices* (2006) for greater critical attention to fiction's antimimetic elements, Richardson expresses his discomfort with the tendency of Rabinowitz and Bancroft's model of mind-reading to conflate fictional characters with real people, potentially creating an environment for "the worst kind of conventional moralizing" (2014: 76). Lest we overlook the fact that "poetic justice is not the same thing as legal justice" (2014: 77), Richardson cautions, "the mimetic aspect of fiction must not be overemphasized; its limitations need to be identified and its significance balanced by the work's other aspects. These include the work's formal concerns and parallels, its genre status [...], and even antimimetic gestures that proclaim the fictional nature of the narrative" (2014: 77). Responding to Richardson in the final essay in the *Style* issue, Rabinowitz and Bancroft again combine the terminology of the cognitive and rhetorical paradigms to insist on the importance of allowing students to assume moral positions "through their own mind-reading" and of ensuring that discussions "include the individual and particular way each student relates to the constellation of characters and the implied author" (2014: 99). This rejoinder continues to tie the reader's ethical engagement to relationships among real and imagined minds, and it still risks occluding the ethical potential inhering in fiction's specific strategies of rhetorical address, which are not limited to the discursive role of the (supposedly mind-like) implied author. As I explain in the next section, this objection to what I, along with Richardson, see as a confining mimeticism in the mind-reading model of ethical engagement emerges from the theoretical and practical challenges I have confronted (and still confront) in my effort to contribute to an ethics-focused curriculum at my home university.

3. Institutional context: Fiction and professional ethics

Since 2001 the University of Hawai'i at Mānoa has required all undergraduates to complete at least one course, preferably within their major programs of study, with a focus on ethical questions.[5] In the years following that mandate, I have developed several "Contemporary Ethical Issues" literature classes for undergraduate English majors and students in the university's campus-wide Honors program. Although they are not billed as classes in "applied ethics," the reading and writing assignments explicitly seek to link students' disciplined, conscientious reading of fiction with their conscious deliberation about moral questions relating to more or less specific types of real-world professional conduct.[6] A class on post-2008 American novels, for example, focuses in part on business ethics, especially in banking and finance, while a class designed for Honors students places a set of novels and stories in the contexts of historical events that led to the consolidation of present-day codes of conduct governing the various academic disciplines in which these students are developing their thesis projects and, ultimately, seeking careers.

In addition to developing these classes, I have served on the campus-wide faculty committee that reviews proposals for courses aiming to fulfill the "Contemporary Ethical Issues" requirement and oversees procedures for evaluating these courses. Examining proposals for ethics-focused courses in fields like Anthropology, Business Administration, Environmental Studies, and Sociology, I began to notice that while it is not uncommon for teachers in these disciplines to incorporate novels, stories, and films into their ethics-oriented classes, the texts are invariably treated as *representations* of ethical dilemmas – essentially surrogate case studies. These proposals represented a conception of fiction's contribution to ethical reflection in which, as Adam Zachary Newton puts it in *Narrative Ethics* (1997: 9), "narrative form functions as a vehicle for substantive ethical 'content.'" I realized that my own proposals were also marked by this impulse to translate "literary discourse into moral recourse" (Newton 1997: 9); in an effort to meet the prescribed hallmarks for these classes, I chose fictions that, as stories, invited dynamic comparisons among different frameworks for ethical deliberation, such as virtue ethics, deontology, consequentialism, and the ethics of care. I did not initially give much thought to how these stories, as fictional discourse, might provide students with ethically challenging experiences arising from what Dorrit Cohn (1998: 130) has called the "uniquely stressful interpretive freedom" with which fiction burdens its readers.[7]

It is of course completely natural and pedagogically expeditious for teachers to turn to fiction for illustrations of moral problems. In the kinds of the classes I

---

[5]I should mention that the same reform instituting this ethics requirement also eliminated the mandate that all undergraduates at UHM take two classes in the English department's Introduction to Literature Program, a scaling-down symptomatic of the waning prestige of literary studies in the American model of higher education.

[6]The criteria for evaluating the substantive content of proposed "Contemporary Ethical Issues" classes are (i) Contemporary ethical issues will be presented and studied in a manner that is fully integrated into the main course content; (ii) The disciplinary approach(es) used in the class will give students tools for the development of responsible deliberation and ethical judgment; (iii) Students will achieve basic competency in analyzing and deliberating upon contemporary ethical issues to help them make ethically determined judgments. (Hallmarks 2014).

[7]Within the discipline of literary studies, as Terry Eagleton has noted, this tendency to reduce literary texts to case studies or reportage manifests itself whenever works are read primarily as illustrations of the real-world social and political problems with which teachers and scholars wish to engage. "To read like this," Eagleton cautions, "is to set aside the 'literariness' of the work – the fact that it is a poem or play or novel, rather than an account of the incidence of soil erosion in Nebraska" (2013: 2).

describe above, fiction can "put a human face" on abstract principles that undergird professional ethical codes, such as respect for persons, beneficence, and justice. It can "bring to life" serious ethical issues, for example Nazi medical experiments in Martin Amis's *Time's Arrow* (1992), or human cloning in Kazuo Ishiguro's *Never Let Me Go* (2005), or the corrupting influence of globalized capitalism in Mohsin Hamid's *How to Get Filthy Rich in Rising Asia* (2013). My concern, however, is that by treating works of fiction exclusively as second-hand case studies, we promulgate an impoverished conception of fiction's capacity to cultivate the moral imagination, because such treatment fails to account for almost everything that differentiates the ethical agency of fiction *as fiction* from that of any other document (a news story, for example, or an oral history, or a witness statement) depicting ethically challenging situations.[8] When we allow this to happen, the question of what makes fiction an *indispensable* rather than a merely convenient component of these classes – a question that echoes some administrators' skepticism about the present and future value of programs in literature – becomes difficult to answer.

My discomfort with mind-reading as a central tenet of literary education is partly rooted in this broader concern about the risk of weakening literature's claim to a privileged position in a course of study that compels students to grapple with ethical questions. In my view, it is important to strengthen our claims for literature's distinctive contributions to the moral imagination, not only in order to secure a place for literary studies within the required curricula of schools and universities but also, more broadly and perhaps more nobly, to promote the study of literature as a means by which people can come to recognize and palpably experience their responsibilities as members of a highly diverse and stratified society in which mindsets, allegiances, and values are decidedly not shared. In pursuit of this goal, it seems important to disconnect at least some facets of fiction's ethical agency from its invitation to read minds.

4. Theoretical rationale: Two views of fiction's invitation

My desire to identify an ethical agency inherent in fictional texts that is independent of mind-reading has led me to weigh the rhetorical and cognitive paradigms against each other to assess each one's capacity to account robustly for fiction's ethical agency. When it comes to questions of ethics, it appears to me that the cognitive paradigm's emphasis on mind – expressed, for example, in Alan Palmer's claim in *Fictional Minds* (2004: 5; see also 177 and 184–85) that "narrative fiction is, in essence, the presentation of fictional mental functioning" – typically results in a conception of fictional texts largely as representations of mindsets, intentions, and behaviors that might prompt moral judgments. On the other hand, the rhetorical paradigm's conception of fiction as an essentially communicative act puts it in a better position to analyze the *prompting itself* as an effect of specific configurations of the fictional discourse, which mediate and manipulate readers' encounters with morally provocative elements of a story world, and, even more important, with their experience of their own morally consequential responses to those encounters. James Phelan captures the key elements of this rhetorical function in his formulation of "position," which he

---

[8]A notable exception is Rita Charon's (2008) description of how studying literature enriches the training of physicians, which privileges the experiential dimension of reading over the edifying effects of morally relevant scenarios represented in literary texts.

describes as "*a concept that combines being placed in and acting from an ethical location*" (2005: 23). For Phelan, fiction exerts its ethical effects by positioning its reader simultaneously within the nexus of four orientations: toward the characters, toward the narrator, toward the implied author, and toward the values embodied in the actions of the first three components. The impact on the reader's moral imagination of this global rhetorical orientation is at least as important as the local impact of any of the story world's represented elements.

To try to pinpoint what I see as the most relevant aspect of this divergence between the two critical orientations for the present discussion, I will compare David Herman's (2008) adoption, on behalf of the cognitive paradigm, of Michael Tomasello's model of the "joint attentional scene" (or "frame") with Richard Walsh's redeployment in *The Rhetoric of Fictionality* (2007) of Louis Althusser's concept of "interpellation." Although they are not exactly symmetrical in terms of how they operate within their respective conceptual systems, both ideas attempt to account for fundamental aspects of a reader's experience of fictional discourse, in particular the alignment of a reading consciousness with an agent of narration. Comparing them in light of the question of how fictional texts might mobilize their reader's ethical agency by means other than mind-reading, I am led to prefer the explanatory power of Walsh's formulation.

In his influential essay "Narrative Theory and the Intentional Stance," Herman critiques what he views as the "anti-intentionalist bias" (2008: 240) in many strands of contemporary narrative theory, arguing in particular against the theoretical validity of the "implied author," which he deems a now-outdated "compromise formation" to avoid the strictures of the intentional fallacy (2008: 242). Herman's own model of reading unapologetically takes for granted that stories are fundamentally the products of intentional acts and that readers make sense of stories by inferring those intentions. To model this alignment between intentions and interpretations, Herman adopts Tomasello's notion of "joint attentional scenes" which bring together, in a situation of human communication, one person's communicative intentions with another person's ascription and construal of those intentions: "In short, in multiple domains and activities, people regularly take up the intentional stance toward persons, objects, or artifacts that they construe as instantiating or emanating from intentional systems – as a heuristic, problem-solving strategy that allows for inferential shortcuts and streamlined judgment protocols" (2008: 237). "Judgment" here does not seem to carry a predominantly ethical valence, as the word typically does when rhetorically oriented theorists use it (see Phelan 2007), but it seems reasonable to include moral evaluations in the scope of these world-constructing construals.

In the domain of fictional narrative, Herman argues, story worlds emerge in these attentional scenes as a result of the reader's inferences about the intentions the text encodes: "Intentions are enacted by interpreters in tandem with the textual structures that afford blueprints for world construction, even as, on the production side of things, communicative intentions are not just instantiated in but enacted in concert with particular textual designs" (256). These blueprints – another metaphor for fiction's "invitation" to its audience – allow readers to "construct," in their own minds, the story world along the lines its creator intended.[9] In this article and throughout his work, Herman offers an especially thoroughgoing and forceful theoretical contribution to the cognitive paradigm.

---

[9]Caracciolo (2012: 217–218) points out that while Herman's recruitment of cognitive models like the joint attentional scene allow Herman to account for the reader's reconstruction of the intended story world, they are less enlightening in regard to the reader's freedom to elaborate interpretations of that world.

Walsh, for his part, seeks in *The Rhetoric of Fictionality* to defend "an understanding of fiction in rhetorical rather than representational terms" (2007: 9). A component of his project involves disambiguating three uses of "voice" in narrative theory. He distinguishes among meanings of voice as "instance" (the agent effecting the narrative), voice as "idiom" (the characteristics of voices represented in the narrative), and voice as "interpellation," which he associates with the reader-orienting effects of focalization, "in which the rhetorical effect is one of alignment with a subject position rather than objectification of a representational subject" (2007: 10). He explains further:

> In every case, the act of narrative comprehension requires an imaginative alignment between the reader (or viewer) and the implied subject position of the discourse. Such alignment may, to an extent, be conscious and qualified by reservations of several kinds; but to the extent that it is unconscious, it has the ideological effect of making the implied subject position seem to constitute the authentic selfhood of the narrative recipient. (2007: 98–99)

Walsh might be understood to be aligning "interpellation" with Wayne Booth's (1983) notion of the implied reader who is invited to subscribe to the implied author's value system.[10] I see his position as less "personalized" than that, however, and I want to emphasize Walsh's effort to separate "interpellation" from the originating function of "instance" and the representational functions of "idiom." Interpellation, he explains, "is a distinct sense of voice not only because it need not be representationally embodied or owned by a character, or a narrating character, or indeed the author, but also because its scope extends well beyond the category of the discursive, or even the perspectival in any limited perceptual or cognitive sense (the domain of focalization), to become an organizing concept for ideology" (2007: 100). For me, it is precisely this extension of interpellation's scope and its "depersonalizing" liberation from representations of identifiable narrative entities that distinguishes Walsh's concept from Herman's "joint attentional frames" and accounts for its considerable analytical power – as well as for its considerable challenge to critical practice.

In the domain of fiction, no less than in real life, is difficult not to take interpellation personally. Robyn Warhol (Herman et al. 2012: 147) offers an especially clear example of how interpellation is "personalized" in the act of reading:

> If a twenty-first-century college student picks up *Persuasion* to find herself effectively interpellated by the narration – if some part of herself answers the call the narrator sends out to the implied reader – her reading experience will be absorbing; if she is offended by class snobbery or can't bring herself to care about the aggregation of tiny faux pas and miniscule interpersonal triumphs that add up to Austen's plot, this can be attributed to her own inability to identify with the implied reader.

Is interpellation always the purview of a narrator, or, for that matter, an author? Is it always a message originating in an identifiable mind, whether actual or invented? Is a reader's response to a fiction's interpellation always a matter of identification with an implied reader? As I interpret Walsh's refinement of the concept, it seems possible to answer these questions in the negative, recognizing that fictional discourse itself can issue an essentially impersonal, anonymous appeal, triggering a response in the reader that does

---

[10] I thank David Ciccoricco for this suggestion.

not involve affirming (or rejecting) the values of narrators and/or implied authors, or identifying (or not) with characters, or any form of mind-reading.

In the admittedly circumscribed context in which I teach fiction, where I aim to draw students into learning experiences that will help prepare them for the ethical challenges of their professional lives, some of which will be governed by formal ethical codes, I find tremendous value in this idea of an impersonal – or, better, transpersonal – interpellation via the discourse of fiction, however abstract, counter-intuitive, and elusive the notion may initially appear. Professional codes of conduct, like moral codes in general, make us at once responsible to everyone and to no one in particular. We do, of course, enact and concretize our responsibilities whenever we respond to specific moral challenges, in which the responsible parties have faces and names, but the codes don't simply switch on in these situations. They run constantly in the background, ceaselessly interpellating us, and most of the time "conforming" to the codes is a matter of sensing their persistent gravitational pull. By the same token, ethics education cannot simply familiarize students with ethical rules and regulations; it must also give them opportunities to attune themselves to the pervasive appeal of what is, in the end, their own sense of responsibility.[11] Though hardly a guarantee of good conduct, that attunement is nevertheless an essential component of a "pro-social" professional life (the investment bankers and subprime lenders who instigated the global financial crisis seem to have tuned it out). As a means of conceptualizing fiction's capacity to provoke such a sensation of obligation, independent of telepathy or empathy, Walsh's formulation of interpellation, especially as it "need not be representationally embodied," seems better suited than Herman's joint intentional frames, in which readers infer intentions on the basis of the representations that signal them.

The moral dimension of interpellation is especially apparent in some forms of digital fiction, especially those that exploit the logical structures of computer-programming languages to create scenarios in which decisions on the part of readers or players have direct consequences for the outcome of narrative events. As Ciccoricco notes, "in digital fictions we must augment what we see and what we hear with *what we do* and what the text does in turn" (2012: 262). In the context of computer games in particular, I see "interpellation" overlapping significantly with the "enaction" Simon Penny (2004: 79) describes:

> … in interactive media a user is not simply exposed to images that may contain representations of things and actions. The user is trained in the enaction of behaviors in response to images, and images appear in response to behaviors in the same way that a pilot is trained in a flight simulator.

I am drawn to Penny's description of enaction because he emphasizes the ethical ramifications of virtual-reality environments, such as flight simulators, that are used to train military personnel for combat. In his view, "games and interactive media in general can be powerful inculcators of behaviors, and these learned behaviors can be expressed outside the realm of the game" (82). Some of these

---

[11] Although my use of "attunement" here alludes Immanuel Kant's "respect for the moral law," I indicate below that students and professionals alike draw from a range of philosophical traditions to describe the sense of personal responsibility that infuses their alignment with formal ethical codes. For a compelling exploration of "attunement" as an ethical resource, connected in particular with the skill of listening, see Lipari (2014).

behaviors, Penny notes, can be anti-social (he does not dismiss the hypothesis that playing violent computer games can encourage violent acts in the real world), but his argument supports the possibility of enactment's "pro-social" effects, and in any case the key point here is that enaction, like interpellation, stimulates the reading subject's sense – that is, recognition and *sensation* – of moral agency.

For an illustration of a salutary interpellation activated in the discourse of digital fiction, I will turn now to Kate Pullinger and Chris Joseph's electronic novel *Inanimate Alice*, a work of digital fiction that in my view interpellates the reader/player as a morally responsible subject via its rhetorical structures, without requiring a telepathic link to its characters' minds or a construal of its authors' intentions.

5. Minds and messages in *Inanimate Alice*

The web-based multimedia novel *Inanimate Alice* combines a verbal text organized in a basic hypertext format (readers can follow links to move among the story's individual scenes), still images, quasi-cinematic animation, music, and built-in computer games to trace the development of a girl named Alice into a successful game designer. The first of its projected ten episodes, "China," launched in 2005, followed by "Italy," "Russia," and "Hometown," with Pullinger contributing the text of the story and Joseph designing the interface, composing the soundtrack, programming the games, and assembling the final product with the Flash platform. The project's producer, Ian Harper, initially conceived the novel as a freely distributed promotional vehicle for a commercial feature film and game venture (Pullinger 2008: 122), but *Inanimate Alice* is now being widely promoted to schools as means of fostering digital literacy. As students proceed through the episodes, which increase in complexity in pace with Alice's growing prowess as a designer, they are expected to build skills in reading, playing, and reflecting on digital texts and games.[12]

In the context of Rabinowitz and Bancroft's critique of the Common Core, *Inanimate Alice* is a particularly opportune test case, not only because it explicitly aligns itself with the Common Core State English Language Arts Standards ("Curriculum"), but also because the theory of reading implicit in its pedagogical claims seems to fall in line with the mind-reading model, though without the skepticism regarding empathy: "As young people almost immediately feel empathy towards Alice and her changing circumstances," Harper writes in an online promotional brochure (Harper n.d.), "it is not difficult to involve, motivate, and engage them in Alice's world, where, along with Alice, the smart teacher can support the child to develop in any number of ways – socially, emotionally, and intellectually." As I elaborate below, this embedding of the novel in the discourse of education standards provides much stronger external evidence of its authors' intentions than do most works of fiction.

---

[12]The project's web site offers a wide range of downloadable teaching resources and activities developed by Jess Laccetti, including lesson plans aligned with the curriculum standards of Australia, Canada, the United Kingdom, and the United States. Gavin Stewart (2010) offers a compelling analysis of these materials along with the many other paratextual elements surrounding the novel.

Alice's circumstances are indeed pitched to solicit powerful emotions. Because her father, John, works in the petroleum industry, her family is constantly relocating, and consequently she is home-schooled by her mother Ming, a painter. Precocious and adept with technology, Alice copes with the instability and isolation of her life by creating a virtual companion named Brad, who sometimes functions as Alice's avatar in the games she designs for a multi-function hand-held device she calls her Player. Furthermore, as Pullinger (2008) explains and both Ruth Page (2008) and David Ciccoricco (2013a: 42–43) analyze, the cinematic focalization shaping the visual narrative often restricts the visual field to what Alice sees, though the novel does not appear to sustain this convention consistently (Ciccoricco 2013a: 42–43).[13] Accounting for these apparent shifts in focalization represents one of the novel's interpretive challenges, and I take them up below to compare the explanatory power of Herman's "joint attentional frames" and Walsh's "interpellation."

I focus on the third episode, "Russia," in which Alice is thirteen and living in Moscow. She wants to attend the International School, but her father's fears of kidnapping keep her at home with Ming. As the "Russia" episode opens, her father is in danger: he's being blackmailed in connection with an oil spill, and some ruffians have shown up at the family's apartment to intimidate him. Alice hides in her bedroom closet, where she finds solace in Brad and one of her games. In this one, a Russian matryoshka doll drops from the top of the screen, and the object of the game is to position Brad on his skateboard so he can catch it before it breaks. It is essentially a version of the old *Space Invaders* console game, except here the falling objects are rescued rather than shot down (Fig. 1).

The image of the matryoshka comes to play a complex semiotic role in "Russia." At the start of every episode of *Inanimate Alice*, a screen of instructions explains that readers must follow links or perform other actions to keep the story moving along, and on the next screen Alice introduces herself – "My name is Alice" – and then states her age. In "Russia," an additional set of instructions gives me two options: I can either read the story *and* play the embedded game or read the story without playing, but as Ruth Page (2008) has pointed out, the

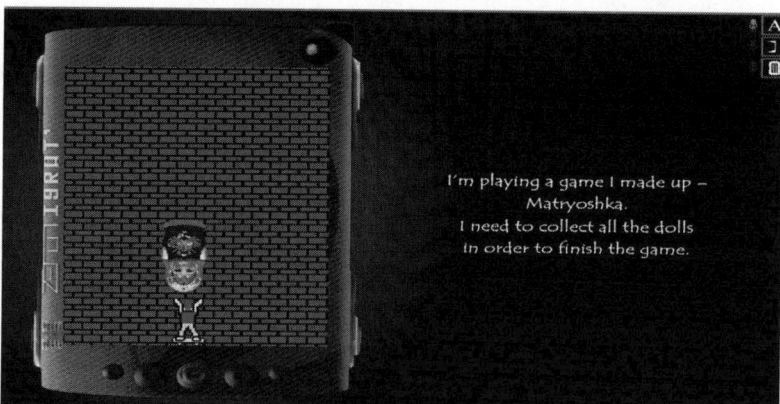

Figure 1. The matryoshka game in the "Russia" episode of Inanimate Alice. *Reproduced with permission.*

[13]See Pullinger (2008) for an account of Pullinger and Joseph's decisions regarding the representation of Alice's perspective.

novel's instructions never explain *how* to play its games or indicate *why* the reader should bother to play them; in "Russia," this omission eventually becomes especially significant for readers who choose to play.

If I elect to play, the text on the opening screen substitutes a matryoshka for the pronoun "I" in the sentence "I'm 13 years old," apparently establishing the doll as an index of Alice's narrating subjectivity. The following screen seems simultaneously to perpetuate and disrupt this focalizing strategy, showing the doll in Alice's closet as the door closes. If I've read previous episodes, I immediately recognize a departure from the novel's Alice-is-the-camera convention: the doll can't "be" Alice because Alice is "looking at" it. Even if I'm new to the novel, as I proceed through the following screens, which recount Alice's parents' decision to flee Moscow that very night, the family's hurried packing, and their anxious drive to an airfield, the *indexical* link (to use Peirce's terminology) between the doll and Alice's consciousness becomes attenuated, but the doll's resonance as a *symbol* of Alice's vulnerability intensifies. I begin to notice that a small image of the matryoshka appears, often fleetingly, in every scene, once in the pocket of an imaginary kidnapper (Fig. 2).

Exploring the screen with the cursor reveals that these dolls are *icons* in both semiotic and functional terms: clicking them lets me enter and play Alice's matryoshka game, in which the doll's semiotic values are coupled with an essentially *economic* value as the token I must collect to win the game. Each time I succeed in rescuing the matryoshka, a doll gets added to a running tally of scenes along the right side of the interface, which also functions as a set of hyperlinks allowing me to jump back into any previous scene (see Fig. 2). As Page indicates, at this point the novel gives me no motivation to play Alice's matryoshka game beyond my own curiosity about the girl's world and whatever ambition I might have to take on the challenge simply for the entertainment of playing and the satisfaction of winning.

When Alice and her parents reach the gates of the airfield, however, the status of my decision to play or not (and to win or not) dramatically changes: it is

Figure 2. One of the partially hidden matryoshka dolls the player is required to collect. Reproduced with permission.

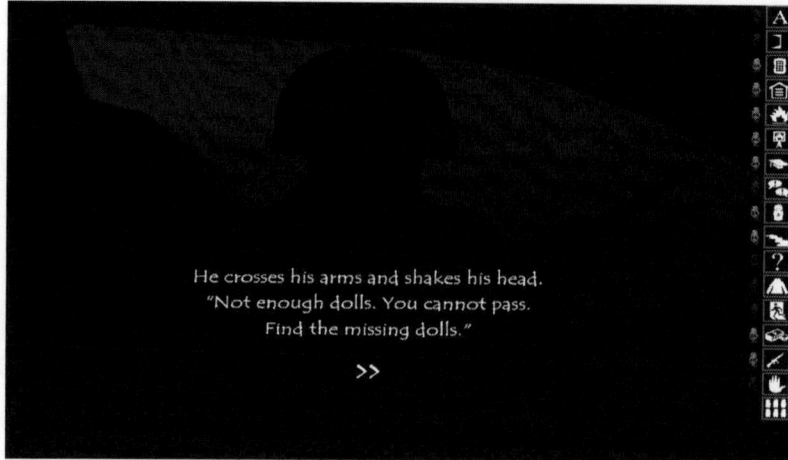

Figure 3. The game requires the player to return to previous screens to collect the remaining matryoshka dolls. Reproduced with permission.

retroactively assigned a crucial role in what rhetorically oriented theorists have called the narrative progression (see Phelan 2007). Aggressively seeking a bribe, the armed guard at the gates seizes Alice's player, examines the matryoshka game, and determines, based on the number of dolls she has collected, whether to allow them to pass, thus transforming what was a largely realist depiction of Alice's experience into a fairy-tale quest (Fig. 3). At the level of the "cybernetic narration" (Ciccoricco 2012: 256) structuring *Inanimate Alice*, the following conditional statement in Chris Joseph's ActionScript programming carries out the guard's command:

```
if ((_parent.dolllevel ≥ 17)||(_parent.gameplay==0)){
gotoAndPlay('onourway');
}14
```

If (and only if) all the dolls have been collected, the narrative may advance to its conclusion, and Alice and her family can be "on their way." If any dolls are missing, I – cinematically positioned in the locus of Alice's subjectivity and the "you" of the guard's command – have the option of clicking back through the previous scenes to collect them or forfeiting the chance to achieve an experience of Alice's story as a (potentially) coherent narrative.

As Phelan and Rabinowitz explain, "completion/coherence refers to the authorial audience's final and retrospective sense of the shape and purposes of the narrative as a whole, which may or may not require a significant reconsideration of earlier hypotheses about configuration" (Herman et al. 2012: 61). At this crux in the narrative, I am indeed compelled to reevaluate my initial assumptions about the matryoshka's value and the stakes of Alice's game, which have suddenly taken on moral significance: what was initially a pastime for Alice has now become a passport, so what was initially merely an *option* for me (to

---

[14]I thank Chris Joseph for his permission to reproduce this code.

complete the game) has become an *obligation* (to help rescue Alice and her family).

Turning back to my comparison of Herman and Walsh's formulations, I want to ask what insights each can offer into the specifically ethical dimension of this narrative turning point. In one sense, Herman's model of joint attentional scenes certainly enables such a reading. If I adopt, in Herman's (2008: 250) words, "an intentional stance toward the textual blueprint, which would otherwise remain a vacuous, non-referring assemblage of symbolic representations," I can infer that the creators of the novel intend that I reconcile the inconsistencies in the story's semiotics, focalization structures, and generic conventions in the logic of fantasy, and, as a result, to experience *Inanimate Alice* as a psychological novel in which the borders of the story world are the borders of Alice's anxious imagination.[15] I can, moreover, infer that the creators incorporate a game in which the player's actions have morally relevant consequences as a means of building the young reader's digital literacy and ethical awareness, emphasizing the point Miguel Sicart (2011: 212) makes in *The Ethics of Computer Games* "players' values and choices make them ethical agents in the game experience – and, by extension, this makes the game experience a moral one." I can also combine these inferences to surmise that Alice, like many children in families undergoing crisis, has psychically assumed responsibility for the problem and its resolution.

Although Herman's model accounts for how I might make sense of the novel's representations of Alice and her world, I find it difficult to use it to isolate any *specific* textual feature that might indicate how *Inanimate Alice*, as a particular kind of communicative situation, enlists my moral imagination.[16] I think Walsh's deployment of "interpellation" does a better job of accounting for how the particular combination of Joseph's conditional statement and the novel's focalizing strategies effect the precipitous transformation of my sense of myself as a moral agent, shifting my aims from the egocentric commitment to (or disinterest in) winning the game to the more altruistic, "pro-social" commitment to winning the game *for Alice*. I don't need access to the authors' intentions or the characters' thoughts and feelings to experience, pleasurably or otherwise, the sense of obligation the text stimulates in me at this moment. I am *structurally* obligated by virtue of the interpellating rhetorical appeal configured in the narrative's patterns of focalization and progression, whether or not I ultimately fulfill that obligation. It is encoded in the novel's narrative discourse, just as, I would argue, obligations are encoded in formal protocols of professional conduct.

Affirming N. Katherine Hayles's (2003: 263) conviction that "the advent of electronic textuality presents us with an unparalleled opportunity to re-formulate

---

[15]Ciccoricco (2013a: 42–43) questions this notion that all the images and animations in the novel can be ascribed to Alice's imagination by pointing to what appear to be depictions of places and events that are crucial to the plot but which Alice herself could never have seen nor likely imagined.

[16]In this regard I share Brian McHale's (2012: 120) questions, which he directs to Alan Palmer's work in particular, about the centrality of "mind" in the cognitive paradigm: "If narrative is essentially identical to mental functioning, one is tempted to wonder what, if anything, is left over. Is there anything in a narrative that is *not* mind?" McHale goes on to point to the methodological limitations arising from this lack of conceptual granularity: "Ultimately, if everything in narrative is mind, then hasn't the very category of *fictional consciousness* or *representation of consciousness* been rendered redundant? Under the "whole mind" hypothesis, is it even useful any longer to maintain a separate category of *represented consciousness*?" (120).

fundamental ideas about texts and, in the process, to see print as well as electronic texts with fresh eyes," I want to suggest that although it may appear that the visual, kinesthetic, and algorithmic affordances of games and digital fictions like *Inanimate Alice* outstrip the capacities of print fiction to put readers in palpably ethical situations, all fictions, in all media, interpellate their audiences in ethically significant ways by virtue of their status as rhetorically configured messages. To provide a few examples of this ethical interpellation via the rhetorical structures of ink-on-paper narratives, I want to return briefly to the three print novels I mention above – Amis's *Time's Arrow*, Ishiguro's *Never Let Me Go*, and Hamid's *How to Get Filthy Rich in Rising Asia* – to point out that they are all "programmed" to lure the reader's imagination into morally fraught situations comparable to the obligation I confront at the checkpoint in *Inanimate Alice*. Although they cannot offer me the option to go back and alter the conditions of the story world, as does Alice's matryoshka game, they all oblige me to make an imaginative effort with significant consequences not only for my intellectual comprehension of the story's ethical ramifications but also for my affective *experience* of those ramifications. Moreover, as I argue in the case of *Inanimate Alice*, these texts' appeals to my moral imagination – their interpellations – cannot be comprehensively described as invitations to read their characters' minds or infer their authors' intentions.

Amis's *Time's Arrow* depicts the life of Odilo Unverdorben, a Nazi doctor exiled in the United States, in a painstakingly reversed chronological order, from his death to his birth, and to complicate matters further, the story is narrated by the doctor's own alienated "soul" – or perhaps his conscience – who for most of the novel refers to Unverdorben in the third person. In his essay on *Time's Arrow*, Phelan (2010: 223–224) describes how the novel's unconventional progression and focalization work in tandem to produce a complex juxtaposition of reliable and unreliable narration that in turn serves to complicate and intensify the reader's experience of Unverdorben's actions: "Amis uses the interrelation between the ethics of the telling and the ethics of the told to activate his audience's ethical imagination about both the condition of the Nazi doctors and the horror of what they did" (226). Here Phelan precisely identifies the features of the novel that led me to assign it in a class focused on literature and the responsible conduct of scientific research. The atrocities represented in *Time's Arrow* spurred the first internationally recognized statutes on research ethics, the 1947 Nuremburg Code, but for my purposes the pedagogical value of Amis's novel derives neither from the details it provides about these violations nor from its insights into the psychology of the perpetrators. Its value, rather, comes from its mobilization of what Maria Mäkelä calls "the peculiarly textual and con-structed nature of *literary experientiality*" (2014: 130). The disorienting narrative structures in *Time's Arrow* require readers to make an effort to retain both their temporal and moral bearings. Focalized in the odd character Phelan calls "Soul," Amis's narrative interpellates its readers into a position of intimate proximity alongside but only rarely congruent with Unverdorben's consciousness. As I see it, this interpellation represents less an invitation to enter into Unverdorben's thoughts than an obligation to witness his actions from an excruciatingly close vantage point, which narrows but never entirely closes the historical distance that can render twenty-first-century readers' horror at the Nazi atrocities perfunctory rather than profoundly felt.[17] Many texts do a far better job of teaching us about

---

[17]For more extensive analyses of the relationship between the narrative form of *Time's Arrow* and its ethical impact on the reader, see Phelan (2012: 2010) and Martínez-Alfaro (2011).

what made those atrocities possible, but few can match Amis's novel's capacity to stimulate not only outrage but also the urge to step back and to set boundaries that inspired the Nuremburg Code and informed subsequent protocols such as the Declaration of Helsinki and the Common Rule.

One of the core principles of these codes of conduct is "respect for persons," a commitment closely associated with the practice of securing informed consent from human subjects prior to their involvement in a research project. Reading Ishiguro's *Never Let Me Go* offers students a compelling opportunity to reflect on the limitations of informed consent, which has long been the target of critique among ethicists. The novel is narrated by Kathy H., a girl who, like all her classmates at her boarding school, has been cloned – and will ultimately be killed – to supply organs for transplant. Strikingly, although her destiny is revealed to her early in the novel, Kathy narrates her story as if the conditions of her existence were natural and inevitable, however sad, even after two of her closest friends succumb to the lethal harvesting. Unlike Unverdorben, Kathy is a victim rather than a perpetrator, but her unreliable narration has a disorienting effect similar to that of Unverdorben's soul in *Time's Arrow*: readers must work to keep their moral bearings and imagine alternative values to those Kathy has accepted. Some of this work certainly involves attempting to read the minds of the characters of Miss Emily and Madame, who advocate – unsuccessfully – for the abolition of the cloning program, but speculating about their good intentions can only partially resolve the frustration of witnessing what is essentially Kathy's complicity in her own murder at the hands of medical science. Here I would return to Walsh (2007: 100) and argue that the narrative discourse of *Never Let Me Go* interpellates the reader in a way that exceeds "the perspectival in any limited perceptual or cognitive sense (the domain of focalization), to become an organizing concept for ideology." While the focalization in Kathy's consciousness permits me to know that she is resigned to her fate, my futile impulse to reject her resignation is a response to the ideological apparatus within which she experiences her victimization as rational and legitimate. My conflicted ethical positioning in this novel's discourse dramatizes the problem of placing too much confidence in informed consent in real-world research, which, according to Susan Sherwin (2005: 159), "relies heavily on the privatized practice of obtaining informed consent from fully briefed individual subjects to protect against the abuse of subjects." Writing from a feminist perspective, Sherwin argues that in the context of marginalized social groups, in particular, such an emphasis on individual autonomy risks overlooking the complex interconnections between indivi-duals' choices and the welfare of the communities to which they belong. Faced with these uncertainties, Sherwin suggests that "an explicit discussion of the relationship between oppression and research would make clear why even the best efforts at obtaining informed consent cannot be sufficient to establish that the research is morally acceptable" (159). Training in the responsible conduct of research must address the pitfalls of informed consent, which have serious implications for researchers and their subjects across a wide range of disciplines. *Never Let Me Go* offers students a particularly compelling opportunity to confront this issue; grappling with Kathy's unreliable narration powerfully attunes them to the potential unreliability of the protocol.

Like *Time's Arrow*, Hamid's *How to Get Filthy Rich in Rising Asia* positions its reader uncomfortably close to a character whose actions most of us would condemn, achieving this effect by way of its relentless second-person address. Framed as an instruction manual for aspiring entrepreneurs in an unnamed South Asian country, the novel methodically tracks the ascendance of the protagonist – "you" – from an impoverished boy in a rural village to the owner of a powerful bottled-water company, providing rationalizations all along the way for the unscrupulous and sometimes brutal behavior that make "your" success possible. The novel does allow – and in a sense dictates – access to "your" mental life, but I would argue again that a significant measure of the moral force of *How to Get Filthy Rich* comes from its rhetorical summoning of the reader into an disturbing position vis-à-vis an ideological system that is only partially conveyed in the form of characters' thoughts. For Walsh (2007: 99), second-person address in fiction constitutes "perhaps the most overt example of interpellation": as he explains,

> a narrative audience is unlikely to feel specifically and individually addressed by a narrative's use of the second person: certainly they do not generally respond as if they were. But to feel interpellated, certainly; in the sense that the second person can generate a subject position specified in terms of imaginative collaboration with the authorial address, with which an individual reader may engage, responsively or resistantly, in a more or less conscious exercise of perspectival engagement.

Although I recognize that *How to Get Filthy Rich* is not a real self-help book and appreciate the ethical cushioning of Hamid's essentially comic deployment of that genre, the novel's narrative structure nonetheless prompts me to resist the profit-at-any-cost ideology to which it encourages me to subscribe. Like the inventively displaced focalization in *Time's Arrow* and the profound unreliability of Ishiguro's Kathy H., the second-person address in Hamid's novel provokes me not only to dissociate from the moral values represented in the story world but also to affirm, if only in inchoate ways, alternative values. All of these rhetorical strategies are akin to the conditional statement in the ActionScript of *Inanimate Alice*, insofar as they are specific features of the narrative discourse that obligate readers to recalibrate their own moral sensibilities in response to the fiction's ethically charged appeals.

In pedagogical terms, each of the scenarios these novels present – the torture of human beings in the name of "science," the cloning of human beings to serve as disposable organ donors, the manipulation and betrayal of human beings for personal financial gain – are tailor-made for comparisons among philosophical frameworks for ethical reasoning, for example Immanuel Kant's categorical imperative to treat other people as ends in themselves, Jeremy Bentham's utilitarian "Greatest Happiness Principle," and Carol Gilligan's feminist model of the ethics of care. At the same time, the creeping sense of unease, frustration, and revulsion students experience as a result of their captivation by the focalizing structures and narrative progressions of these novels presents an equally rich focus of ethical reflection: alongside the question "How do we apply the available ethical frameworks to identify and address the moral problems represented in this text?" students can be led to address the question "Which of the available ethical frameworks best describes my subjective response to this text's appeal to my emotions and values in relation to the moral problems they represent?" For some of them, that experience will resonate with Kant's "respect for the moral law,"[18] others with what David Hume (1995: 87) calls the "sentiment of disapprobation, which, by the structure of human nature, we unavoidably feel at the

---

[18]In the context of my present discussion of ethically oriented literary pedagogy, I find Ido Geiger's (2011: 163) description of Kant's idea particularly resonant: "This feeling of respect for the moral law, or better, the capacity for feeling respect for the law – this *affective attunement to the claims of morality* – is a necessary condition of moral agency. It is not our duty to acquire this capacity – although it is our duty to cultivate it."

apprehension of barbarity or treachery," still others with the disturbance of the ego's equanimity that for Emmanuel Levinas heralds the advent of the Other.[19] The differences among students' affinities for particular descriptions of moral impulses make for provocative and productive class discussions, and they often vary from text to text. Attending in this manner to the rhetorical appeals of novels and stories, in addition to the fictional worlds and minds they represent, not only permits students to "talk about their feelings" in a rigorous way, but also encourages them to step back from and reflect on their initial, habitual responses, subjecting them to critique, and assessing them in relation to the demands of the formal codes of ethics that will govern their future professional activities.

In light of the examples of *Inanimate Alice* and these three print novels, Palmer's definition of narrative fiction, which I quote above, as "in essence, the presentation of fictional mental functioning" seems to me analogous to asserting that the Jewish Museum in Berlin is, in essence, a collection of historical artifacts. Both assertions are correct, of course, but in the case of the museum the description sidelines the essential role Daniel Libeskind's innovative (and controversial) architectural design plays in organizing those artifacts into a narrative of Jewish history while at the same time introducing voids and enclosures that complicate the visitor's physical, emotional, and moral progress toward whatever sense of coherence, completion, or obligation that story might inspire in them. In the case of fiction, any text's invitation to take an ethical stance in relation to the fictional world it represents presupposes, as Herman suggests, an invitation to assume an intentional stance vis-à-vis the text itself as the product of a human mind. The invitation does not, however, presuppose that reading the mind of the text's creator, or the minds of the characters inhabiting its world, will be the reader's only means of ethical engagement. As I have tried to show, the discursive architecture of the narrative itself exerts its own shaping effect on the reader's experience and plays a crucial role in activating the fiction's moral agency.

6. Readdressing the invitation

As I indicated at the start, I do not wish to discount the power of mind-reading in the experience of fiction; I have instead tried to point out that the model overlooks a valuable capacity of fictional discourse to attune readers to a sense of responsibility – to their own capacity to feel responsible – that does not require them to construe characters' thoughts or authors' intentions. I recognize, of course, that the austere, abstract, "impersonal" rhetorical appeal I have been describing, like the abstract codes of conduct with which I have associated it, actualizes its full ethical potential only in the context of particular lived experiences, in which our ability to ascribe intentions, thoughts, and feelings to others

---

[19]Given my focus on Walsh's redeployment of Althusser's concept of interpellation, it is striking to note that Levinas at times uses the term "interpellation" to describe the appeal of the Other, as in this passage from "Phenomenon and Enigma" (1987: 64–65): "Across the unbreakable chain of significations, standing out again the historical conjuncture, was there not an expression, a face facing and interpellating, coming from the depths, cutting the threads of the context? Did not a neighbor approach?" Martínez-Alfaro's (2011) compelling reading of *Time's Arrow* draws heavily on Levinasian ethics.

is indispensible. Francisco Varela (1999: 73) is right to argue, in the course of his effort to integrate cognitive science with a range of wisdom traditions, that "compassionate concern cannot be created merely through norms and rationalistic injunctions. It must be developed and embodied through disciplines that facilitate the letting-go of ego-centered habits and enable compassion to become spontaneous and self-sustaining." Reading fiction is certainly one of those disciplines, but making the most of fiction's resources means accounting, critically and pedagogically, for all of them. Avoiding the reductive formalism of the Common Core by grounding a literary pedagogy in the mind-reading model risks distracting teachers and students from the ethical resources inherent in the structural, rhetorical features of fictional discourse. In an earlier essay (Bancroft and Rabinowitz 2011: 334), Bancroft and Rabinowitz themselves note how "the joy students get from reading characters' minds is so powerful that it sometimes deflects their attention from other important details – and from what they already know." Overlooking any of the distinctive ethical resources embedded in the discourse of fiction and, as a consequence, under-utilizing the discipline-specific strategies for identifying and *activating* those resources seems ill-advised at a time when the field of literary studies, at least in the American school system, is faced with proving its irreplaceable pedagogical value while simultaneously maintaining its intellectual integrity.

To come back to the pedagogical concerns with which I started, when I try to imagine the ethical benefits of a disciplined, conscientious engagement with fiction for not only students on their way to becoming English teachers, novelists, and game designers but also those who are on their way to becoming attorneys, bankers, and biomedical researchers, I think of that benefit as deriving from a visceral, often pleasurable, sometimes disturbing experience of a shift from a sense of themselves as people with options to a sense of themselves as people with obligations. Fiction facilitates such a shift not only because it invites readers into a web of interpersonal relationships, all of which depend upon a robust Theory of Mind to function adequately, but also because it summons them into a circuit of transpersonal appeals embodied in the social contract, the law, and the various moral codes, formal and informal, governing large and small social groups.

The emphasis on utility, productivity, and "career readiness" at all levels of American education directs the bulk of resources and energy to maximizing students' options, but for many Americans those options are neither as plentiful nor as promising as they used to be, a situation that is provoking American students and teachers alike to recalibrate their goals and reassess their values. "Before the financial crash," Andrew Delbanco (2012: 148) observes, "students were 'fleeing' from useless subjects such as literature or the arts, and flocking to 'marketable' subjects such as economics. Now, in the lingering aftermath of the global financial crisis, the flight continues; many students are also wondering what, in fact, is useful for what." The current instability of so many institutions in American society, a precariousness that is prompting many Americans to do some soul-searching, may actually offer teachers of literature opportunities to reassert the value of their contribution to individual and collective flourishing. The Great Recession has raised the stakes considerably; one of the challenges of an ethically engaged literary pedagogy today is to make the reading of literature an occasion for students to imagine the *dwindling* of their personal options as an *expansion* of their interpersonal obligations. Amidst the extreme economic asymmetries, intense anxieties, and smoldering conflicts of contemporary American society, that challenge, daunting as it is, seems well worth taking on.

REFERENCES

Amis, Martin. 1992. *Time's arrow*. New York: Vintage.

Bancroft, Corrine & Paul J. Rabinowitz. 2011. Cats, dogs, and social minds: Learning from Alan Palmer–and sixth graders. *Style* 45(2),333–338.

Bok, Derek. 2013. *Higher education in America*. Princeton, NJ: Princeton University Press.

Booth, Wayne C. 1983. *The rhetoric of fiction*. Chicago: University of Chicago Press.

Caracciolo, Marco. 2012. On the experientiality of stories: A follow-up on David Herman's "Narrative theory and the intentional stance." *Partial Answers: Journal of Literature and the History of Ideas* 10(2),197–221.

Charon, Rita. 2008. *Narrative medicine: Honoring the stories of illness*. Oxford: Oxford University Press.

Ciccoricco, David. 2012. Focalization and digital fiction. *Narrative* 20(3),255–276.

Ciccoricco, David. 2013a. Digital fiction and worlds of perspective. In Alice Bell, Astrid Ensslin & Hans Rustad (eds.), *Analyzing Digital Fiction*, 39–56. New York: Routledge.

Ciccoricco, David. 2013b. Focalization and digital fiction. *Narrative* 20(3),255–276.

Cohn, Dorrit. 1998. *The distinction of fiction*. Baltimore: Johns Hopkins University Press.

The common core state standards for English language arts and literacy in history/social studies, science, and technical subjects. 2014. Common Core State Standards Initiative. http://www.corestandards.org/ (last accessed 26 October 2014).

Curriculum. n.d. In Inanimatealice.com, http://www.inanimatealice.com/curriculum.html (last accessed 10 October 2014).

Delbanco, Andrew. 2012. *College: What it was, is, and should be*. Princeton, NJ: Princeton University Press.

Eagleton, Terry. 2013. *How to read literature*. New Haven, CT: Yale University Press.

Geiger, Ido. 2011. Kant on the affective moods of morality. In Hagi Kenaan D & Ilit Ferber (eds.), *Philosophy's moods: The affective grounds of thinking*, 159–173. New York: Springer.

Hallmarks of contemporary ethical issues classes. 2014. Office of General Education, University of Hawai'i at Mānoa, http://www.hawaii.edu/gened/focus/e.htm (last accessed 22 October 2014).

Hamid, Mohsin. 2013. *How to get filthy rich in rising Asia*. New York: Riverhead.

Harper, Ian. n.d. Digital literacy on whiteboards. *Alice's School Report* (3), http://issuu.com/inanimatealice/docs/school_report_3, (last accessed 10 October 2014).

Hayles, N. Katherine. 2003. Translating media: Why we should rethink textuality. *Yale Journal of Criticism* 16(2),263–290.

Herman, David. 2004. *Story logic: Problems and possibilities of narrative*. Lincoln: University of Nebraska Press.

Herman, David. 2008. Narrative theory and the intentional stance. *Partial Answers: Journal of Literature and the History of Ideas* 6(2),233–260.

Herman, David. 2013. *Storytelling and the sciences of mind*. Cambridge, MA: MIT Press.

Herman, David, James Phelan, Peter J Rabinowitz, Brian Richardson & Robyn Warhol. 2012. *Narrative theory: Core concepts and critical debates*. Columbus: Ohio State University Press.

Hogan, Patrick Colm. 2003. *The mind and its stories: Narrative universals and human emotion*. Cambridge, MA: Cambridge University Press.

Hogan, Patrick Colm. 2011. *Affective narratology: The emotional structure of stories*. Lincoln: University of Nebraska Press.

Hume, David. 1995. *An enquiry concerning the principles of morals*. Edited by J. B. Schneewind. Indianapolis, IN: Hackett.

Ishiguro, Kazuo. 2005. *Never let me go*. New York: Knopf.

Jay, Paul. 2014. *The humanities "crisis" and the future of literary studies*. New York: Palgrave Macmillan.

Keen, Suzanne. 2007. *Empathy and the novel*. Oxford: Oxford University Press.

Levinas, Emmanuel. 1987. Phenomenon and enigma. In Emmanuel Levinas, *Collected philosophical papers*, translated by Alphonso Lingis, 61–73. Dordrecht: Martinus Nijhoff.

Lipari, Lisbeth. 2014. *Listening, thinking, being: Toward an ethics of attunement*. University Park, PA: Penn State University Press.

Mäkelä, Maria. 2013. Cycles of narrative necessity: Suspect tellers and the textuality of fictional minds. In Lars Bernaerts, Dik de Geest, Luc Herman & Bart Vervaeck (eds.), *Stories and minds: Cognitive approaches to literary narrative*, 129–151. Lincoln: University of Nebraska Press.

Martínez-Alfaro, Maria Jésus. 2011. Where madness lies: Holocaust representation and the ethics of form in Martin Amis's *Time's arrow*. In Susana Onega & Jean-Michel Ganteau (eds.), *Ethics and trauma in contemporary British fiction*, 127–154. Amsterdam: Rodopi.

McHale, Brian. 2012. Narrative minds revisited. *Narrative* 20(1),115–124.

Murphy, T. 2014. The tragedy of the common core. *Mother Jones* (September/October), 37–68.

Newton, Adam Zachary. 1997. *Narrative ethics*. Cambridge, MA: Harvard University Press.

Page, Ruth. 2008. Inanimate Alice by Kate Pullinger & Chris Joseph. *Magazine Electronique du CIAC* 30, http://magazine.ciac.ca/archives/no_30/sommaire.htm (last accessed 22 October 2014).

Palmer, Alan. 2004. *Fictional minds*. Lincoln: University of Nebraska Press.

Penny, Simon. 2004. Representation, enaction, and the ethics of simulation. In Noah Wardrip-Fruin & Pat Harrigan (eds.), *First person: New media story, performance, and game*, 73–84. Cambridge, MA: MIT Press.

Phelan, James. 1996. *Narrative as rhetoric: Technique, audiences, ethics, ideology*. Columbus: Ohio State University Press.

Phelan, James. 2005. *Living to tell about it: A rhetoric and ethics of character narration*. Ithaca, NY: Cornell University Press.

Phelan, James. 2007. *Experiencing fiction: Judgments, progressions, and the rhetorical theory of narrative*. Columbus: Ohio State University Press.

Phelan, James. 2010. Teaching narrative as rhetoric: The example of *Time's arrow*. *Pedagogy* 10(1), 217–228.

Phelan, James. 2012. The ethics and aesthetics of backward narration in Martin Amis's *Time's arrow*. In Jakob Lothe, Susan Rubin Suleiman & James Phelan (eds.) *After testimony: The ethics and aesthetics of Holocaust narrative for the future*, 120–139. Columbus: Ohio State University Press.

Pullinger, Kate. 2008. Digital fiction: From the page to the screen. *Communications in Computer and Information Science* 7, 120–126.

Pullinger, Kate & Chris Joseph. 2005 (continuing). *Inanimate Alice*, http://www.inanimatealice.com/ (last accessed 22 October 2014).

Rabinowitz, Peter. J. & Corinne Bancroft. 2014. Euclid at the core: Recentering literary education. *Style* 48(1),1–34.

Richardson, Brian. 2006. *Unnatural voices: Extreme narration in modern and contemporary fiction*. Columbus: Ohio State University Press.

Richardson, Brian. 2014. Learning to read. *Style* 48(1),76–78.

Sicart, Miguel. 2011. The Ethics of Computer Games. Cambridge, MA: MIT Press.

Sherwin, Susan. 2005. Belmont revisited through a feminist lens. In James F. Childress, Eric M. Meslin & Harold T. Shapiro (eds.), *Belmont revisited: Ethical principles for research with human subjects*, 148–164. Washington, DC: Georgetown University Press.

Stewart, Gavin. 2010. The paratexts of *Inanimate Alice*: Thresholds, genre expectations and status. *Convergence: The International Journal of Research into New Media Technologies* 16(1),57–74.

Varela, Francisco J. *Ethical know-how: Action, wisdom, cognition*. Palo Alto, CA: Stanford University Press, 1999.

Walsh, Richard. 2007. *The rhetoric of fictionality: Narrative theory and the idea of fiction*. Columbus Ohio State University Press.

Zunshine, Lisa. 2006. *Why we read fiction: Theory of mind and the novel*. Columbus: Ohio State University Press.

Zunshine, Lisa. 2008. *Strange concepts and the stories they make possible: Cognition, culture, narrative*. Baltimore: Johns Hopkins University Press.

Zunshine, Lisa. 2014. What reading fiction has to do with doing well academically. *Style* 48(1),87–92.

"Take that you intellectuals!" and "kaPOW!": Adam Thirlwell and the Metamodernist Future of Style

ALISON GIBBONS

Passing the postmodern

The future has always been a controversial place, a melting pot of possible and impossible worlds at which we can only guess. In cultural and artistic terms, the present moment itself is also not without critical debate. Nevertheless, among international scholars of contemporaneity, a critical consensus does appear to be forming – a consensus that we have in some way laid postmodernism to rest.

In 1990, John Frow was asking the question, already in the past tense, "What was postmodernism?" while Linda Hutcheon, in the epilogue to the second edition of her seminal book *The Politics of Postmodernism*, admits, "the post-modern may well be a twentieth century phenomenon, that is, a thing of the past" (2002: 165). She continues, "The postmodern moment has passed, even if its discursive strategies and its ideological critique continue to live on – as do those of modernism – in our contemporary twenty-first-century world" (2002: 181). As Toth and Brooks (1999: 1) point out, despite Hutcheon's definitive claims that postmodernism has "passed," that "it's over" (Hutcheon 2002: 166), there is an ambiguity to her words: while she claims that the temporal specificity of post-modernity is "a thing of the past," she also suggests that aspects of its style and epistemology "live on." This is why, although the latter intimates that a new cultural epoch that utilizes postmodern discursive strategies may be upon us, Toth (2002) and Toth and Brooks (1999) suggest that it is more accurate to think of postmodernism not as in the past but as *passed* or better, as *passing*.

Since the mid-1990s, Toth and Brooks claim, "we have been engaged in a process of mourning, a process that sees us trying to break (finally) with postmodernism – or, at the very least, to break (finally) with postmodernism's apparent solipsism and irresponsibility, its ethical and social vacuity" (1999: 3–4). Interestingly, and perhaps also deliberately, Toth and Brooks' own articu-lation contains the very same slippage as Hutcheon's, speaking as they do of a "process" but one that seeks finality.

Of course, making conclusive remarks about the here and now as part of a paradigm shift into a new cultural epoch is difficult, to say the least. As Gąsiorek and James write in the introduction ("Fiction since 2000") to a 2012 special issue of *Contemporary Literature* on post-millennial fiction, "it can be tricky to obtain some critical purchase on a body of writing that's so close to us, so immediate that it sounds contrived to say that we can retro-spectively frame the first decade of the 2000s with the same coherence as we can, for instance, the 1980s or 1990s" (2012: 609–610). For Gąsiorek and James, the way around this is to examine post-millennial writing not through cultural periodization but "through the optic of *commitment*" (2012: 610; original italics). Whether one takes the critical position that postmodernism is past/passed or passing, the recent fervor for ethical, political, social, and environmental commitments is telling in that it appears to indicate, at the very least, an epistemological shift away from the superficiality of postmodern irony and, at its greatest, the onset of a more substantial post-postmodern turn.

Linda Hutcheon ends the epilogue to the second edition of *The Politics of Postmodernism* with a provocation: "Post-postmodernism needs a new label of its own, and I conclude, therefore, with this challenge to readers to find it – and name it for the twenty-first-century" (2002: 181). This challenge has not gone without response. Indeed, a number of scholars have christened the post-postmodern by developing a critical framing, and it is possible to group such framings into five thematic strands. Firstly, Lipovetsky (2005) conceives of the contemporary as "hypermodern," which he sees as a period of hyperconsumerism and of great anxieties. Secondly, Kirby's (2009) "digimodernism" and Samuels's (2008) "automodernism" foreground the digitalization of twenty-first-century society, particularly in terms of its impact on textuality. Jessica Pressman (2014) also considers the digital, but her book *Digital Modernism* provides a bridge from the digital into the third strand in which a modernist legacy is traced within contemporary literature (Walkowitz 2006; James 2012; James and Seshagiri 2014). The fourth strand represents a reactionary and troubled rapport with postmodernism, calling instead for a return to realism, humanism, and an ethical relation to the social world: in McLaughlin's (2004; 2012) and Timmer's (2010) "post-postmodernism," in Green's (2005) "late postmodernism," and in related discussions of David Foster Wallace's work as "new sincerity" (Kelly 2010) and "postirony" (Konstantinou 2012), this is a response to the self-referential nature of postmodernism amidst a TV generation of authors seeking to reconnect fiction to social reality. In Moraru's (2011) "cosmodernism," literary works press for relationality to others in the globalizing world, while for Giles (2012) and Holland (2013) it takes the form of "post humanism" and "postmodern humanism" respectively. In the fifth and final strand are approaches that situate themselves somewhere between the ideologies and critical practices of modernism and postmodernism, namely Eshelman's (2008) "performatism," Bourriaud's (2009a; 2009b) "altermodernism" (see also Gibbons 2012), and Vermeulen and van den Akker's (2010) as well as Martin's (2012) and Contos'(2013) "metamodernism."

These strands are not entirely disparate; the boundaries between them are fuzzy. While the present and future moment is read through differing interpretive lenses, taken together, these framings help to build a critical vision of the recent shift in commitments and the contemporary *Jetztzeit* that succeeds postmodernism. This article offers an account of the cultural moment as metamodern. In doing so, it does not subscribe inflexibly to the term but presents a considered synthesis of the aforementioned strands of contemporaneity. In the next section, I introduce "metamodernism" as the term is employed within this article. Despite the growing prevalence of metamodernism as a term to denote the cultural *Jetzteit* of the late twentieth and early twenty-first centuries, a comprehensive study of the ways in which contemporary literature relates to the metamodern paradigm has yet to be written. This paper therefore offers a pioneering look at the textual devices used by metamodernist writers by presenting a detailed case study. This takes the form of a stylistic analysis of a piece of metamodernist fiction, namely Adam Thirlwell's (2012a) novella *Kapow!*

The metamodern present

In their 2010 article "Notes on metamodernism," Vermeulen and van den Akker present the first account of metamodernism. Like many critical commentators previously and subsequently, they argue that the "postmodern years of plenty, pastiche, and parataxis are over" (2010: 2) and acknowledge the plethora of positions as to why and when this cultural shift took place. Indeed, various factors are frequently mentioned. In terms of events, critics repeatedly point to the 1989 fall of the Berlin Wall, the 9/11/2001 terrorist attacks on the World Trade Center, the 2007–2008 financial crisis, and the ensuing anarchic forms of global revolution (the Arab Spring, the 2010 London student riots against austerity, and the rise of the Occupy movement since 2011), while cultural factors such as economic turbulence and inequality, digital and technological development, and climate change are oft cited. All of this, it should be said, is (even if only implicitly) set against a backdrop of late globalization.

In her epilogue to the second edition of *The Politics of Postmodernism*, Hutcheon was careful not to relegate "the discursive strategies" or "ideological critique" (2002: 181) of postmodernism – or of modernism for that matter – entirely to the past, as mentioned in the introduction to this article. Indeed, it is not that the textual tricks of the postmodern have perished into history, but that its archetypes and ideals have lost their potency. As Lipovetsky argues in his account of the hypermodern, the "increasing insecurity of people's lives has supplanted the carefree 'postmodern' attitude" (2005: 40). As a result, the dominant character of metamodern artistic practice is a shift to what Vermeulen and van den Akker call the "aesth-ethical" (2010: 2). Aesth-ethical commitment pervades what I am here calling metamodernist writing: it is opposed to the injustices of global capitalism, concerned by the increased digitalization and hyper-reality of society, conscious of the shifting social relationships in a globalizing world, and it hopes for a shared sustainable future, however untenable that may be. In other words, metamodernism is concerned with global ethics. What I am arguing, essentially, is that metamodernist writers share with global ethicists a commitment to justice, though while global ethicists seek to shape debates and find solutions, the writing of metamodernist authors has the ability to raise the consciousness and conscience of the general public: fiction thus becomes a vehicle through which to increase awareness of contemporary insecurities – environmental, social, political. And, as Widdows powerfully states in her introduction to global ethics as a discipline, these "things matter in terms of how we understand human beings now and into the future and are at the heart of creating a world where human beings are treated ethically" (2011: 1–2).

This humanist aspiration is articulated in the allied issues of relationality and complicity. "Relationality," put forward by Moraru in his book *Cosmodernism* is "a strong ethos of cultural-epistemological and existential indebtedness" (2011: 21). Relationality signifies our human connectedness in the globalizing world and consequently our ethical obligations to each other. In Moraru's words, this is "another way of saying that 'we' owe it to others, but also to ourselves, to own up to how much we owe them, by behaving accordingly" (2011: 21). In metamodernist writing, this means acknowledging our complicity in the state of global affairs (from intersubjective memories to awareness of our participation in various political, economic, and environmental networks: for instance, of capital in the purchase of commercial goods or of the ecological in our decisions to recycle or not). Stylistically, this humanist commitment can be seen in metamodernist fiction in the way writers employ perceptual deixis, free indirect discourse, and modes of address, particularly in their play with the possibilities of pronominal positioning.

Vermeulen and van den Akker suggest that in order to communicate aesth-ethical commitment, metamodernist artworks "oscillate" between modernism and postmodernism. More specifically, metamodernism "oscillates between a modern enthusiasm and a postmodern irony, between hope and melancholy, between naiveté and knowingness, empathy and apathy, unity and plurality, totality and fragmentation, purity and ambiguity" (2010: 5–6). Lipovetsky similarly identifies a contemporary *Jetztzeit* that is "a paradoxical combination of frivolity and anxiety, euphoria and vulnerability, playfulness and dread" (2005: 40). While modernism was fuelled by an enthusiasm for utopian thinking and an enlightened idealization of reason, and while postmodernism rejects such optimism in favor of nihilistic irony and distrust, metamodernism is flavored by the simultaneous and paradoxical sense of hope and future failure. Irony in metamodernist writing is, therefore, not a derisive apolitical performance but unreservedly committed to both promises that the locutionary act sets forth, both the surface meaning and its intended opposite. Another means in which metamodernism achieves its oscillation is through the assimilation of high and low cultural references. As a technique this might appear rather postmodern, yet it is employed in metamodernist writing not merely to create eclectic textuality but to present juxtapositions that evoke a reflection on contemporary culture. Similarly, metamodernist writing often contains everyday references, such as the explicit use of brand names, in a cloaked acknowledgement and criticism of commercialized culture.

While Vermeulen and van den Akker do not explicitly reference the changing order of the globalizing world, they do speak of three "geopolitical tendencies": "a deliberate being out of time, an intentional being out of place, and the pretense that that desired atemporality and displacement are actually possible even though they are not" (2010: 12). Placelessness and timelessness are illusory projects, but even so there is a sense that time and space operate differently under metamodern conditions. Nicolas Bourriaud, in describing altermodernism in *The Radicant* (2009b), similarly claims that the "major aesthetic phenomenon of our time is surely the intertwining of the properties of space and time, which turns the latter into a territory every bit as tangible as the hotel room where I am sitting right now or the noisy street that stretches beneath the window" (2009b: 79). On the surface, it might appear that there is a contradiction here: that time and space have been compressed *and* that time and space have been displaced. However, in its oscillating form metamodernism in fact embraces both of these seemingly competing urges. On the one hand, it emphasizes the specificity of time and place, while also denying it through what Bourriaud calls "the aesthetics of heterochrony" in which "delay (analogous to the 'pre-recorded') coexists with the *immediate* (or 'live') and with the anticipated" (2009a: 21; original italics). Vermeulen and van den Akker conclude "Notes on metamodernism":

> the metamodern should be understood as a spacetime that is both-neither ordered and disordered. Metamodernism displaces the parameters of the present with those of a future presence that is futureless; and it displaces the boundaries of our place with those of a surreal place that is placeless. For indeed, that is the destiny of the metamodern wo/man: to pursue a horizon that is forever receding. (2010: 12)

In their concluding remarks, the metaphor of time as space (in this case a "horizon") is evidently at play while the reference to displaced "parameters" and "boundaries" intimates an intermixing of temporal chronologies. In meta-modernist writing, heterochrony is often created through frequent temporal deictic shifts (e.g. changes in tense), while specificity is made manifest through the use of proper nouns providing specific geographical locations. Moreover, the breakdown of national borders and geographical boundaries in the globalizing world is often enacted in metamodernist writing through integrating lexis from different languages while the idea of the "glocal" (Robertson 1995) can be seen in the use of dialectical variants.

The discussion of the features of metamodernism provided in this section of the article is by no means exhaustive, but serves to suggest some of the cultural shifts of thought and emphasis that metamodernism entails. In the remainder of the article, close stylistic analysis will be used to demonstrate how Adam Thirlwell engages with the stylistic traits of metamodernism, as well as how he uses them as part of a metamodernist socio-political critique. The analysis progresses through the novella chronologically: section 1 studies the opening of *Kapow!* and specifically the way Thirlwell manipulates temporal and spatial deixis to create heterochrony; section 2 discusses the novella's multimodality and Thirlwell's notion of a "pure international"; section 3 considers the use of code-switching and shifts of register; section 4 focuses on reader address and point of view; and section 5 examines Thirlwell's use of free indirect discourse in relation to notions of "ethical kitsch." I start, though, with an introduction to *Kapow!* and to Adam Thirlwell as a writer.

Adam Thirlwell, metamodernism, and *Kapow!*

Adam Thirlwell is a British novelist whose debut novel *Politics* (2006) won him international recognition. This was followed by an award-winning critical work *Miss Herbert* (2007) and a second novel *The Escape* (2010), and by the time he wrote *Kapow!* Thirlwell had already established himself as an important novelist in the opening years of the twenty-first century. He describes himself in an interview (Gibbons, forthcoming) as a "mischievous radical," and his political affiliations – which he does not explicitly disclose – are evidently more socialist than they are neoliberal. Indeed, it seems fitting in this sense that Thirlwell's novella *Kapow!* focuses on what journalist Paul Mason (2012), in relation to such recent unrests as the Arab Spring, the student riots, and the Occupy move-ment, has called the "new global revolutions." Thirlwell's novel is therefore a time-specific work, grounding itself in the metamodern by engaging with truly contemporaneous issues. Moreover, in considering such global conflicts, Thirlwell constructs a narrative in which a self-conscious London-based narrator is writing a story set against the backdrop of the violent civil uprisings in Cairo, a story that has been told to him by Faryaq, a London taxi driver and brother of one of the central Egyptian characters. This recursive narrative structure of nested worlds creates multiplicities of place and time that sit alongside and within each other, thus creating a heterochronic topos. Moreover, the layering of worlds and space-time parameters is all the more tricky because *Kapow!* is a multimodal novella.[1] It is told in forty-nine short chapters, with throw-out pages

---

[1] As such, and with "footnoted" text traversing the page in various directions, the extracts presented in this article do not reproduce the novella visually. Rather, they are laid out in such a way as to allow ease of reading here.

and bifurcated footnotes that disrupt the central traditional block layout of text, traversing the page in alternate directions to the main body of the narrative.

1. Digital media and "the cartoon sounds for violence"

Kapow! begins with "As you will recall, folks, it seemed like everywhere they were starting revolutions" (Thirlwell 2012a: 5; all further quotations from the novella will be identified with page numbers alone). The opening immediately summons reader involvement through direct address in the form of a generalized second person. It also contains multiple temporal parameters through its temporal deictic structure: the verb phrase "will recall" encodes future time in the habitual modal auxiliary "will" while the main verb "recall" suggests a recent past, known by narrator and readers alike. This is followed by the simple past in "seemed" and the past continuous in "were starting." In temporal terms, then, not only does *Kapow!* immediately encode the heterochrony of metamodernist art, it depicts these "everywhere revolutions" as vague and ongoing and part of a shared global history to which readers, like us all, are witnesses. Thirlwell's labeling of his readership as "folks," however, is somewhat jarring – the low-culture tone of the register does not entirely fit with the semantics of the sentence; while "revolutions" carries serious connotations of violence and social conflict, the colloquial "folks" is reminiscent of the *Looney Tunes* closing slogan, "That's all folks!" Such shifts in register are characteristic of the linguistic games Thirlwell plays in *Kapow!*, but these are not games for games' sake as they might have been in postmodern playfulness. Rather, they form part of the author's metamodernist critique of the socio-political climate of contemporary times. Indeed in interview with Toby Lichtig, Thirlwell speaks of his admiration for "serious playfulness" (2011: 34), a phrase certainly in keeping with the metamodern oscillating aesthetic set out by Vermeulen and van den Akker (2010) and described above.

The narrator continues, "Everyone who was everywhere was using a videophone" (5) and later adds, "While in the miniature movies on the internet people were gathering in squares and ripping up pavements. It surprised me how easily you could do this – just prise up pavement, like a lawn" (5). Repetitions of "everyone" and "everywhere" emphasize the widespread scale of unrest, as does the way in which Thirlwell frequently starts sentences in *Kapow!* with the conjunction "while" functioning temporally to set up a syntactic structure of a subordinate clause followed by a main clause (as in "while X, Y"), only to omit that main clause. This gives the impression of events constantly happening somewhere else and simultaneously. Thirlwell's reference to "miniature movies on the internet" and the simile of ripping up "pavement, like lawn" suggests the ways in which, in the Western world, our understanding of such politically charged events is filtered through new technologies. The news and images reach us through second-hand media-saturated experiences, seemingly no more authentic than an animation.

Indeed, Thirlwell concludes *Kapow!*'s opening chapter with poignant critical reflection:

> Everywhere I looked I saw the cartoon sounds for violence: Wham! for instance, or Kapow! It sometimes scared me. Because you might want justice, or you might also want peacefulness. But then again, maybe you can't have true peacefulness if you also don't have justice. All of which might mean, I was simply thinking, that it might not be obvious how revolutionary you wanted yourself to be. You might not know where a revolution began. Or if you did, then where it ended. (5–6)

Not only does Thirlwell foreground how to a privileged Westerner (in his narrator's case a young and fairly politically naive London hipster) the ferocity of the violence happening elsewhere seems unreal and almost fantastical in its stylized media portrayal, but such events are also shown to challenge easy cognizance in that their status as events (both self-contained and as part of a larger chain of events) is intellectually contestable. This can be seen in the narrator's uncertainty about the desired goals of the uprising. Linguistically, this is clear from the use of the modal verb phrase "might want"; the frequency of epistemic modality in lexis such as "might," "maybe," and "might not know"; and the cluster of conjunctions – alternative "or" and adversative "but." The closing words of chapter one are vital for framing the polemics of the entire novella: "You might not know where a revolution began. Or if you did, then where it ended." In *Kapow!* Thirlwell uses linguistic style and multimodal design to comment on the entanglement of revolution and counter-revolution, and how literary form can participate in present and future debates on the nature of the ethical, social, and political injustices of the contemporary world.

2. The global, the multimodal, and imagining "new forms"

Thirlwell intends for his readers to identify the narrator of *Kapow!* as himself: Adam Thirlwell. There is no doubting this since early in *Kapow!* the narrator begins to expound his theories of the potentialities of language and literature as vehicles of travel through their capacity for immersion, adding the bifurcated footnote, "In my first book I'd played with space, then in my second I had the same kind of fun with time. But now I was done with these major categories. I was hoping that I could go minutely everywhere" (10). Like many metamodernist writers, Thirlwell sees form and style as central in enabling literature to engage with world affairs. In chapter seven, which features the first throw-out page in *Kapow!* Thirlwell's extra-textual and narratorial counterpart claims, "... as I listened to Faryaq I was still beginning to wonder if I could in some way construct my own Arabic novel. Or at least a pulp novelette, a zoom of pure joyfulness. Maybe the cartoon sound effects were right. The era was world-historical, so why couldn't I describe whatever stories I wanted and claim they were real?" (17). Underlying the narrator's thought processes are questions of nationhood and cultural belonging. As a white British author, is Thirlwell *allowed* to adopt the modes, conventions, and settings of an "Arabic novel"? In an introduction to a special issue of *McSweeney's* on translation (issue 42), Thirlwell advocates a literature that is "pure international" in its ability to borrow literary genres and cultural techniques (2012b). Thirlwell's qualms in undertaking what, in the *McSweeney's* introduction, he calls "the pure, unembarrassed inauthentic" are clearly expressed when he downgrades his own Arabic novel to a lower culture "pulp novelette" or a filmic "zoom." Ultimately though, Thirlwell advocates a "world-historical" aesthetic, one in which forms of culture and cultural production become global property.

As a novella about the Arab Spring, however, *Kapow!* is not a globalized appropriation of the Arabic novel that reinforces Western imperialism in some form of literary colonial rule. Certainly not, as Thirlwell defends *Kapow!* saying:

> I didn't want to be *topical*. I think instead it just had something to do with this new mania for connections, my idea of integrity that meant you had to follow every thought as far as you could, into all the sad dead ends. And to present this new way of thinking I began to imagine

new forms, like pull-out sentences, and multiple highspeed changes in direction. I imagined concertina pages of stories, pasted pictures. And why not? (18)

This is, of course, an accurate description of *Kapow!*, its multimodal innovations doing exactly what the narrator therein imagines. Moreover, Thirlwell's recognition of "this new mania for connections" might be read as an awareness of the "complex connectivity" (Tomlinson 1999) of the globalized world – that is, the way in which contemporary experience is characterized by the global interconnectedness of social, political, environmental, and economic interaction.

3. Switching codes and registers, "And you? Could you?"

Thinking about *Kapow!* in terms of "this new mania for connections," Thirlwell is not solely interested in composition but also the impact this has on the reading experience:

> I wanted to make reading an experience that aged you. If I'd had a slogan, that slogan would have been stolen from a poem by Mayakovsky. It would have been, dear reader, *And You, Could You?* So yes, it was at around this time that I was trying to read the newspapers as if everything was a possible sign, or symptom. I read *The New York Times* and *Le Monde* and *The Guardian* and the *New York Review of Books* and tried to think differently. I pasted things up. I made what in another line of work would be called my montages. All of which could lead to the very obvious $10,000 question: what was I avoiding, via this freestyle imagination, this crisis in which I found myself? I amn't, dear reader, going to say. Let's say that I just cherished this idea of writing something that would keep unfolding out of itself, a story that would take in as many other stories as possible. **Y**
> And of course one problem with this would be that the conversations in particular would be totally unreal because the words these people like Faryaq and Rustam used were French or Arabic or Uzbek or whatever, but so what? I wanted to enter a new era of world description. And if you begin to worry about these kind of limits, well why not worry about them all? Why not worry about, say
>
> > A. dying
> > B. things
> > C. thinking.
>
> And so on. You think any of those are verbal, buster? But basta.
>   **Y** So I began there, with Faryaq, in the freezing city of London, telling me about what was happening elsewhere, in the place of revolution. (19)[2]

Fittingly, this is the first concertina page in *Kapow!*, occurring immediately after Thirlwell's mention and introduction of the idea of writing as "new forms, like pull-out sentences." In this passage, Thirlwell continues to develop his notion of a "pure international," of a "world historic." This is particularly evident in the bifurcated footnote that digresses horizontally across the main body of text and then down the throw-out pages. Here, Thirlwell admits a potential problem with creating his own take on the Arabic novel: "that the conversations in particular would be totally unreal because the words these people like Faryaq and Rustam used were French or Arabic or Uzbek or whatever, but so what? I wanted to enter a new era of world description." While he admits that a certain level of multiculturalism or transnationality is not completely possible, the list of

---

[2]My use of **Y** within quotations from *Kapow!* is a close visual rendering of the actual symbol used to indicate the bifurcated footnotes in *Kapow!* These essentially occur in *Kapow!* as a footnote marker in place of the numerical footnote system that one might be more accustomed to seeing in academic writing.

abstract nouns that follows and the pointed question "You think any of those are verbal . . ?" suggest the narrator believes that, in form and thematic, his topical narrative itself will be universal enough. Or perhaps pluriversal might be more accurate, since the tale unfolds and proliferates, both in narratological terms with its web of stories and in material terms with its throw-out pages. In discourses that are keen to resist the standardizing forces of globalization, there has been a strong move towards "pluriversality" (Mignolo 2011): that is, rather than aiming for a universal world which carries with it connotations of cultural standardization, the favored approach moves towards a pluriversal world which embraces critical dialogues of and between diversity.

Thirlwell's final comment in the footnote demonstrates such a dialogue of diversity: not only does he call the reader "buster," another colloquial address that might lend itself to the language of cartoons, he writes, "You think any of those are verbal buster? But basta." Thirlwell employs both alliteration and code-switching. "Basta" is a word found in Italian, Spanish, and Portuguese, and means "stop," "enough." By code-switching, Thirlwell's prose engages with issues of language, globalization, and linguistic diversity not only on a theoretical level but in its stylistic composition.

The intermixing of different registers often found in metamodernist writing is also at work in this passage: the high-brow is acknowledged in the list of literary publications but counterbalanced by the mention of a "slogan" and "the $10,000 question," bringing to mind advertising campaigns and game shows respectively. The intertextual reference to Mayakovsky is similarly duplicitous: on one hand, as a central figure in Russian futurism, Mayakovsky seems to be an elitist literary allusion, while, on the other hand, the poetic line out of which the narrator extracts his slogan, "and you, / Could you play a nocturne On a flute of water-pipes?" itself blends high and low culture with the image of a classical musical composition potentially emerging from a domestic object.[3] Literary allusion similarly features in the narrator's address, "dear reader," a marked change from the colloquial "folks" of the opening, bringing with it a literary history of use in such canonical texts as Charlotte Bronte's *Jane Eyre* and James Joyce's *Finnegan's Wake*. Its second context of usage, "I amn't, dear reader, going to say" is interesting, though, due to the presence of linguistic deviation in Thirlwell's choice of "amn't,". This is a contracted form of the first-person singular present tense negative of the copula verb "to be," in this instance manifested as "am." From the perspective of historical linguistics, "amn't" dates back at least as far as the seventeenth century but, probably because the proximity of the nasals constrict ease of articulation, it fell out of common use. Found today only in Scottish and Irish [Hiberno] English (though it may also be a feature of West Yorkshire), its absence in Standard English is known as the "amn't gap" (Broadbent 2009). Thirlwell's use of the highly non-standard contraction therefore adds a dialectical or local variety to the text.

Direct address to the reader seems to be particularly fitting, since it places the reader in a relationship not just with *Kapow!*'s author/narrator but with the local and global events at its heart. As mentioned, Thirlwell's self-disclosed slogan to *Kapow!* is a duplicitous mixture of high and low culture. Yet it is not just a borrowed quotation. Thirlwell plays on an irony or sarcasm that he claims to be dubious about in *Kapow!* when he wonders, "Are you really still allowed this multiple sarcasm, I was thinking, when you haven't, let's say, earned it?" (73).

---

[3]From the poem "And You Think You Could?" by Vladimir Mayakovsky.

Kapow!'s slogan is underwritten by Thirlwell's cynicism and mockery in order to pose a serious question to the reader: *"And You, Could You?"* Interrogating global civil unrest, the nature of revolution, the discrepancies across and between the Western and Eastern worlds, *Kapow!* is multimodal and disruptive to the sort of immersive reading traditional literary layouts might allow. This is because Thirlwell wants to evoke solemn thought from the reader. He wants reading *Kapow!* to "age you" because he wants to elicit contemplation from the reader of their awareness and/or ignorance of global injustices. In asking the reader, *"And You, Could You?"* Thirlwell is asking the reader to acknowledge their complicity in world affairs and their global responsibilities.

4. The Reader, "It's always been about you"

Towards the end of *Kapow!* Thirlwell increasingly makes the reader's role more explicit. He opens chapter forty-three by disclosing:

> It's always been about you, dear reader. If you want to know what is really a digression and what isn't, in a story, then you have to wait until the end. Or, to put it another way: if you want to know which stories are within the stories, you have to wait until the end. And this might seem like the purest realism, but there is also, I was starting to think, a more magical way of thinking. **Y**
> But then, it all depends who is looking. From a certain height, if you can only get there, in your jet pack, maybe premonitions are visible everywhere.
> **Y** Because if a story's extended in one direction it might mean that the story you thought was real, in which all the other stories were contained, was in fact – like, wham! – part of another story, of which you knew nothing. Just as the reader is part of a story, of which the reader knows nothing. (71–72)

Placing the reader at the center of both the book and the greater aesthetic politic he is expounding, Thirlwell demonstrates the difficulty in understanding the significance of world events through clever stylistic constructions. There is inexact syntactic parallelism in the sentences, "If you want to know what is really a digression and what isn't, in a story, then you have to wait until the end. Or, to put it another way: if you want to know which stories are within the stories, you have to wait until the end." Thirlwell sets up a vague opposition through negation in the phrase "what is really a digression and what isn't" and complicates meaning in "which stories are within stories," with both phrases using indeterminate determiners ("what," "which") to thwart concrete meaning.

All of this, really, returns to Thirlwell's metamodernist critique of the real and unreal, the way in which the prolific reshaping of events by media discourses, such as television news reporting, prevent us from really knowing what is going on in the world. As he writes, "the story you thought was real, in which all the other stories were contained, was in fact – like, wham! – part of another story, of which you knew nothing. Just as the reader is part of a story, of which the reader knows nothing." Correspondingly, for all Thirlwell's emphasis upon the reader, this final comment in which the "reader knows nothing" is rather cutting, gesturing not only to readers' misinformation by the media but also perhaps their complacent role in this symbolic structuring of world knowledge. After all, the repeated conditional "If you want to know" is a hypothetical construction that questions both readers' knowledge *and* their desire for such knowledge.

Complicity and relationality (our involvement and our responsibility in the global systems, the social and political realms, that define the globalized world of the twenty-first century) are not effortless cognizance. They are ethical burdens (they "age" us), and so it's hardly surprising that sometimes we choose to ignore them. As Thirlwell writes casually: "it all depends who is looking. From a certain height, if you can only get there, in your jet pack, maybe premonitions are visible everywhere." The reference to "your jet pack" contains a metaphorical compression of time and space. The mention of height and the use of the spatial adverb "there" suggest the jet pack will transport its user up to a vantage point where they can see an entire terrain, and thus see how localities are connected. However, the jet pack, with its futuristic connotations, enables "premonitions," a noun that suggests potential temporal knowledge of that which is to come.

To put it another way, this is, on one hand, a cloaked critique of the notion of a panoramic, omniscient narrative perspective, found for example in "purest realism." On the other, it is an impossible aspiration, omniscience being something the narrator knows cannot be realized. For the reader of *Kapow!,* a jet pack view is certainly not achievable. In terms of their own reality and their place within the global systems of our time, readers cannot ever truly escape from their own positioning in relation to those systems. Similarly in reading *Kapow!,* readers are continually presented with shifting vantage points – of perspective, of place, of time, and of form in the novella's multimodality. It is not accidental that the bifurcated footnote "But then, it all depends who is looking" requires the reader to rotate the book ninety degrees to read the horizontal text. In style, narrative, and design then, *Kapow!* works against a singular, uncomplicated perspective, offering instead a proliferating panorama that can only be achieved through a (re)construction of its multiplicities and its connections.

5. *Against ethical kitsch, "because they know he's one of them"*

The idea of working against an uncomplicated perspective applies not only to *Kapow!*'s style and form, but also to its ideological engagements. Thirlwell clearly intends to question his readers and their political and ethical motives, and while he does this repeatedly and insistently, it is important to recognize that he does not let himself off the hook either. As the narrator's meetings and conversations with Faryaq, the London taxi driver, about the civil unrest in Cairo filter out, he tells his readers:

> As for me I went to watch some hipster Joe Swanberg movie where he asks sadly at the end Do Movies Matter? and it seemed so misplaced, this question, so full of pity. **Y**
> And as I left the cinema going up to Waterloo Bridge I was treated to my own version of crude montage, as I walked behind two people saying that they could only text if they were using predictive text except maybe the iPhone if you used the qwerty keyboard, while passing a guy begging on the bridge's steps. I looked at him and he looked at me. It was like that moment in the book where the aristocratic poet realises that all the clochards in Paris are grinning at him, because they know he's one of them. (74)

In this scene, Thirlwell juxtaposes the nonchalance of Western privilege with an image of Western poverty. This is inscribed in the lack of awareness of the two walkers whose unashamed discussion of the elite telecommunication brand iPhone appears to render them oblivious to the contrast in socio-economic circumstances. Thirlwell demonstrates this in his depiction of their conversation: "they could only text if they were using predictive text except maybe the iPhone if you used the qwerty keyboard." This is highly colloquial in its unwieldy and improper use of grammar as well as being written as free indirect speech. In the context of *Kapow!*, it gives the impression both of Thirlwell as narrator overhearing the dialogue as well as representing the intersubjective, and absorbed, perspective of the two speech participants. In contrast, and foregrounded due to its brevity, the visual exchange between narrator and beggar is loaded with significance: "I looked at him and he looked at me." Moreover, its syntactic parallelism is indicative of the mutual or shared moment of compassion that Thirlwell describes. The stylized juxtaposition of these two self-absorbed technophiles with the meaningful exchange between beggar and narrator (who represents an extratextual counterpart of Thirlwell himself) might be construed as a depiction of the author's own knowing benevolence. Indeed, it might be tempting to read this scene, and perhaps the novella more generally, as ethical kitsch.

In recent times, the term "ethical kitsch" has been called upon, and the phenomenon frowned upon, by a number of scholars. It appears to have been first used in the 1969 translation of Gillo Dorfles' essay collection *Kitsch: An Anthology of Bad Taste* (published in its original Italian a year earlier) in which Dorfles defines it as a "kind of bad taste which does not so much affect the work of art, as dress or moral attitude" (1969: 129). As such, ethical kitsch is cast as a sentimental moral position. Dorfles employs the term very generally, and his book, as he acknowledges in the opening note, neglects the domains of theatre, television, and literature. "Ethical kitsch" has, however, been employed by scholars of the literary, namely Leo Bersani (1995), Amos Oz (2010 [2005]), Ewan Fernie (2007: 2013), and Walter Benn Michaels (2013). In his discussion of contemporary fiction, Michaels declares, "it's this insistence on the right attitude that produces the dominant form of kitsch today – ethical kitsch" (2013: 922–923). Ethical kitsch serves to exhibit the moral conscience of the writer and to guide and reinforce the appropriate ethical judgment in the minds of readers.

While the reverence inscribed in Thirlwell's parallelism "I looked at him and he looked at me" might suggest a shift into ethical kitsch, *if* this is so, it is a performance. For although in the extract Thirlwell's narrator continues to claim that he and the beggar are akin, Thirlwell's words once again brim with sarcasm. Indeed, he has framed the bifurcated footnote in which these words occur with cultural references, having started by namedropping indie movie director Joe Swanberg and closing the scene with a high literary allusion. Doing so is deliberate in that it serves to undercut the validity of any moralizing that may be interpreted. These "hipster" references demonstrate the complexity of Thirlwell's position, since they go some way towards equating him as narrator with the technophiles, and they enable an acknowledgment of his own complicity within the contemporary cultural order. In this extract, Thirlwell is not parading his own moral stance with the view that readers concur with its sanctity. The purity of any ethical attitude is often inescapably diluted by our actions in our lived realities. Thirlwell is therefore showing recognition of the convoluted nature of a definitive moral stance and accordingly intimating that readers might also question and critique their own.

Conclusion: "In a future beyond me"

Ultimately, in *Kapow!* Thirlwell offers a metamodernist vision of the present and future of literature, both in theory and practice, as a poetics of multimodal form that engages with the social, ethical, political, and economic circumstances of the twenty-first century and the globalizing world. *Kapow!* is metamodernist in its use of stylistic devices – namely heterochronic spatio-temporal deixis, second-person address, intermixing of high and low register and code-switching – to express its aesth-ethical commitment: a refusal to accept the current state of the world, asking readers instead to think critically and defiantly about the ways in which world events are connected and how their own involvement figures in such a world.

Metamodernist writing does not neglect issues of global ethics. In Fernie's words, without such matters "art is unthinkable; and so is love, whether sexual or religious – to say nothing of any kind of reformation or revolution and therefore hope for the future" (2013: 33). Fernie's mention of "reformation or revolution" is clearly apt. In an interview, Thirlwell admits: "Sadly, I'm a very moral writer. But I do want to get away from niceness" (Lichtig 2011: 35); Getting "away from niceness" means that rather than telling readers how he feels or what is right for them to think and feel, Thirlwell chooses instead to provoke awareness and consideration. *Kapow!*'s narrator reflects, "But did this mean I knew anything, or that I could see an end? Amigos, no!" (76). Not knowing the answers, though, clearly does not mean losing sight of the questions.

Like all of us, Thirlwell cannot predict the future. Writing prior to *Kapow!*'s 2012 publication, he did not know how the Arab Spring and its uprisings would play out, whether a resolution to larger world problems could be found. At the end of *Kapow!*, Thirlwell offers an uncertain conclusion to the turbulent relationship of two characters, the married couple Nigora and Rustam. He writes:

> He would tell his wife that he loved her. She would tell him that she loved him back – and she'd be lying, thought Nigora. She would be lying to Rustamjon. But I'm not convinced that this is true. Because in the darkness a final thought would cloud and cling to her – that the problem was time travel. The problem was that you would only know that you had been married to the wrong person when it was way too late to change. If, in fact, you would ever know at all. Just as I also knew that only in a future beyond me, and beyond you, dear reader, will it be obvious what has really happened to my characters in the epoch of revolutions, if this is an epoch at all, which isn't at all what I'm saying, so I'm not saying anything so definite. I am leaving them there, while the military council develops its schemes and power grabs. (79–80)

To conclude this article, I want in a sense to leave you as my reader in exactly the same place Thirlwell leaves his reader: "there, while the military council develops its schemes and power grabs." Or rather, I want to leave you here in the twenty-first century, since this is the global world we live in. Metamodernist writing hints at a future of literature and literary innovation that uses stylistic forms not for innovation's sake. Instead, metamodernism offers a literature that is accountable, just as we ourselves are accountable. Therefore, my closing words, which are in fact Adam Thirlwell's words from *Kapow!*, are designed to both lighten the mood and to age you, to use our thinking about the literature of today and of the future as a means to get us thinking about the present and the future of our globalizing world: "Take that, you intellectuals! Or, in my favorite cartoon term of the moment, kaPOW!" (79).

REFERENCES

Bersani, Leo. 1995. *Homos*. Cambridge, MA: Harvard University Press.
Bourriaud, Nicolas. 2009a. Altermodern. In Nicolas Bourriaud (ed.), *Altermodern: Tate triennial*, 11–23. London: Tate Publishing.
Bourriaud, Nicolas. 2009b. *The radicant*. New York: Lucas & Sternberg.
Broadbent, Judith M. 2009. The amn't gap: The view from West Yorkshire. *Journal of Linguistics* 45(2), 251–284.
Contos, Ashlie M. 2013. *Nomina Nuda Tenemus*: Jonathan Safran Foer, finding meaning within empty names, or (re) construction of deconstruction. In Marie Hendry & Jennifer Page (eds.), *Media, technology, and imagination*, 53–66. Newcastle upon Tyne: Cambridge Scholars Publishing.

Dorfles, Gillo. 1969. *Kitsch: An anthology of bad taste*. London: Studio Vista.

Eshelman, Raoul. 2008. *Performatism or the end of postmodernism*. Aurora, CO: Davies Group Publishers.

Fernie, Ewan. 2007. Dollimore's Challenge. *Shakespeare Studies* 35, 133–157.

Fernie, Ewan. 2013. *The demonic: Literature and experience*. New York: Routledge.

Frow, John. 1990. What was postmodernism? In Ian Adams & Helen Tiffin (eds.), *Past the last post: Theorizing post-colonialism and post-modernism*, 139–152. Calgary: University of Calgary Press.

Gąsiorek, Andrzej & David James. 2012. Fiction since 2000: Postmillennial commitments. *Contemporary Literature* 53(4): 609–627.

Genet, Jean. 1971. [1969] *Funeral rites*. London: Panther.

Gibbons, Alison. 2012. Altermodernist fiction. In Joe Bray, Alison Gibbons & Brian McHale (eds.), *The Routledge companion to experimental literature*, 238–252. London: Routledge.

Gibbons, Alison. An interview with Adam Thirlwell. Forthcoming in *Contemporary Literature* 55(4).

Giles, Paul. 2012. All swallowed up: David Foster Wallace and American literature. In Samuel Cohen & Lee Konstantinou (eds.), *The legacy of David Foster Wallace*, 3–22. Iowa City: University of Iowa Press.

Green, Jeremy. 2005. *Late postmodernism: American fiction at the millennium*. New York: Palgrave.

Holland, Mary. 2013. *Succeeding postmodernism: Language and humanism in contemporary American literature*. New York: Bloomsbury.

Hutcheon, Linda. 2002. [1995] *The politics of postmodernism*. 2nd edn. New York: Routledge.

James, David. 2012. *Modernist futures: Innovation and inheritance in the contemporary Novel*. New York: Cambridge University Press.

James, David & Urmila Seshagiri. 2014. Metamodernism: narratives of continuity and revolution. *PMLA* 129(1),87–100.

Kelly, Adam. 2010. David Foster Wallace and the new sincerity in American fiction. In David Hering (ed.), *Consider David Foster Wallace: Critical essays*, 131–146. Austin: SSMG Press.

Kirby, Alan. 2009. *Digimodernism: How new technologies dismantle the postmodern and reconfigure our culture*. New York: Continuum.

Konstantinou, Lee. 2012. No bull: David Foster Wallace and postironic belief. In Samuel Cohen & Lee Konstantinou (eds.), *The legacy of David Foster Wallace*, 83–112. Iowa City: University of Iowa Press.

Lichtig, Toby. 2011. An interview with Adam Thirlwell. *Wasafiri* 26(3),34–37.

Lipovetsky, Gilles. 2005. *Hypermodern times*. Cambridge: Polity Press.

Martin, Paul Eve. 2012. Thomas Pynchon, David Foster Wallace and the problems of "metamodernism." *C21 Literature* 1(1),7–25.

Mason, Paul. 2012. *Why it's kicking off everywhere: The new global revolutions*. London: Verso.

Mayakovsky, Vladimir. 1998. And you think you could? In Donald Allen, Fred Jordan, Dick Seaver & Barney Rosset (eds.), *Evergreen Review reader: 1957–1966: A ten year anthology*, 160. New York: Blue Moon Books.

McLaughlin, Robert L. 2004. Post-postmodern discontent: Contemporary fiction and the social world. *Symploke* 12(1–2), 53–68.

McLaughlin, Robert L. 2012. Post-postmodernism. In Joe Bray, Alison Gibbons & Brian McHale (eds.), *The Routledge companion to experimental literature*, 212–223. London: Routledge.

Michaels, Walter Benn. 2013. Forgetting Auschwitz: Jonathan Littell and the death of a beautiful woman. *American Literary History* 25(4),915–930.

Mignolo, Walter. 2011. *The darker side of Western modernity: Global futures, decolonial options*. Durham, NC: Duke University Press.

Moraru, Christian. 2011. *Cosmodernism: American narrative, late globalization, and the new cultural imaginary*. Ann Arbor: University of Michigan Press.

Oz, Amos. 2010. God, Satan and human: A speech delivered on August 25, 2005 on the occasion of being awarded the Goethe Prize in Frankfurt, Germany. *Southern Cross Review* 72, no pagination, http://southerncrossreview.org/72/pz-evil-god.html (last accessed on 14 April 2014).

Pressman, Jessica. 2014. *Digital modernism: Making it new in new media*. New York: Oxford University Press.

Robertson, Roland. 1995. Glocalization: Time-space and homogenous-heterogeneity. In Mike Featherstone, Scott Lash & Roland Robertson (eds.), *Global modernities*, 25–44. London: Sage Publications.

Samuels, Robert. 2008. Auto-modernity after postmodernism: Autonomy and automation in culture, technology, and education. In Tara McPherson (ed.), *Digital youth, innovation, and the unexpected*, 219–240. Cambridge, MA: MIT Press.

Thirlwell, Adam. 2006. *Politics*. London: Vintage Books.

Thirlwell, Adam. 2007. *Miss Herbert*. London: Jonathan Cape.

Thirlwell, Adam. 2010. *The escape*. London: Vintage Books.

Thirlwell, Adam. 2012a. *Kapow!* London: Visual Editions.

Thirlwell, Adam. 2012b. Introduction. In *McSweeney's 42, Multiples of Twelve Stories appearing in up to six versions each*. Special Issue of *McSweeney's Quarterly Concern*, ed. Adam Thirlwell. San Francisco: McSweeneys.

Timmer, Nicoline. 2010. *Do you feel it too? The post-postmodern syndrome in American fiction at the turn of the millennium*. Amsterdam; New York: Rodopi.

Tomlinson, John. 1999. *Globalization and culture*. Cambridge: Polity.

Toth, Josh. 2010. *The passing of postmodernism: A spectroanalysis of the contemporary*. Albany: State University of New York Press.

Toth, Josh, & Neil Brooks. 1999. Introduction: A wake and renewed? In Neil Brooks & Josh Toth (eds.), *The Mourning After: Attending the Wake of Postmodernism*, 1–13. Amsterdam: Rodopi.

Vermeulen, Timotheus & Robin van den Akker. 2010. Notes on metamodernism. *Journal of Aesthetics & Culture* 2.

Walkowitz, R. L. 2006. *Cosmopolitan style: Modernism beyond the nation*. New York: Columbia University Press.

Widdows, Heather. 2011. *Global ethics: An introduction*. Durham: Acumen.

The Paradoxes of "Unnatural" Mimesis in Gordon Sheppard's *HA!*

DANUTA FJELLESTAD

What is an "unnatural" narrative? In a fascinating book on narrative theory – or, more correctly, a book that explains four distinct strands in narrative theory – written by five leading figures in the field (David Herman, James Phelan, Peter J. Rabinowitz, Brian Richardson, & Robyn Warhol 2012) an eager reader like myself finds that "unnatural" is used as a synonym for "antimimetic" (Richardson 2012: 21). Mimesis here is taken to be the natural/standard mode of narrative. Granted, Richardson admits that there are other definitions of the term; these are at the core of another volume, *A poetics of unnatural narrative* (2013), edited by Jan Alber together with Henrik Skov Nielsen and Richardson himself. In the introduction (Alber *et al.* 2013: 6), the editors point out that while Alber designates "physically, logically, or humanly impossible scenarios and events" as characteristics of "unnatural" narratives, Nielsen proposes that the term be used to refer to narratives that in the real world would be judged as "physically, logically, mnemonically, or psychologically impossible or implausible." Suspecting perhaps that the differences between the various definitions appear to be hair-splitting in nature, the editors point out that "the same basic features and qualities of narrative fiction" are common ground for unnatural narratology: "the impossible, the unreal, the preternatural, the outrageous, the extreme, the parodic, and the insistently fictional" (2013: 9). Such a generous definition leaves somewhat troublingly few fictional narratives outside the realm of the unnatural; what matters, it seems, is the *degree* to which a given narrative deviates from mimesis.

Although like many others I too flinch at the word "unnatural," I do welcome this relatively recent turn toward a narratological study of experimental narratives, not least because I have been teaching and researching experimental literature for several decades. As a corrective to a "pronounced mimetic bias" of narrative theory which is declared to be "largely useless" when dealing with innovative texts (Alber *et al.* 2013: 4), I find unnatural narratology appealing in its promise to help me better understand and articulate the type of experiments I have been encountering with increased frequency in the past decade or so. The experiments that concern me here do not reside in the fictional worlds (the represented or, if you wish, the content), but rather in the material and physical aspects of the narrative – the mode of representation that deviates from what is conventionally regarded as "natural" in literary production. The type of "unnaturalness" that I want to draw attention to is paradoxical in its resolute adopting of mimesis to materially foreground such "natural" channels of communication as the letter and the postcard.

Given narratology's preoccupation with narrative rather than modes of its embodiment, it is not surprising that this type of mimesis has hardly registered on the narratological radar. However, it is high time to expand the corpus of texts for unnatural narratology beyond fantasy and science fiction and venture into what is often referred to as multimodal literature, defined by Kress and van Leeuwen (1996: 183) as "any text whose meanings are realized through more than one semiotic mode." Commonly, in multimodal literature the narrative is interspaced with the use of a broad range of images, typographic variations, and other graphic elements. Although by no means a new historical phenomenon (think Laurence Sterne's *Tristram Shandy* [1759–1767] or Raymond Federman's *Double or nothing* [1971]), the multimodal novel has become so common in the early twenty-first century that it is an inextricable feature of post-postmodernism.[1] Of the large corpus of post-postmodern novels I want to mention but two, Mark Z. Danielewski's *House of leaves* (2000) and Jonathan Safran Foer's *Extremely loud & incredibly close* (2005). In what follows I want to focus on a narrative that has been unjustly neglected in discussions of multimodality, experimental literature, and post-postmodernism: *HA! A self-murder mystery* (2003) by Gordon Sheppard. This text will serve as my entry point into the discussion of "unnatural mimesis."

Published in 2003, *HA!* is a gargantuan volume of close to nine hundred pages. It tells of the life and death of Québécois separatist intellectual, novelist, and film-maker in the late 1960s and the 1970s, Hubert Aquin (1929–1977), the author of *Prochain épisode* (*Next episode*, published 1963). Or, to be more precise, it is the story of Gordon Sheppard's quest, in Sherlock Holmes fashion, to understand the 1977 suicide of this Québécois cult figure through interviews with those who knew Aquin: friends, family members, lovers, artists, witnesses, cleaning personnel, etc. Transcriptions of recorded interviews are played off against a combination of extracts from fictional works; period newspaper clippings are given side by side with excerpts from Aquin's own novels and documentary writing as well as from a great many other literary works. Classified by the publisher as a novel and regarded as a *documentary* novel by Sheppard himself, that *HA!* draws on the genre of detective fiction is clearly signaled by the subtitle ("A self-murder mystery"). Its affinity with biography, suggested by the acronym HA (Hubert Aquin), is far less obvious to begin with: none of the four definitions of the combinations of the two letters (Ha; Ha!; Ha! ha!; HA) refers to Aquin.[2] Apart from biography and detective fiction, the book makes use of the conventions of psychological study, encyclopedia, historiography, political pamphlet, metafiction, literary criticism, and hypertext, to name just a handful of the staggering number of genre affiliations that *HA!* riffs on. Throughout, the documentary and factual are extensively braided with the fictional and fantastical, a strategy established right from the beginning, on the "Dedication" page (a paratextually placed page that comes after the title and the page with definitions of "ha") explaining that *HA!* is dedicated to all who have committed suicide and offering a list of close to two hundred names, making Hedda Gabler, Anna Karenina, and Othello rub shoulders with Yukio Mishima, Socrates, and Virginia Woolf in Dante's second ring of the seventh circle of Hell.

Generically and ontologically a hybrid text, *HA!* is also graphically promiscuous. Even at first glance it presents itself as an aggressively – perhaps even oppressively – visual narrative that could be called an "iconotext" (Louvel 2011; Wagner 1996), "imagetext" (W.J.T. Mitchell 1994), "mixed" (Bernier 1990), or "hybrid" (Sadokierski 2011) text, that is, one that creates its meaning through

---

[1] For a definition and review of post-postmodernism see Fjellestad & Engberg 2013.

[2] These definitions, listed on a paratextually placed page immediately after the title, range from self-evident (an exclamation or expression of surprise) to obscure ("derived from the Mi'kmaq word 'Hescuewaka' meaning 'an unexpected place' ") to irrelevant ("New York Stock Exchange symbol for Hawaiian Airlines, Inc."). Even at this micro-level Sheppard mocks the reader's expectations.

complex and intricate intersections of words with images.[3] Maps, diagrams, music notations, EEG records, reproductions of postcards, photographs, film posters, film stills, handwritten letters and notes, classical paintings (by, for instance, Michelangelo and Goya), *I Ching* hexagrams, bills, etc. inhabit virtually every page. It is indeed not difficult to understand why one reviewer called *HA!* "the wildest scrapbook" (Homel 2003).[4]

That the reader is to anticipate an "unnatural" narrative is signaled as early as the title page: we learn that *HA!* is "written and directed" by Gordon Sheppard. While we do expect books to be written, they cannot be said to be directed: this is reserved for such non-print media as performances and films. Surprising in the context of a print book, the word clearly indexes the novel's multimodal nature. For instance, a number of features of the narrative turn out to mimic film conventions: the dialogue-heavy narrative has in many places a distinct flavor of film-script; juxtapositions of various parts of the text resemble the filmic technique of quick cuts; after the narrative proper is finished, we are faced with rubrics such as "Cast" and "Credits." And then there are of course the abundant references, both verbal and visual, to a variety of films. Sheppard's own *raison d'être* for this self-fashioning as a director is offered in the section "Authorized comments" at the end of the book. He explains his use of a graphically varied montage, his "Copy and Paste salute to hypertext," as an attempt to reflect the multimedia environment that has shaped the lives of people in the West for more than fifty years and in which both Aquin's suicide and the investigation of his death took place (Sheppard 2003: 857). Sheppard, then, presents himself as what can be called a creative director whose imprint is omnipresent in the narrative's every aspect. He is also, we need to remember, an actor, not only when interviewing those who knew Aquin, but also when in a "typically postmodern" fashion he playfully writes himself into the narrative when he offers such personal details as being "off-pink in colour" with "a half-full head of half-black hair, and a blue-eyed gaze which, according to the mirror, is both ravishing and impenetrable" (Sheppard 2003: 858). This self-mocking tone stands in stark contrast to a later admission that while working on the book about Aquin's self-murder, he found out that the prostate cells in his own body "refused to commit suicide," putting his life "in jeopardy" (Sheppard 2003: 861). A book about death, *HA!* turns out to have been written in the shadow of the approaching literal death of its author.[5] Such weaving together of gravity and triviality, gaiety and morbidity, the momentous and the negligible orchestrates the narrative's every aspect.

---

[3] These terms, it needs to be observed, are not synonymous. For instance, iconotexts tend to be seen as integrating the verbal and the visual into one artifact, while the concept of the mixed text is often used to refer to texts in which there is a hierarchical rather than integrative relationship between images and words. However, the usage of these terms is far from rigorous; all of the terms overlap, at least partly.

[4] Compared to *Moby Dick*, *Ulysses*, *Gravity's Rainbow*, and the film *Citizen Kane*, *HA!* was immediately pronounced a literary masterpiece and a work of genius, reviewers competing with each other in their use of adjectives such as amazing, extraordinary, monumental, magnificent, magisterial, brilliant, staggering, mesmerizing, riveting, and profound. The McGill-Queen's University Press webpage offers a representative sample of the reviews of *HA!*; see http://mqup.mcgill.ca/book.php?bookid=1674. Many of the unsolicited comments can be found on Gordon Sheppard's home page, http://www. gordonsheppard. com/bottom/bHA.html. Considering the enthusiasm with which the publication of *HA!* was greeted, the critical neglect of Sheppard's novel is quite surprising.

[5] Sheppard died of prostate cancer in 2006, three years after the publication of *HA!*.

As must be clear from the above, Sheppard's text fashions its "unnaturalness" through all kinds of language- and genre-games as well as the unconventional graphic layout and inclusion of images. But side by side with such obviously antimimetic strategies *HA! amplifies* mimesis so that through its excess it is, as it were, *undermined from within and denaturalized.* This process of turning mimesis against itself reaches a kind of climax in two physical inserts that the reader finds in the narrative. These inserts, I want to propose, serve as but one exemplar of a different type of "unnaturalness" than unnatural narratology has dealt with thus far.

After close to seven hundred pages crowded with images the reader may not be surprised to find an image of an envelope with the caption "Facsimile of Hubert Aquin's farewell letter to Andrée dated March 16 1977." A single handwritten word, "Amour," is placed in the middle of the envelope. The surprise comes as the reader turns the page and discovers a three-dimensional envelope glued to the bottom of the page.

Once the envelope is opened, two sheets of yellow legal paper filled with Aquin's handwriting can be pulled out (Sheppard 2003: 697). This physical letter turns out to be the French "original" of the one printed two pages earlier, its content rendered in English (and in italics). Above the letter in English there is a note that it was "written in blue ink on lined yellow notepad paper" (Sheppard 2003: 696); this ekphrastic description is given a material reality in the insert.

The second physical insert comes toward the very end of the narrative. On the top of the page we find the following text: "Addressed to Emmanuel and post-marked Geneve [*sic*], February 25 1977, this postcard arrived in the mail at 3776 rue Vendôme, Montréal, one week after Aquin's death" (849). Below the caption we see a reproduction of the obverse (face) and reverse (back) of a postcard in black and white. Underneath this reproduction there is a physical envelope (without its top flap) glued to the page.

Inside the envelope the reader finds the "original" postcard, a physical object to be pulled out, viewed, and read. The handwritten text in French (Aquin's message to his son Emmanuel) is rendered in English beneath the glued envelope. We read: "A small reminder of Aigle and of our picnics. One difference today: you can't see the mountains and it's snowing up there. I'll wait for you to go back up Leysin. Papa Hube" (Sheppard 2003: 849).

What's going on in these two textual instances? How can we interpret them? To begin with, like many images in *HA!* (for instance maps or newspaper clippings or photographs), the letter and the postcard have a documentary function, very much in line with the biographical thrust of the novel. The letter and the postcard participate in a set of thematic concerns that are built up by the verbal narrative as well as by all kinds of images embedded in *HA!*. For instance, both the letter and the postcard relate to the thematic of remembrance and memory, enhancing it through the question about the function of physical objects in assisting memory. Both instances can be read in the context of the themes of spectrality and ghostliness that saturate the narrative, not least because both messages arrive after Aquin's death; they are messages, as it were, from the grave. The letter resonates with the theme of Aquin's obsessive braiding together of love and death (in particular suicide) throughout his life. Both are traces, mementos, of Aquin who is no more; not unlike Barthes's "ça a été" ("that-has-been"), they arrest a specific temporal moment and lodge it in the present. Both the letter and the post-card participate in the reflections on the role of writing in eternalizing what is mortal and perishable, the human flesh, the traces of which are preserved in the handwritten. They also trigger off reflections on the original and copy: while the physical letter and postcard pass for originals in relation to their reproductions (in English in the case of the letter and as an image in the case of the postcard), they themselves are reproductions of the originals that are not available to the reader; they are facsimiles, duplicates, perhaps in the same way as Aquin's suicide is a duplicate of a number of other self-murders that resonate in *HA!*.[6]

Important as it is to see the letter and the postcard as part of the overall design and thematic of *HA!*, their singularity, their difference from other images and everything else that is going on in the text is what is most compelling. This singularity resides in their palpably mimetic aspects which set in motion a number of questions that pressure narratological concerns.

As I have mentioned, the contents of the letter and the postcard are doubly embedded and twice accessed by the reader: they are part of the narrative that *HA!* unfolds in English in the conventional format of the book but also physically semidetached mini-narratives in French. Thus the surfeit of narrative information or semantic overdetermination that Peter Rabinowitz (1987) discusses in *Before reading* is compounded by the *structural* surplus of the epistolary inserts. It is important to note that the repetition of the narrative content is a repetition with a difference, or, rather, a chain of differences: of the language used (English vs. French), of the medium (the book vs. the letter/postcard), of mode ("impersonal" print font vs. personal handwriting), of placement (within the conventional page parameters vs. outside of these), of space (two- vs. three-dimensional), of visibility (in full sight vs. hidden), of aesthetics (conventional vs. surprising). Such a technique can be likened to the playing of the same tune in different registers; this is, in fact, the orchestration of *HA!*: the telling and re-telling of the story of Aquin's death by various characters and means (documentary, fictional, visual) that – at least partly – arrests progression, underscoring the circular logic of the narrative. The inserts raise the question of the dependence of the diagetic process on the medium. As the reader encounters the letter and the postcard, the flow of diegesis is interrupted; the reader is pulled out of his/her immersion in the narrative, bringing to consciousness the fact that the progression of narrative depends on the tactile/physical engagement with the book/text, an engagement that we have learned *not* to heed.[7] Importantly, the reader's attention is relayed, as it were, from the story to the medium of telling the story; the medium of delivery of the narrative becomes thus part of the narrative world.

The inserts can also be seen as nodal points in which the complex relations between the actual, authorial, and narrative readers are played out. The letter and postcard arrive, as it were, twice to the wrong (that is, unintended) addressee: once as transcribed into the main narrative, and then as "originals," doubling the actual and authorial reader's voyeuristic (unethical?) engagement with what is the property of the other. When the flesh-and-blood reader opens the letter, he or she

---

[6] The fact that the letter and the postcard are present in the narrative as concrete and corporeal entities raises questions about singularity that is in tension with the mass/ mechanical reproduction. (It is tempting to draw parallels with Benjamin's discussion of the aura of art in the age of mechanical reproduction.)

[7] Of course all reading engages the senses and thus the reader's body. However, we have been habituated to disregard the routine of, for instance, turning pages as having no other than a purely pragmatic function. The two inserts – as well as a range of other experiments in contemporary literature – make it simply impossible not to pay attention to the physicality of accessing narratives.

is aligned with its addressee, Aquin's widowed partner Andrée, the letter's legitimate audience. Like her, the reader accesses the letter in full knowledge of Aquin's death. In an interview that precedes the letter Andrée says: "I was somewhat apprehensive about reading it [the letter], not because I was expecting there to be revelations in it, but knowing he was dead it gave me an odd feeling seeing Hubert's handwriting. . ." (Sheppard 2003: 695). Like her, the reader too encounters Aquin's handwriting, this trace of Aquin's body, and is expected to *experience* Andrée's "odd" feeling, not just *read* about it. In being programmed to repeat what Andrée did and felt, the reader acts as her (uncanny, anonymous) alter ego. The reader, in a way, bestows his/her own flesh onto the character that exists as a textual construct. Another way of putting it would be to say that the physicality of the letter calls forth the embodied reader and becomes the site of the encounter of three bodies: Aquin's, Andrée's, and the reader's. This overlap is indeed a moment of an uncannily "visceral reading" (Cranny-Francis 2005: 37).[8]

To say that, however, is to bracket the fact that this (physical) meeting of the reader with the letter is staged by Sheppard: it is he who has re-directed the letter and the postcard from its "natural" context of Andrée's home to the "unnatural" context of a book. Aquin's messages reach the reader through the intervention of the authorial agent. Thus on the one hand the material letter and postcard eject the reader from the state of immersion in the narrative and, in a metaleptic moment offer a *surfeit* of mimesis. On the other hand both artifacts draw the reader's attention to the process of mediation and expose the "unnaturalness" of the fictional mimesis. They thus simultaneously and paradoxically bridge and widen the gap between the fictional world and the world of the flesh-and-blood reader.

Physical inserts of the kind discussed above can be encountered in a number of narratives today. Duane Swierczynski's *The crimes of Dr. Watson* (2007), for instance, contains several glued-in envelopes that enclose objects such as a postcard, an arrest ledger, a post-office telegraph, a matchbook, etc. In *Cathy's book* (2006) by Sean Stewart and Jordan Weisman, the reader finds an envelope containing some thirty physical objects, all from hand-written cards to newspaper clippings and receipts to a paper napkin.[9] Somewhat less spectacular moments of "de-naturalization" through what I would like to call, for lack of a better term, "kinetic interruption" are encountered in narratives that do not demand that the reader extract a physical artifact but instead unfold pages to get access to the narrative. This is the case in Steve Tomasula's novel *VAS: An opera in flatland* (2004) or in Adam Thirlwell's *Kapow!* (2012). In the latter, the unfolding from the main body of the book results in words dizzyingly running across accordion-like strips, the linearity of which mockingly clashes with the chunks of narrative printed in various directions. *Kapow!* is also a good example of yet another "unnatural" narrative mode: reading that involves a physical rotation of the book. Such rotation is the organizing principle of Danielewski's *Only revolutions* (2006). Praised both for its literary merit and its typographical innovation, the

---

[8] Cranny-Francis uses this phrase in passing when discussing the impact of images on readers (37).

[9] It is worth mentioning that issue 16 of *McSweeney's Quarterly* contains two inserts. The first one, a comb, seems to me to be gratuitous, while the second, a deck of fifteen oversized cards backed and cornered like playing cards that can be shuffled and read in any order, are highly functional, since they are the conduits of Robert Coover's short story, "Heart Suit" (2005), and the order in which the chunks of text are read radically impacts the plot.

novel tells the stories of its two main characters, Sam and Hailey, in such a way that they cohabit each page in an upside-down fashion. The reader has to physically rotate the book by 180 degrees to read either Sam's or Hailey's narratives, although other reading paths are possible too: reading one character's narrative from beginning to end or following the publisher's recommendation to read the first eight pages from one story, then eight pages from the other, and so on. Each choice has an impact on the narrative plotting, whether the two story lines meet on a page, or are run in parallel, or are intermittently interwoven. Yet another type of kinetic interruption is constituted by the flipbook technique. In Steven Hall's *The raw shark texts* (2007) the reader comes across a section of some fifty pages that, when flipped, show a shark made of fragments of the main character's life-story racing right at the reader. "In flipping pages 335 through 373," observes Kiene Brillenburg Wurth (2011: 131), "the reader *engenders* the shark's approach" (emphasis added). At the end of Jonathan Safran Foer's *Extremely loud & incredibly close* (2005) we are faced with a sequence of fifteen pages which, when flipped, show the famous figure of the falling man from 9/11 moving upward, back to the safety of the not-yet-destroyed tower.[10]

We must ask ourselves if such experimentations are gratuitous, if we are dealing with negligible gimmicks, and if critics such as Madelena Gonzales (2008), for instance, are justified in their indignant claims that when writers compete with the Internet – a common enough take on the rationale of experimentation in contemporary fiction – they offer but excess and banality.[11] Such unequivocal dismissal of narrative experiments is foolish, even if, admittedly, some of the experiments are more interesting and successful than others; the function of some is easier to discern, while others evade naturalizing efforts. But leaving aside the question of value, such texts are important objects of narratological attention, not least because they are part and parcel of contemporary – post-postmodern – literature and symptomatic of current re-configurations of fictional narratives. It is new kinds of narratives that emerge or take a more central stage in the ecology of narrative forms that propel the "ongoing remodulation of narrative analysis" (Herman 1999: 3) as much as the theoretical debates. When the literary landscape is reconfigured, so too the analytical needs to be adjusted.

It could of course be argued that as non-verbal, such techniques are justifiably outside the realm of narratological concerns. However, in all types of the kinetic interruption I have mentioned above the reader's engagement with the physical object is non-trivially involved in meaning-making processes and thus must be considered as intrinsic to the study of narrative. For instance, in demanding the reader's physical interaction, these "kinetic" devices interrupt and often relay

---

[10] Gibbons (2012: 164) reads the flipbook as creating "doubly deitic subjective alignment for the reader with Oskar." Reading Foer's novel for its representation of trauma, Gibbons (2012: 165) sees the flipbook working to "direct the readers to perform curative procedures for post-traumatic stress."–Nørgaard (2010: 123) also sees this segment of Foer's novel as inviting the reader "to play an active role in the creation of meaning"; flipping through the pages makes the figure "float from Real to Ideal." At this moment, I would say, the reader participates in Oskar's fantasy to reverse time.

[11] Gonzales (2008), I hasten to explain, does not deal with any of the techniques that I present here; her strictures are directed at narratives such as Jeanette Winterson's *The powerbook* (2001) and Martin Amis's *Yellow dog* (2003). However, since she sees such narratives as embodying the aesthetics of post-realism, her comments can be extended to the type of narrative I am interested in.

narrative progression, although in an "unnatural" way. In narratives such as Coover's "Heart suit" (2005) they magnify the already complex story-plot relation.

I am happy to register signals – however vague – that non-verbal narrative techniques of the kind discussed above are beginning to attract the interest of leading narratologists. For example, in his explication of antimimetic strategies Richardson (2012: 77) opens up for the inclusion of one type of "unnatural" techniques I have described, even if he does so only in passing. Discussing the *fabula – sjuzhet* distinction, he notes:

> In the work of many contemporary authors, the text from which the story is extracted has become increasingly unusual or unlikely. Such narratives may . . . even consist of piles of unbound or unnumbered pages, which the reader must arrange into an order for it to be apprehended (B.S. Johnson's *The unfortunates*, 1969) or take the form of thirteen large playing cards that can be arranged in multiple possible orders (Robert Coover's "Heart suit," 2005).

As we see, the format of the book, the physical platform of the narrative that is unconventional, enters Richardson's field of vision when dealing with antimimetic narratives. By extension, then, a conventionally shaped book should perhaps be considered to be part of the mimetic tradition and thus subject to narratological scrutiny. Whereas Richardson places the physical platform of narrative on the radar screen, James Phelan (2013: 215) gestures toward an inclusion of images into narratological considerations when he registers the thematic importance of an angelic female figure that the reader finds on the title page of Toni Morrison's *Beloved*. Clearly, non-verbal features of narratives have entered the field of narratological investigation.

Narratology has always been tested by the particularities of narrative forms. Unnatural narratology, we are informed in the introduction to the volume edited by Alber *et al.* (2013: 2), aims "to challenge general conception of narrative by accentuating two points: (1) the ways in which innovative and impossible narratives challenge mimetic understanding of narrative, and (2) the consequences that the existence of such narratives may have for the general conception of what a narrative is and what it can do." The innovative techniques discussed above pose a challenge of a different order than even the most experimental texts that unnatural narratologists have dealt with so far; they may actually be the testing grounds for the limits of unnatural narratology. It remains to be seen if more capacious and flexible models of analysis can be developed to include such experimentation.

REFERENCES

Alber, Jan, Stefan Iversen, Henrik Skov Nielsen & Brain Richardson. 2013. Introduction. In Jan Alber, Henrik Skov Nielsen & Brain Richardson (eds.), *A poetics of unnatural narrative*, 1–15. Columbus: Ohio State University Press.

Bernier, Silvie. 1990. *Du texte à l'image: Le livre illustré au Québec*. Sainte-Foy: Presses de l'Université Laval.

Coover, Robert. 2005. Heart suit. *McSweeney's Quarterly* 16, n. pag.

Cranny-Francis, Anne. 2005. *Multimedia: Texts and contexts*. London: SAGE.

Danielewski, Mark Z. 2006. *Only revolutions*. New York: Pantheon.

Fjellestad, Danuta & Maria Engberg. 2013. Toward a concept of post-postmodernism or Lady Gaga's reconfigurations of Madonna." *Reconstruction: Studies in Contemporary Culture* 12(4).

Gibbons, Alison. 2012. *Multimodality, cognition, and experimental literature*. New York: Routledge.

Gonzales, Madelena. 2008. The aesthetics of post-realism and the obscenification of everyday life: The novel in the age of technology. *Journal of Narrative Theory* 38(1),111–133.

Herman, David. 1999. Introduction: Narratologies. In David Herman (ed.), *Narratologies: New perspectives on narrative analysis*, 1–30. Columbus: Ohio State University Press.

Herman, David, James Phelan, Peter J. Rabinowitz, Brian Richardson & Robyn Warhol. 2012. *Narrative theory: Core concepts and critical debates*. Columbus: Ohio State University Press.

Homel, David. 2003. Attempting to explain a suicide. Review of *HA! A self-murder mystery* by Gordon Sheppard. *The Gazette* (1 Nov.). http://gordonsheppard.com/review/attempting-to-explaina-suicide-the-gazette-2003/ (last accessed on 5 Dec. 2008).

Kress, Gunther & Theo van Leeuwen. 1996. *Reading images: The grammar of visual design*. London: Routledge.

Louvel, Liliane. *Poetics of the iconotext*. 2011. Karen Jacobs (ed.), Laurence Petit (trans.). Farnham: Ashgate.

Mitchell, W.J.T. 1994. *Picture theory*. Chicago: University of Chicago Press.

Nørgaard, Nina. 2010. Multimodality and the literary text: Making sense of Safran Foer's *Extremely loud and incredibly close*. In Ruth Page (ed.), *New perspectives on narrative and multimodality*, 115–126. New York: Routledge, 2010.

Phelan, James. 2013. *Reading the American novel 1920–2010*. Malden, MA: Wiley-Blackwell.

Pressman, Jessica. 2009. The aesthetics of bookishness in the twenty-first century literature. *Michigan Quarterly Review* (Fall), 465–482.

Rabinowitz, Peter J. 1987. *Before reading: Narrative conventions and the politics of interpretation*. Ithaca, NY: Cornell University Press.

Richardson, Brian. 2012. Antimimetic, unnatural, and postmodern narrative theory. In David Herman, James Phelan, Peter J. Rabinowitz, Brian Richardson & Robyn Warhol, 20–28. *Narrative theory: Core concepts and critical debates*. Columbus: Ohio State University Press.

Sadokierski, Zoe. 2011. Visual writing: A critique of graphic devices in hybrid novels, from a visual communication design perspective. Ph.D. dissertation, University of Technology, Sydney. https://opus.lib.uts.edu.au/research/handle/2100/1042 (last accessed on 10 Oct. 2011).

Sheppard, Gordon. 2003. *HA! A self-murder mystery*. Montreal: McGill-Queen's University Press.

Stewart, Sean, Jordan Weisman & Cathy Brigg. 2006. *Cathy's book: If found call (650) 166–8233*. Philadelphia: Running Press.

Thirlwell, Adam. 2012. *Kapow!* London: Visual Editions.

Wagner, Peter. 1996. Introduction: Ekphrasis, iconotexts, and intermediality: The state(s) of the art(s). In Peter Wagner (ed.), *Icons – texts – iconotexts: Essays on ekphrasis and intermediality*, 1–40. Berlin: Gruyter.

Wurth, Kiene Brillenburg. 2011. Posthumanities and post-textualities: Reading *The raw shark texts* and *Woman's world*. *Comparative Literature* 63(2),119–141.

Utopia, Sort of: A Case Study in Metamodernism

TIMOTHEUS VERMEULEN & ROBIN VAN DEN AKKER

Quite unexpectedly, the figure of utopia has reappeared across the arts in the past few years, often alongside a renewed sense of empathy, reinvigorated constructive engagement, a reappreciation of narrative and a return to craftswo/manship. In the last decade there have been numerous international exhibitions and symposia, anthologies and monographs reappraising utopia, ranging from a big budget three-year exhibition program at the Arken Museum in Denmark (2009–2011) to Hans Ulrich Obrist's popular Manifesto Marathon at the Serpentine Gallery in England (2008), to the controversial performances by the Israeli artist Yael Bartana which call for the realization of a Jewish utopia in Poland (2010–present). Indeed, Obrist, following Immanuel Wallerstein (1998), explicitly called for a return to thinking in terms of utopia, eutopia and utopistics so that we can once again conceive of the future. In this essay, we wish to examine the return of utopia in contemporary art by deliberating on the practices of three artists – David Thorpe (1972, UK), Ragnar Kjartansson (1976, Iceland) and Paula Doepfner (1980, Germany) – within the broader context of post- and metamodernism. We argue that the utopian turn is part and parcel of the shift from postmodernism to metamodernism that took place in the 2000s. Each of our analyses concentrates on one particular aspect to this shift: the discussion of Thorpe's collages concentrates on the reappropriation of postmodern conventions of intertextuality to create a sense of community; the discussion of Kjartansson's performances focuses on the adoption of postmodern irony to generate a feeling of sincerity; and the discussion of Doepfner's installations engages with the use of postmodern melancholy in order to invoke hope.

The re-emergence of utopia out of the spirit of metamodernism

Our analysis takes as its starting point the premise that around the turn of the millennium postmodernism (as Fredric Jameson conceptualized it) receded and another cultural dominant emerged: metamodernism. Jameson described postmodernism as a hegemonic "structure of feeling" (1991: xiv) characterized by senses of an end – of History, social class, art, the subject, etc. We conceive of metamodernism as structure of feeling typified by the return of many of these debates, foremost among them History, the grand narrative, *Bildung* and the agent.[1]

The notion of the "structure of feeling" is borrowed from the British cultural theorist Raymond Williams. Williams defined it, cryptically, as our social

---

[1] We do not have the space here to elaborate in detail on our notion of metamodernism and its various tendencies. We refer the reader to our previous publications for further discussion. See, for instance, Vermeulen & van den Akker (2010) or Vermeulen & van den Akker (2014).

"experience ... in solution" (2001: 33), which lies "deeply embedded in our lives; it cannot be merely extracted and summarized. It is perhaps only in art – and this is the importance of art – that it can be realized, and communicated, as a whole experience" (2001: 40). In other words, a structure of feeling is a sentiment or, rather, still a sensibility that many people share, that many are aware of, but which cannot easily, if at all, be pinned down. If this today, after decades of (post)structuralism and the quantification of the humanities, sounds vague, it is precisely what Williams intended: it is that element of culture which circumscribes it but nonetheless cannot be traced back to any one of its individual ingredients, that element which eludes, or is left after, structuralist analysis. The tenor of the structure of feeling, however, can be traced in art, which has the capability to express a common experience of a time and place.

As the prefix "meta" (i.e. after, beyond) suggests, the case for metamodernism depends on a break with – or, rather, the sublation of – a postmodern moment, which, as so many others already argued (Eshelman 2008; Kirby 2009; Bourriaud 2009; Moraru 2010; Nealon 2012), has lost its sway on contemporary aesthetics and culture. We think, here, of the waning of a host of different impulses, which nonetheless share some kind of family resemblance – Jameson's "senses of an end," if you will – such as pop art and deconstructive conceptual art (from Warhol to Hirst, by way of Koons); punk, new wave and grunge's cynicism in popular music; disaffected minimalism in cinema; spectacular formalism in architecture; meta-fictional irony in literature, as well as the whole emphasis on a dehumanizing cyberspace in science-fictions of all kinds. Since the turn of the millennium, however, we have seen the emergence of various "new," often overlapping, aesthetic phenomena such as the New Romanticism in the arts and the New Aesthetic in design, the New Sincerity in literature and the New Weird or Nu-Folk in music, Quirky Cinema and Quality Television, as well as the discovery of a new terrain for architecture, each of them characterized by an attempt to incorporate postmodern stylistic and formal conventions while moving beyond them.[2] Meanwhile, we witness the "return" of realist and modernist forms, techniques and aspirations (to which the metamodern has a decidedly different relation than the postmodern).

If postmodernism must be associated with socio-economic developments that Jameson described, following Mandel, as late capitalism, metamodernism can be seen to be intertwined with social and economic tendencies that have come to be labeled under the cognomen of global capitalism. The various preconditions for this shift from late capitalism to global capitalism – gradually set in place in preceding decades – all converged and coagulated around, or after, the turn of the millennium. It was in the 2000s, after all, that the maturity and availability of "digital" technologies and "renewable" technologies reached a critical threshold; the millennial generation came of age determined to recreate the world in its own image; the BRICs rose to prominence; the era of cheap oil and fantasies of nuclear abundance gave way to fracking-induced dreams of energy independence; "Project Europe" got derailed; immigration policies and multicultural ideals backlashed in the midst of a revival of conservative nationalism; US hegemony declined; the Arab Spring toppled many a dictator that had long served as a puppet for Western interests; bad debts became, finally and

---

[2]See, in order of appearance, Konstantinou (2009); Vermeulen &. van den Akker (2010); Allen and McQuade (2011); MacDowell (2012); Sterling (2012); Vermeulen & Rustad (2013); Poecke (2014).

inevitably, as much a problem for the First World as it always has been for the Third World; and the financial crises inaugurated yet another round of neoliberalization (this time by means of austerity measures of all sorts), exposing and deepening the institutionalized drive towards economic inequality and ecological disaster. Each in their own way, these developments gathered momentum in the 2000s, and "jelled and combined" – to use Jameson's (1991: xix) apt expression – to kick-start History (Vermeulen & van den Akker 2011).

The re-emergence of the figure of utopia in contemporary art is related to all of these developments (in capitalism as well as in culture and aesthetics). This is to say that "Utopia" – as a trope, individual desire or collective fantasy – is once more, and increasingly, visible and noticeable across artistic practices that must be situated in, and related to, the passage from postmodernism and metamodernism.

Under postmodernism, to wit, the figure of utopia was avoided as something suspiciously totalitarian while it morphed into its generic "dystopian" cousin (in cyberpunk, for instance) or turned into debris after the operations of deconstruction (in, say, pop art and conceptual art); both forms should be seen as critiques of the actually existing Communism or Capitalism of that day and age rather than attempts to evoke an image of a possible future. It has led Jameson, among others, to search for what he described after Ernst Bloch as the "utopian impulse" in social phenomena or cultural forms that are seemingly devoid of utopianism (such as, indeed, deconstructive conceptual art or dystopian cyberpunk) by means of a dialectical excavation process that he half-jokingly described as "utopology" (2010: 434).[3] The most pressing example of this type of dialectical criticism is his essay "Utopia as Replication" (2010: 410–434), in which he, ingeniously and maliciously, seeks to lay bare the utopianism of the retail leviathan Wal-Mart, which is without a doubt the most repressive and depressive multinational firm around (though, by now, Amazon might have caught up on the international ranking of exploitation). In so doing, he aimed to contribute

> to the reawakening of that historicity which our system – offering itself as the very end of history – necessary represses and paralyzes. This is the sense in which utopology revives long-dormant parts of the mind, organs of political and historical and social imagination which have virtually atrophied for lack of use, muscles of praxis we have long since ceased exercising, revolutionary gestures we have lost the habit of performing, even subliminally.

For Jameson, then, this kind of excavation has been a very necessary intervention in the debate about postmodernism, as – simply put – the figure of Utopia had disappeared from sight and, consequently, was threatening to disappear from the mind and our very much incomplete cognitive maps, as some kind of endangered species barely surviving in the pockets of encroaching capitalism.

Under metamodernism – and this is perhaps the most paradoxical aspect of our current social situation or historical moment, which, as has been widely noticed, is characterized by a deepening of the neoliberalization of the institutional constellations surrounding (a hence purer form of) capitalism– there is no need to dig deep or look far and wide for the figure of utopia.[4] It appears everywhere and nowhere across the arts and contemporary culture. If anything,

---

[3]See this excavation process in relation to deconstructive conceptual art and dystopian cyberpunk in Jameson's *Postmodernism, or, the cultural logic of late capitalism* (1991: 154–179) and *Archaeologies of the future. The desire called Utopia and other science fictions* (2005: 383–394).

[4]For a particularly original take on this situation see Williams & Srnicek (2013).

we could say, after Gramsci's adagio, that nowadays there is, and very much so, a pessimism of the intellect and an optimism of the will. (We wouldn't go so far as to claim that the opposite was true for the postmodern years, but it is an interesting thought exercise). The millennials know too much of today's exploits, inequalities and injustices to take any meaningful decision, let alone position themselves on a convenient subject position, yet they appear – from the political left to the political right – to be to be united around the *feeling* that today's deal is not the deal they signed up for during the postmodern years (with its promise of the end of conjunctures, careless consumerism, and eternal growth; see for instance Castells, Caraça & Cardoso 2012). That this feeling is translated into various movements that neatly bookend the 2000s (as a period, that is) such the Alter-globalists and the Indignados / Occupy or the European populist right and the Tea Party – which are, of course, as diverse in their aims as they are similar in their libidinal investments, modes of organization and, indeed, utopian longings – is just another indication of the re-emergence of the figure of Utopia today.

David Thorpe: Intertextual reimaginations

Born in 1972, working and living in London, his art part of the Saatchi collection (generally associated with the postmodern Young British Artists), David Thorpe is too old to belong to the millennials. Yet Thorpe's work – like Doig's, Hatoum's, Eliasson's and Bas Jan Ader's – has been pivotal in carving out, or cutting and pasting rather, the aesthetic and semiotic sphere that many of the millennials, including artists like Cyprien Gaillard, Armin Boehm, and Guido van de Werve and, indeed, Ragnar Kjartansson and Paula Doepfner, have been making their own over the past few years – the realm of the metamodern.

In many respects, Thorpe's work resonates with postmodern sensibilities, or rather, indeed, sensibilities that over the past few years have come to be associated with postmodernism but are not necessarily postmodern. Discussions of his work often center on its eclectic reappropriation, its generic hybridity, or what one might call its multimediality or intertextuality, or as one critic put it, "corrupt etymology" (Wood 2004: 89). Indeed, throughout his career, Thorpe has worked with a wide variety of materials, within a diversity of styles and genres, borrowing conventions and ideas from often-incompatible traditions. In his earlier works, for instance, he pitted with and against each other techniques of collaging, glass-painting and paper-cutting. Works like *Out from the night, the days are beautiful and filled with joy*, from 1999, and *Good people*, from 2002, are put together through collaging pieces of colored glass, leather, bark, dried flowers, paper, as well as by the painstaking processing of cutting and folding paper. Thorpe's later work in this sense is even more "corrupt." Works such as *The defeated life restored* (2005), *The collaborator* (2010) and *Endeavours* (2010) incorporate methodologies ranging from oil painting, soundscaping, light installations, sculpturing with metal, wood, leather and organic materials like barks and twigs, as well as ceramic crafts.

Besides adopting diverse methods and techniques, these works also eclectically appropriate conventions and gestures from a wide variety of traditions. *Out from the night, the days are beautiful and filled with joy*, for instance, appears to appropriate motifs from mid-century science fiction, German Romanticism, nineteenth-century American landscape painting and traditional Japanese wood cuttings, while *Good people* adds new-age and sectarian iconography and populuxe. Later works, like *The defeated life restored* and *Endeavours*, incorporate religious imagery, pagan elements, but also IKEA and other DIY features. Thorpe also makes reference to very diverse philosophical concepts or figures such as Nietzsche's Zarathustra, Foucault's Panopticon or the Messiah.

For Fredric Jameson, eclecticism was a sign above all of ahistoricity, depthlessness, inauthenticity and the waning of affect of the postmodern. In his discussions, reappropriation becomes a symbol not only of the withering of art's critical potential, but also of art's ability to be art for art's sake. Eclecticism, Jameson asserts, turns the original, inimitable practice of a William Faulkner or D.H. Lawrence into a code, a "field of stylistic and discursive heterogeneity without a norm" (1991: 17). Eclecticism, however, let alone appropriation, is certainly not exclusive to postmodernism. There are plenty of examples of eclectic reappropriation prior to the postmodern paradigm or alongside it in non-Western cultures. One simply needs to think of works from the mannerist era, or of certain eastern perceptions of art and art-making, where copying is not an anomaly but an asset.

Thorpe turns Jameson's assertion upside down. Not only does he turn multi-mediality and intertextual eclecticism from an unimaginative and craftless trick into a new form of making art that makes claims of affect, historicity, depth and even authenticity; he also uses eclecticism precisely to directly engage with the distinction between *l'art pour l'art* and art as social salvation. For far from adapting and reappropriating simply in order to play the poststructuralist semiotician, Thorpe engages with fragments from past movements and genres precisely in order to discover a new field of hitherto uncharted, that is, as of yet unsignified, possibilities. Similarly, far from masking his own critical or creative capacity, he precisely draws attention to his talent as a craftsman.

In the mixed media collage *Good people*, for instance, Thorpe appropriates a great diversity of diverging stylistic conventions, methods and materials to create a recognizable yet also strange, seemingly utopic world. The collage depicts a wooden building set amidst bare, autumnal trees, green moss and grass. The building at once evokes a space ship, transported from another galaxy; the frontispiece of a large boat, putting ashore in undiscovered lands; the architecture of new ageism; a church; a sectarian sanctuary; and a drifter or hermit's home, put together from found pieces of wood, scrap metal and glass. The woods, with its bare trees, most obviously resemble the woods of Caspar David Friedrich, alive yet melancholic. Circled mysteriously around the building, closing it off from all sides, they appear to harbor some hidden secret. In stylistic terms, the wooden building hovers somewhere between the utopias of Star Trek and the new ageists, the religious, the sectarians and the hobos, without landing anywhere in particular. It floats in a zone that is both instantly recognizable, because it reminds one of all these earlier traditions, but also strange, since its logic adheres to no tradition in particular. Thorpe reimagines from former utopias – none of which can be ascertained, some of which have been proven impossible – another utopia that is literally nowhere, a noplace. Indeed, the intertextual structure posing as a building cannot be entered: it lacks a door.

However, the utopia that emerges from Thorpe's eclectic reappropriation is not only impossible, it is also problematic. For the traditions the work appropriates are certainly not compatible. Indeed, however alike traditions such as science fiction and Romanticism, new ageism and Christianity may be, however much they may historically be related, they cannot coexist. They all propose their own ideal of utopia, of transcendence, that is mutually exclusive. The scientific utopia of, say, *Star Trek*, for instance, cannot coexist with the biblical utopia of Christianity, because they are based on contrary assumptions with respect to utopia, truth and the myth of origins. In addition, the sectarian imagery invokes as many negative connotations as the other references might incite positive feelings. In this respect the trees recall a shrine as much as a prison, guarding each side, its bark pasted over the paper and glass of the building. It may well be the witch from Hansel and Gretel that Friedrich's wanderings lead to eventually. *Good people* stylistically creates an impossible unity, imagines a harmony that cannot be.

Other works like *You are nothing* (2005) and *Great isolate* (2010) appear to use religious, Romantic and especially organic conventions and materials like light, bark, twigs, leaves and flower petals, traditionally used to show the transcendent, only in order to put the spectator back in his or her plane of immanence. In the watercolor painting *Great isolate*, a twig shaped somewhat like a menorah forms a thorny fork, while a branch of leaves resembles a shield, problematizing its material's natural and still present promise by turning the flexibility of nature into a cultivated fixation. In *You are nothing*, a lyrical poem chanting the lines "The inner light, the inner light is within me. Ecstasy is here" turns into a rather more ambiguous genre when it declares: "You are nothing. This world is not for you. Go!" Again, Thorpe's intention is unclear. Is he advocating a utopic promise? Or is he bullying us into suicide? Or both at once? Thorpe reappropriates conventions associated with postmodernism, yet redirects and resignifies them towards new horizons. His eclecticism is not, however, simply a matter of ahistorical or disaffected nostalgia, presentism, or futurism. In Thorpe's work, the contexts of the styles he adopts linger, their sensibilities resonate, precisely because they are each forced into a harmony with styles whose contexts and sensibilities they are incompatible with. In so doing, he shows us the possibilities of the future precisely by drawing attention to the intertextual limitations of the multifarious past.

Ragnar Kjartansson: Between hope and despair

Thorpe's legacy is increasingly visible across the arts. The likes of Charles Avery, Bettina Krieg, Jorinde Voigt and Jenny Michel, for instance, follow in Thorpe's footsteps by imagining impossible alternate worlds from various intertexts. Cyprien Gaillard turns modern housing blocks into incomprehensible, impenetrable, mysterious Stonehenges, that is, creates a hauntology of the modern by evoking Romantic paintings. Rob Voerman produces from scrap utopic yet only temporarily habitable sites and buildings, while Kaye Donachie's paintings, modeled after videos from 1968 and Woodstock, intimate secret societies and sects that are as idyllic and inviting as they are uncertain. Another artist who may be said to tread in Thorpe's footsteps is the Icelandic performance artist Ragnar Kjartansson. Kjartansson shares Thorpe's predilection for eclectic, intertextually composed utopias that make it immediately obvious that they are impossible to inhabit. In Kjartansson's case, influences appear to range from Marina Abramovic to Bas Jan Ader to Samuel Beckett, from folk music to blues to metal, and from Romanticism to Icelandic mythology. But where Thorpe works primarily with static materials, Kjartansson engages with utopia by way of performances incorporating live music, live theatre, installations and even live painting.

In this essay we will look at Kjartansson's utopias from another angle, however. For the element that is most important in his engagement with utopias is not intertextuality but another typically postmodern convention: irony. Now, over the past few postmodern decades, irony has, by and large, become synonymous with sarcasm, cynicism and even nihilism. Or at least in the visual arts it has. In the works of the Young British Artists, Damien Hirst, the Chapman brothers and Tracey Emin foremost among them, as well as in the works of artists related to them, like Jeff Koons and Cindy Sherman, irony has been utilized almost exclusively as a tool to deconstruct contemporary culture until there is neither anything contemporary nor anything remotely cultural left: broadly speaking, what remains is either something shiny, something sexually polymorphous (or, in non-psychoanalytical terms, vernacular, perverse) or something involving excrement. In the works of the Young British Artists and their contemporaries, irony is used to cancel out utopianism. In the work of Kjartansson and the Young Berlin artists, however, it is used to counterbalance it, to keep it in check.

Kjartansson's work oscillates continuously between sincerity and irony. Or as one reviewer put it: Kjartansson has "made a career of turning the deepest Icelandic traditions into works of performance that are part myth, part put-on, and part spontaneous adventure" (Byles 2009: 49). In his most famous work to date, *The end*, a six-month-long performance piece performed at the 2009 Venice Biennale, Kjartansson locked himself in one of the palazzo's lavish rooms together with a friend. Each day, as visitors carefully treaded around them, they drank beers and smoked cigarettes while Kjartansson painted his friend, who was wearing nothing but speedos. One might say that the performance underlined the baroque and bourgeois sensibility of the environment, reflecting the palace's grotesque architecture, critiquing the public's decadence and eventual self-destruction. Similarly, it seems feasible that the artist intended to parody the classical model of the artist's studio. However, there was also a rather Romantic, even hopeful element to the performance. Drinking himself into a state of trance or deliriousness, Kjartansson painted a new painting of his friend each day. It was as if by inducing himself into a state of semi- or subconsciousness, by being together with him, and by painting him again and again, Kjartansson tried to find something about his friend that he had not discovered before, something unknown to him one day that might reveal itself the next. Whatever else Kjartansson intended with *The end*, one outcome appears to have been that critical inquiry must always necessarily be infused with empathy.

Repetition is pivotal to Kjartansson's reimagination of utopia. Whether it is in the form of a famous Icelandic comedian walking in the snow shooting a gun for days on end (*Guilt trip* 2007), or a mother spitting in her son's face at repeated intervals (*My mother and me* 2005), or the artist himself singing a fifteen-couplet opera for hours on end (*Schumann machine* 2008), repetition is used by Kjartansson as a means to push, à la Beckett, the boundaries of the comedic to their tragic limits and vice versa, the beautiful to the ugly, and vice versa. By repeating one gesture to the extent that it becomes absurd, he tries to reveal the transcendent within the immanent.

One performance is particularly illustrative here. In *God* (2007), Kjartansson looks into the camera, dressed in an immaculate black suit, standing against a tasteless bright pink background. Backed by an orchestra of twelve cellists and violinists, he sings the same line, uninterrupted, for half an hour. The line is "sorrow conquers happiness." On the one hand, by repeating the line over and over, in a soft, sad, voice, Kjartansson affirms its meaning. In this sense, one may say that he is literally singing the last remaining gasps of happiness out of him. On the other hand, however, by changing the tempo, the notes, or the tone of voice slightly with each new utterance, he suggests that he is attempting to get something else out of the sentence each time he articulates it afresh. He appears to be seeking some sort of revelation or redemption even. It is almost as if he is saying: I realize sorrow conquers happiness, but might there be a possibility that

I can find some happiness or truth in it? The piece's title adds to the performance's confusion. The God of the title may refer to Kjartansson himself, as he sings about his creation as a place of misery and disappointment. But it may also be the case that the artist is calling for God, asking him whether this is really all there is.

Kjartansson here oscillates between melancholy, or even apathy, and hope. He realizes that sorrow conquers happiness, i.e. that the ways of the world are one way, yet nonetheless hopes in spite of his better judgment that sorrow does not necessarily conquer happiness, i.e. that the ways of the world are not necessarily as they seem but are the opposite. We have called this double-bind oscillatory, but one may even say that, like Thorpe's, his performance is not so much an oscillation as it is a multistability, a performance that we call oscillatory simply because we do not have the critical capacity to perceive both categories, melancholy and hope, at once. For *God* is never no longer melancholic, and always already hopeful.

Of course, Kjartansson is part of a larger aesthetic tradition. The tradition he appears to fit in with – one that may be called either Romantic Conceptualism or simply Romantic Irony – is above all embodied by Bas Jan Ader. The Dutch-American Ader was a performance artist working throughout the 1970s whose performances played out impossible scenarios. In one performance, he tried to defy gravity by hanging onto a branch, in another by riding a bicycle onto the water, and in yet another, by bending over without falling. Of course, each and every one of Ader's attempts failed. But that was his point, to try in spite of its inevitable failure. It is this double-bind, to try in spite of one's better judgment, that also characterizes Kjartansson's work. A crucial difference between Kjartansson and Ader, however, is that while Ader was a lone voice emerging in a still predominantly postmodern artscape, Kjartansson finds himself singing amidst numerous other metamodern tenors and sopranos like Olafur Eliasson, Michail Sailstorfer, Susanne Burner and Mariechen Danz.

Where Thorpe reimagines utopia as an impossible possibility through his use of the hitherto almost exclusively postmodern convention of intertextuality, Kjartansson reimagines utopia by incorporating into his performances both hope and irony. What they share, however, is their use of techniques and tropes associated with the postmodern precisely in order to surpass the postmodern. The way in which they both do this is by bringing the postmodern into the realm of what one might call the modern (Vermeulen & van den Akker 2011), and vice versa by dragging the modern into the realm of the postmodern: *metamodernism*. Thorpe's mixed media installations, collages, paper cut-outs and paintings no longer distinguish between pastiche and historicity, or between eclecticism and authenticity. Similarly, Kjartansson's performances do not distinguish between hope and irony, or between immanence and transcendence. Each of these artists believes that they can do both, at once.

Paula Doepfner: Utopia revisited

The last artist we wish to discuss is Paula Doepfner. Doepfner is part of a talented group of young artists affiliated with Galerie Tanja Wagner, the Gertrude Stein, or Goldsmiths, if you will, of the Young Berlin art scene (other artists exhibiting with Tanja Wagner are Mariechen Danz, Angelika Trojnarski, Ulf Aminde and Sejla Kameric). Like Thorpe and Kjartansson, Doepfner works across traditions and genres, eclectically adopting styles, methods and materials. In her latest solo show, *Promessus* (2010), she used anything from video, photography and painting to installation art, reappropriating materials as diverse as trees, twigs, thorns, branches, moss, ice, pieces of paper, rusting metal, celluloid, clay, paint and canvas. The aspect of Doepfner's work we want to focus on is her reimagination of utopia as a place that is unthinkable. Considering its title, it seems appropriate to take her latest show as our point of departure.

Judging from the show's title, Doepfner holds an ambivalent position towards utopia. On the one hand, *Promessus* invokes the word *promise*. Yet, on the other hand, it also infers the word *messy*. I will make you, the spectator, a promise, it says, but a promise that is messy, that has – not unlike the #occupy movements or the indignados – no clear form or future. The title brings up several other connotations that further complicate the inherent promise. The tragic figure of Prometheus instantly comes to mind, the trickster who stole fire from the Gods so as to offer mankind the gift (or the curse) of technological civilization. He, of course, was severely punished for his hubris. Odysseus (Ulysses) is another mythological figure that is present, the voyager who was regarded as a cunning strategist by the Greeks and as a deceitful con artist by the Romans for his maneuver with the Trojan horse. His journey to Ithaca, his beloved "homeland" (to use Ernst Bloch's metaphor for utopia) was full of despair and travail. And wouldn't James Joyce, the Modern Master, add that the same could be said of every single day of our everyday lives? The exhibition's theme, indeed, seems to be the Janus-faced nature of utopianism. It takes the visitor on an adventurous journey, but it is highly dubitable whether utopia awaits at its end.

Doepfner's reappropriation of the gallery's entrance is illustrative of this dual approach to utopia. Piles of wild bushes above a man's height barricade the entrance door; clouds of thick mist block the view of the space beyond, thorny branches claw at skin and cloth as travelers navigate their way to the unknown. This is less a welcome than a warning. What is she trying to tell us? That pursuing utopian horizons comes with the risk of getting lost? Of getting hurt? Of getting your hands dirty? There is only one piece of advice at the beginning of this voyage: *Whatever you wish to keep, you better grab it fast* (2010), another artwork is titled. Meticulously painted roots, "thick with description", float against a white background in the vacuum between two glass plates. They warn the weary traveler that all things solid may melt in the air, that stable positions should not be taken for granted, that anchors might come loose.

Yet the titular promise urges the visitor to go on, to delve further into this nether world. Once the wilderness has been traversed, the mist has risen and the thorns have been removed, one enters yet another ambivalent space. A rather large chunk of ice dangles from the ceiling (*Ohne mich* 2010). From what was originally a geometrically shaped cube, Doepfner has carved out something that looks as if it just broke off of a glacier. Within a few days the ice will have melted. But for a moment it looks as solid as a rock. For a moment it captures nature in transition. As it melts, the glacier releases citations, frozen in the ice, from Robert Musil's modern masterpiece *The man without qualities*. These citations all speak of utopian longings and the desire to transcend the limitations of man. "In flooding and losing oneself," a typical one reads, "the borders between the I and the world dissolve and a new world appears, in which inside and outside are no longer opposites." Yet these otherworldly hopes are not easily fulfilled, if they are at all. The pieces of paper, barely legible because of the ice water, drop upon a bed of moss placed in the middle of an iron plate. The moss is supposed to safeguard the paper cuttings from the carnivorous plants underneath, but doesn't live up to its task, as the water, after leaking incessantly for days on end, has flooded the plate and the moss has died. Musil's citations will either be exposed to the carnivores or disintegrate in the water.

Interestingly, the artificial organicity of the glacier is juxtaposed to a series of photographs of actual glaciers, hanging on the wall behind the installation (*Höhlung* 2010). Taken together, the installation and these photos betray a fascination with the different phases of the elements and the transitions between these phases. The artificial glacier melts; the ice water leaks on the iron plate, which slowly turns red as a result of oxidation; the leaked water evaporates because of the room's temperature. The natural glaciers, meanwhile, are figuratively frozen in time, brought to a standstill by means of a photographic image. This trope of shifting between shapes, stages and phases is continued as we move to yet another space. Scattered over the floor of the gallery lie several volcanic rocks. Of course these clotted clumps of lava are the inverse of a leaking "glacier," as if to say that things do not necessarily need to perish, that they can also consolidate, that some things can be permanent. By contrasting ice and lava, water and fire, the sea and the sun, Doepfner seems to warn us that we should continuously reposition ourselves between elements and amongst phases, so that our utopian aspirations do not evaporate, solidify or come to a standstill.

Doepfner's exhibition ends, fittingly, with rage. She has taken the visitor on a journey towards utopia, but each time she believed she had it within her sights, it disappeared before her eyes; the moment she articulated it was the moment it eluded all representation. The back wall of Galerie Tanja Wagner is painted with thick, multilayered, unevenly splattered lines. The colors are earthy browns, dark reds and greys, a mixture, it almost seems, of earth, blood and dust. One might be mistaken that Doepfner has returned to the postmodern practice of deconstruction: the picking out and unpicking out of known forms into alienated fragments. Yet the contrary is true. What she appears to be trying to do is not to deconstruct, but to reconstruct. She realizes, at this point, that none of the conventions she has adopted can invoke utopia. Here, screaming paint onto the wall, smearing the red, brown and gray colors of blood, earth and dust, of life and death onto the canvas like a mad alchemist, she is desperately trying to find the language that might represent utopia. It is a language that is unmistakably violent, a language also without direction. For Doepfner, it seems, that is the real, darker nature of the longing for utopia: it opens up an impossible transcendental sphere, more plane of immanence than noumenon, we should always strive to move into but never get to.

Openings and conclusions

The figure of utopia in any one period, Jameson argued, is very much related to the social situation of the historical moment in question. This means, by extension,

> that our imaginations are hostages to our own mode of production (and perhaps to whatever remnants of past ones it has preserved). It suggests that at best Utopia can serve the negative purpose of making us more aware of our mental and ideological imprisonment; and that therefore the best Utopias are those that fail the most comprehensively. (Jameson 2005: xiii)

The metamodern figure of utopia, as it appeared across the arts in the 2000s, represents, then, at least two aspects of the metamodern structure of feeling. We hope to have shown, first, that we witness a utopian turn in the arts that stands for the re-emergence and multiplication of utopian desires of all sorts in contemporary culture. To our mind, artists today are once more taking to reimagining utopia primarily because they are faced with a radically unstable and uncertain world, where political systems and power relations are diffuse and unpredictable, financial security a rare privilege and ecological problems – sometimes quite literally – clog the horizon. By this we do not mean to say that the return to utopia is an escape mechanism. On the contrary. During the postmodern years of relative peace and plenty, few artists felt the need to imagine alternative societies or cultivate a utopian desire. Even those artists that were critical did not look elsewhere but rather set their sights on problems *within* society. Now that conflicts are pending and poverty is increasingly widespread within the West, looking elsewhere for solutions suddenly seems like a viable option again. As an impossible possibility, utopia should not be perceived as a new ideological blueprint, however. Much rather, it should be understood as a tool, say, a looking glass, for scanning this world and others for alternative possibilities. It is not invoked to get us away from something according to this or that dogma; it is evoked out of a renewed utopian desire.

Second, the metamodern figure of utopia indicates that there are no clear utopian horizons after decades of TINA and careless consumerism. Thorpe's collages, Kjartansson's performances and Doepfner's installations radiate with, and oscillate between, decay and transcendence, the permanent and the transitory, melancholy and hope, enthusiasm and despair. Elsewhere we have described this oscillation, after Plato and Voeglin, as *metaxy*, an oscillation between the poles of existence, an attempt to unify a double-bind, an impossible possibility (Vermeulen & van den Akker 2010: 201). Each of these three artists reimagines utopia, whilst lacking the conceptual tools to imagine Utopia in the first place and realizing that it can never be realized in the second instant. For each of them, hope is both natural to the human species and a skill that needs to be learned, a rare good that needs to be fought for. Their struggles are hard (whether in Thorpe's persnickety craftsmanship, Kjartansson's endurance or Doepfner's continual disappointments), and ultimately futile. But they do struggle. Their utopianism does give a sign of life at a time when Fukuyama and Danto and other postmodern doctors had declared the patient dead and buried. Yet it's not an easy struggle. It never will be. They have to reinvent a tradition of utopianism that the postmoderns carelessly neglected. But they do – collage by performance by installation – in spite of themselves.

Now, of course, there is much more to these artists' work than we have been able to discuss here. Kjartansson's performances, for instance, are as interesting for their ironic utopianism as they are for their aesthetic sensibilities, while Thorpe's collages can also be seen in the light of concerns about ecology and climate change. Similarly, Doepfner's work has a philosophical depth that goes far beyond the scope of this essay. What we have wanted to do here is merely look at one aspect of their work that has become particularly prevalent of late.

In a similar vein, the account we have given of metamodernism, too, is highly reductive. If we are correct in asserting that metamodernism has quickly become the Western world's new dominant cultural structure of feeling, there certainly is more to metamodernism than the oscillation between utopia, irony, intertextuality and melancholy. Elsewhere we have argued, for instance, that whereas both the modern and the postmodern were tied, temporally, to a Hegelian understanding of history, the metamodern links itself to a more Kantian proposition of history (Vermeulen & van den Akker 2011: 25–40). The *modi operandi* discussed here should also be understood not along the lines of Hegel's "positive idealism," but with the "negative idealism" of his contemporary. For when Kant says that the history of mankind is the realization of a "secret plan," he also says that it is so only insofar as it is "seen" as such. As he clarifies his position elsewhere: "[e]ach [...] people, *as if* following some guiding thread, go toward a natural but to each of them unknown goal" (1963: 21; emphasis added). History coming to an end – the state he referred to as "Perpetual Peace" or the "Kingdom of ends," i.e. as something that might not exist to begin with coming to an end – would be a contradiction in terms. For Kant, we are not really moving toward a natural but unknown goal, but we (need to) pretend we are doing so that we progress morally as well as politically. Metamodernism adheres to Kant's philosophy of History in that it moves for the sake of moving, making attempts in spite of their inevitable failure; it forever seeks a truth that it never expects to find. Indeed, because it never finds it, it never stops its search.

By bringing up the notions of Utopia and the End of History, one immediately poses another question, one that we hope to engage with in future research: the question of the end of the Grand Narratives. The German philosopher Peter Sloterdijk wrote that the problem with all those grand narratives of the past was not that they were too grand, too all-encompassing, but that they were, in fact, not grand enough (2004: 7). It should be added, however, that any single reason for "incrudelence" towards this or that grand narrative, to use Lyotard's well-known phrase, cannot be sought in a lack of size, but must be found in the fact that one narrative after the other stopped being "contemporary" and consequently lost all explanatory power. The question remains, therefore, whether we can revive, after decades of consensus about the impossibility (undesirablity even) of thinking the past, present and future as a meaningful whole, the ability to conceive of a guiding thread of History, a thread that might function as a guide for all those who struggle – like so many young people today – with a renewed desire for utopia.

REFERENCES

Allen S. and M. McQuade (eds.). 2011. *Landform building: Architecture's new terrain*. Zurich: Lars Muller.

Bourriaud, Nicolas. 2009. *Altermodern*. London: Tate Publishing.

Byles, Jeff. 2009. What do you do with a drunken painter? *Modern Painters* (May), 48–53.

Castells Manuel, João Caraça & Gustavo Cardoso (eds.). 2012. *Aftermath: The cultures of the economic crisis*. Oxford: Oxford University Press.

Eshelman, Raoul. 2008. *Performatism, or the end of postmodernism*. Aurora: The Davies Group Publishers.

Jameson, Fredric. 1991. *Postmodernism, or the cultural logic of postmodernism*. Durham: Duke University Press.

Jameson, Fredric. 2005. *Archaeologies of the future. The desire called utopia and other science fictions*. London: Verso Publishing.

Jameson, Fredric. 2010. *Valences of the dialectic*. London: Verso Publishing.

Kant, Immanuel. 1963 [1784]. Idea for a universal history from a cosmopolitan point of view. In Lewis White Beck (ed. and transl.), *Kant on history*, 11–26. Upper Saddle River: Prentice Hall.

Kirby, Alan. 2009. *Digimodernism: How new technologies dismantle the postmodern and reconfigure our culture*. New York: Continuum.

Konstantinou, Lee. 2009. *Wipe that smirk off your face: Postironic literature and the politics of character*. Ph.D. dissertation, Stanford University.

MacDowell, James. 2012. Wes Anderson, tone and the quirky sensibility. *New Review of Film and Television Studies*. 10(1), 6–27.

Moraru, Christian. 2010. *Cosmodernism: American narrative, late globalization, and the new cultural imaginary*. Ann Arbor: University of Michigan Press.

Nealon, Jeffrey T. 2012. *Post-postmodernism: or, the cultural logic of just-in-time capitalism*. Palo Alto: Stanford University Press.

Obrist, Hans Ulrich. 2010. Manifestos for the future. *E-Flux* 12, 01/2010. http://www.e-flux.com/journal/manifestos-for-the-future/ (last accessed 29 July 2014).

Poecke, Niels van. 2014. De ballast van vernieuwing: Over metamodernisme in de popmuziek. *Gonzo Circus* 122, n.p., http://www.gonzocircus.com/essay-de-ballast-van-vernieuwing-over-metamodernisme-in-de-popmuziek/ (last accessed on 29 July 2014).

Sloterdijk, Peter. 2004. *Im Weltinnenraum des Kapitals. Für eine philosophische Theorie der Globalisierung.* Frankfurt Am Main: Suhrkamp Verlag.

Sterling, Bruce. 2012. An essay on the new aesthetic. *Wired*, 2 April 2012, http://www.wired.com/2012/04/an-essay-on-the-new-aesthetic/ (last accessed on 29 July 2014).

Vermeulen, Timotheus & G. Rustad. 2013.Watching television with Jacques Rancière: US "quality television," *Mad Men* and the "late cut." *Screen* 53(3), 341–354.

Vermeulen, Timotheus & Robin van den Akker. 2010. Notes on metamodernism. *Journal of Aesthetics and Culture* 2, 1–14.

Vermeulen, Timotheus & Robin van den Akker. 2011. Metamodernism, history, and the story of Lampe. In Rachel MagShamrain & Sabine Strumper-Krobb (eds.), *After postmodernism*, 25–40. Konstanz: Hartung Gorre Verlag.

Vermeulen, Timotheus & Robin van den Akker. 2014. Art criticism and metamodernism. *ArtPulse* 19 (5), 22–27.

Wallerstein, Immanuel.1998. *Utopistics: Or, historical choices of the twenty-first century.* New York: The New Press.

Williams Alex & Nick Srnicek. 2013. Accelerated manifesto for an accelerationist politics. *Critical Legal Thinking*, http://criticallegalthinking.com/2013/05/14/accelerate-manifesto-for-an-accelerationist-politics (last accessed 29 July 2014).

Williams, Raymond. 1977. *Marxism and literature.* Oxford: Oxford University Press.

Williams, Raymond. 2001 [1925] Film and the dramatic tradition. In John Higgins (ed.), *The Raymond Williams reader*, 25–41. Oxford: Blackwell Publishers.

Wood, Catherine. 2004. David Thorpe. *Frieze* 84 (June–August). http://www.frieze.com/issue/review/david_thorpe/ (last accessed on 29 July 2014).

Don DeLillo's *Point Omega*, the Anthropocene, and the Scales of Literature

PIETER VERMEULEN

9/11 fiction after trauma

In a widely noted essay from 2009, Richard Gray diagnoses 9/11 literature with a double failure of the imagination. Gray notes that while canonical 9/11 fictions such as Claire Messud's *The Emperor's Children*, Don DeLillo's *Falling Man*, and Jay McInerney's *The Good Life* duly acknowledge that after 9/11 "some kind of alteration of imaginative structures is required," they lack "the ability and the willingness imaginatively to act on that recognition" (2009: 134). The first problem is that their assessment of the psychosocial effects of the ashes of 9/11 rarely moves beyond "the preliminary stages of trauma" (2009: 130); the second is that these ashes are invariably gathered into the domestic domain: time and again, Gray writes, 9/11 fiction "retreat[s] into domestic detail" (2009: 134). The upshot of this preoccupation with domestic trauma is a foreclosure of the *global* dimensions of the affective and political changes that the events of 9/11 have unleashed. Against this tormented home-liness, Gray recommends a literature that is more willing to "open up and hybridize American culture" (2009: 153). In his response to Gray, published in the same issue of *American Literary History*, Michael Rothberg finds himself in broad agreement with Gray's assessment and recommendation, and adds that Gray's call for a hybridized America could be enriched by "a complementary centrifugal mapping that charts the outward movement of American power" (2009: 153). What is needed, according to Gray and Rothberg, is less domes-ticity and more world; what prevents a passage from the former to the latter is a tendency to linger over the disabling psychological effects of trauma.

The characterization of canonical post-9/11 fiction as overly domestic has become somewhat of a critical commonplace, even if Catherine Morley (2011) has shown that attention to the domestic already dominated late 1990s fiction, and Georgiana Banita has observed a growing interest in the global ramifications of the war on terror in what she calls the "second wave" of 9/11 fiction (2012: 166–67). The observations of Gray and Rothberg derive their critical thrust from these critics' shared commitment to transnational and cosmopolitan connected-ness, ideas that still figure prominently on critical agendas in different disciplinary formations such as transnational cultural studies, postcolonialism, or world literature. In the face of the contemporary novel's retreat into the domestic, Gray and Rothberg propose that it extends its scope to a global arena, and that it trains its focus on the sites where the global has inflected the local. Still, this overt transnational commitment is underwritten by a second, and less conspicuous, conviction: Gray's and Rothberg's interventions convey an undiminished belief that the novel form, if only it would begin to live up to its potential, has the capacity to deliver ever more "otherness," and can serve as an appropriate imaginative vehicle for addressing the ethical and political problems that face us in the early twenty-first century.

In this essay, I turn to a number of contemporary critical discourses that unsettle the conviction that contemporary challenges can adequately be addressed by repositioning ourselves along the continuum that ranges from the local to the global – by abandoning the domestic impasses of trauma for more worldly vistas. Ursula Heise has described the "theoretical stalemate" in which debates over the relative merits of the local and the global tend to end (2008: 7–8): it makes exactly as much sense to promote local modes of belonging as forms of resistance against capitalist globalization as to deride them for their refusal to transcend their provincialism. Indeed, phenomena like global warming or the sublime abstractions of financialization can arguably not be captured by merely extending the *geographical scope* of the literary imagination, but may well require a *shift in scale* beyond the scale on which human life is used to operating. In other words, addressing these issues may require from contemporary fiction that it learns to entertain spatiotemporal dimensions that the novel form never imagined it would have to imagine. If the novel form has traditionally been invested in the exploration of the fate of the individual and its relation to its social contexts, the discourses on the Anthropocene and on the geological ramifications of human culture I engage with in this essay present the contemporary novel with a new challenge: that of scaling up its imagining of the human to the dimensions of biological and geological time.

After my discussion of cultural geology and the Anthropocene, I go on to show that contemporary fiction has indeed begun to imagine scales that cannot be located on the spectrum between the domestic and the global. I focus on Don DeLillo's short 2010 novel *Point Omega*, in order to measure its difference from his earlier *Falling Man* (2007), a novel that is often seen as paradigmatic of 9/11 fiction's failure to move beyond "the endless reenactment of trauma" (Versluys 2009: 20; Dunst 2012: 60), as a work that is "immured in the melancholic state" (Gray 2011: 28). *Point Omega* is less fixated on one particular event: it is written against the background of the Iraq campaign, an incomplete, protracted, and non-climactic period that lacks the readability and narratability of the punctual events of 9/11 (Luckhurst 2012: 721). Like *Falling Man*, it is marked by a lack of narrative progress and imaginative resolution, yet it is organized around a very different evocation of space and time, which radically interrupts the domesticating tendencies that foreclose *Falling Man*'s imagining of the global ramifications of contemporary disaster. *Point Omega* does *not* offer a more worldly perspective, but instead negotiates the relations between the human world and spatiotemporal dimensions in which human concerns hardly figure. While *Falling Man* can be read as what Roger Luckhurst has called a "paradigmatic" trauma novel (2008: 90–97) and as a faithful and even formulaic example of what Rothberg calls traumatic realism, *Point Omega* signals a disruption of the protocols of realism – a disruption that trauma fiction, in spite of the rhetoric of unrepresentability and violence that accompanies it, has not managed to effect (Vermeulen 2012: 549–568). *Point Omega* displays what David Palumbo-Liu, in his account of contemporary fiction, has called "the disruption of literary realism by excessive otherness" (2012: 28–29). When "the invasion of otherness" occasions "the failure of the liberal imagination to make good on its aspirations to accommodate it" (Palumbo-Liu 2012: 61–62), we witness the breakdown of one of the crucial technologies through which the liberal imagination has tried to achieve that accommodation: the literary novel. While Palumbo-Liu connects this crisis to "increased and intensified globalization" (2012: 143), the example of *Point Omega* – whose slender shape barely qualifies it as a novel – shows that globalization merges with other decidedly non- or post-human powers to subvert the psychological realism that a novel like *Falling Man* perpetuates.

By emphasizing that *Point Omega* not only breaks open the continuum from the global to the local but also moves beyond the compulsive repetitions of trauma, I want to underline another limitation of calls for transnational or cosmopolitan connectedness. These discourses tend to figure intercultural connectedness as geographical extension, and do not account for the transformative role of temporality in contemporary developments in literary form. In his magisterial survey of *Twenty-First-Century Fiction*, Peter Boxall organizes the disparate set of concerns that animate contemporary fiction around that fiction's commitment to register and shape a new temporal awareness. Boxall observes "the glimmering outline of a new kind of temporality" (2013: 39), "new measures of speed and slowness" (2013: 207). He presents *Point Omega* as one such novel that is concerned with "how to understand the transition from one time zone to another" (2013: 22). My reading makes Boxall's general characterization more specific by showing that DeLillo's novel figures that transition as a move beyond the temporality of trauma, and its foreclosure of *global* extension, to the nonhuman vastness of *geological* time. For Boxall, contemporary fiction's renegotiation of temporality conveys "the perception that the narrative mechanics which have allowed us to negotiate our being in the world, to inherit our pasts and to bequeath our accumulated wisdom to the future, have failed" (2013: 217). *Point Omega*'s tentative narrative innovations make visible the limits of traditional narrative mechanics and intimate imaginative challenges that a mere geographical extension beyond domestic trauma cannot address.

The scales of literature: Cultural geology and the Anthropocene

In a recent essay entitled "The Posthuman Comedy," Mark McGurl commends Wai Chee Dimock's influential work on the "deep time" of literary history for relating American literature to other continents and other times. Dimock's daring juxtapositions of Thoreau and the Hindu *Bhagavad Gita*, for instance, or of Henry James and the *Odyssey*, expand "the tracts of space-time across which literary scholars might draw valid links between author and author" (2012: 533). For McGurl, Dimock instantiates the transnational turn that I have also identified in Gray and Rothberg: for her, as for those critics, an extension of space-time somehow reinvigorates "our very sense of the connectedness among human beings" (2012: 533) across the globe and literature operates as "a remarkably frictionless conduit of transnational sympathy and identification" (2012: 534). Yet if Dimock expands the scope of literary attention to the globe, then for McGurl the globe is not enough, as he argues for the need to supplement the transnational exploration of different locales and temporalities with the more encompassing perspective of a "new cultural geology." This approach would "position culture in a time-frame large enough to crack open the carapace of human self-concern, exposing it to the idea, and maybe even the fact, of its external ontological preconditions, its ground" (2011: 380). Transnationalism, even in its most adventurous forms (as in the work of Dimock), fails to factor in "scientific knowledge of the spatiotemporal vastness and numerousness of the nonhuman world" (2012:

537). McGurl envisions a literature in which this nonhuman vastness "becomes visible as a formal, representational, and finally existential problem" (2012: 537). He does not find these more capacious spatiotemporal parameters in the realist novel, which typically "eddies in an unheroic present" (2013: 632), but rather in the genres of science fiction and horror. Unlike the literary novel, these genres are "willing to risk artistic ludicrousness in their representation of the inhumanly large and long" (2012: 539). For McGurl, "those rare works of literature that set themselves the task of scaling our vision dramatically up or down or both" (2012: 541) define what he calls the "posthuman comedy" – his term "for the appearance of the problem of scale in modern literary history" (2013: 632).

McGurl's term "posthuman comedy" usefully foregrounds questions of genre and of the role that literary form can play in intimating nonhuman scales. Yet even if McGurl explicitly excludes the literary novel – as opposed to genre fiction – from the category of posthuman comedy, it persists in a less conspicuous form in his intervention. For one thing, McGurl's expectation that genre fiction make the problem of scale "visible as a formal, representational, and finally existential problem" (2012: 537) voices a markedly *novelistic* conception of literature. The expectation that literature can recode historical and ontological challenges as existential concerns is traditionally directed at the literary novel, as the main modern literary technology for the management of empathy and desire. To put this point differently, if genre fiction has the means to *evoke* nonhuman otherness, it cannot therefore do the cultural work of making it *matter* as a formal and existential *problem*. Indeed, McGurl's case would be better served by recording the breakdown of the human in the face of the nonhuman in the very form through which the human has traditionally been imagined: in the literary novel. Even if the impact of nonhuman otherness on human life requires that the narrative repertoire of the traditional novel be revised, this shift can be made palpable by confronting the limits of that repertoire in the very form where the reader expects it to operate. As I show below, this is precisely what happens in *Point Omega*, in which the exposure to nonhuman dimensions strains the limits of the novel form. DeLillo's novel tests the form's "elastic powers" only to have these powers radicalized to breaking point through their confrontation with an "excessive otherness" that overwhelms them (Palumbo-Liu 2012: 15, 29). Interestingly, McGurl recognizes that the breakdown of form can evoke the irruption of the nonhuman, even if he again attributes this potential to genre fiction, rather than to the literary novel: if works that aim to scale our visions up or down ultimately "fail to transcend their historical and medial conditions of possibility," this "testifies to the limits of the human imagination … but those limits are also what allow us to know and feel our presence in the world as something in particular" (2012: 541–542). Such a confrontation with the limits of the human imagination is precisely what takes place in *Point Omega*.

The overlap between questions of scale, form, and the human is also explored in discourses on the Anthropocene – and this is the second critical domain on which I will draw. The notion of the Anthropocene has gained a wide currency in the last few years, as its relevance for the study of literature and culture has begun to be assessed. Coined by the chemist Paul Crutzen and the biologist Eugene Stoermer in 2000, the term captures the influence of human activity on the world's geological and ecological make-up, and proposes that man's dramatic impact on the globe's chemical composition and climate since James Watt's development of a practical steam engine in 1784 be recognized as a geochrono-logical unit in its own right.[1] As "in terms of key environmental parameters, the Earth System has recently moved well outside the range of natural variability exhibited over at least the last half million years" (Crutzen & Steffen 2003: 251), it is time to start thinking of humanity "as a geological force" (Chakrabarty 2012: 2). The Anthropocene, in other words, demands that we must "scale up our imagination of the human" (Chakrabarty 2009: 206), as the human now at once participates in "differently-scaled histories of the planet, of life and species, and of human societies" (Chakrabarty 2012: 14).

While the notion of the Anthropocene opens up the same sublime vistas as McGurl's posthuman comedy, the conception of human agency that it entails is very different. While McGurl insists on the vanity of human striving in the face of "an absolutely indifferent, starkly inhuman universe" (2012: 548), the Anthropocene inserts the human into geological deep time as a responsible agent. Deep time, in the Anthropocene, is not the human's other, but rather another plane on which it cannot but exert agency. If anything, it further aug-ments human responsibility and agency: the human is the force that has decisi-vely contributed to global warming, mass extinction of species, and rising sea levels, but it is also the only power that can consciously intervene in the destructive movements it has unleashed. In the Anthropocene, the human needs to think of itself not only as a "human human" (human life as we think we know it), but also as a particularly "nonhuman human" (Chakrabarty 2012: 12), as a force that is of the same order of nonhuman agencies such as rocks, meteors, and volcanoes. We must now think "human agency over multiple and incommensu-rate scales at once" (Chakrabarty 2012: 1) and think "disjunctively about the human" (Chakrabarty 2012: 2). In the Anthropocene, human life is simulta-neously both a geological force and a conscious agent. This is less a question of *evoking* nonhuman dimensions than of figuring the fissure that cultural geology and the Anthropocene locate at the heart of human life. As I will show, this challenge of figuring a disjunction that exceeds the psychological realism of trauma fiction is the one to which *Point Omega* imagines itself to be responding.[2]

---

[1]Dating the start of the Anthropocene to the 18th century is not uncontroversial, and will remain contested as the term awaits official recognition as a distinctive stratigraphic unit. Crutzen's and others' idea that the Anthropocene was inaugurated around 1800 is chal-lenged by the contention that it began with the mass clearing of forests for agriculture about 8,000 years earlier. For a good sketch of these and other issues surrounding the use of the term, including the option of subdividing the period in different stages, see Szerszynski (2012).

[2]Noma Bar's cover illustration for the Picador edition of the novel, which is only one in a series of stunning covers he has made for recent issues and reissues of DeLillo's novels, captures this challenge to present a disjunction at the heart of the human. On the model of the famous "duck-rabbit illusion," it presents a desert landscape with a lizard that, on closer inspection, also outlines two contiguous human faces. The lizard serves as the eye of the most prominent of these faces, which can be read as a way to bend the traditional image of the eyes as a gateway to the soul toward a recognition of evolutionary time at the heart of the human. Bar's illustration points to the necessity as well as the difficulty of seeing human life *simultaneously* in terms of intersubjective relations and in terms of its irreducible implication in biological and geological time.

"Horrible minimalism": *Point Omega*'s slowness

If *Point Omega*, as James Gourley has argued, is "able to engage with the concept [of temporality] at a remove from the pressures of September 11" (2013: 86), it does so through two crucial strategies: its evocation of a contemporary work of art – Douglas Gordon's *24 Hour Psycho* – and its own temporal organization. Significantly, in *Falling Man* these same two elements served to bind the novel to the repetitions and the lack of progression that mark psychological trauma. *Falling Man* begins in the immediate aftermath of the attacks on the Twin Towers, in "a time and space of falling ash and near night" (2008: 3), as Keith, the novel's protagonist, leaves one of the collapsing buildings. Both Keith and his estranged wife Lianne fail to work through the impact of the events as they surrender to parallel lives of numbed disconnection. This lack of progression is sealed by the novel's ending: the last of the novel's intermittent efforts to inhabit the perspective of one of the terrorists ends when the airplane he hijacks enters the building from which Keith will emerge into the street on which the novel had opened. The novel's narrative grammar constitutes a loop of endless repetition.

The novel also features several descriptions of unannounced public performances in New York by the fictional David Janiak, known as Falling Man (2008: 219). Letting himself fall and remain suspended by one leg, Janiak's performances are "painful and highly dangerous," keeping him bound, as we learn late in the novel, to his "chronic depression due to a spinal condition" (2008: 222). The effect of these performances, one of which Lianne witnesses at close range, is equally destructive for its audience: not only is Janiak's bodily discomfort contagious (2008: 168), it also keeps Lianne ensnared in the traumas of her personal life – especially her father's suicide (2008: 169, 218) – as well as those of contemporary U.S. society: Janiak's posture mimics the weirdly serene image of a man falling from the Towers famously captured by Richard Drew and popularized under the name "Falling Man." *Falling Man*'s *evocation* of Janiak's *reenactment* of this iconic image is then, in a sense, a double ekphrasis. In this way, DeLillo's evocation of art itself obeys a rhythm of contagious and compulsive repetition that does not allow the individuals it affects any sense of progression, and keeps them captured in an existence lived "in the spirit of what is ever impending" (2008: 212).

Point Omega also evokes a work of art that is itself an evocation of another iconic work: the four central chapters of this decidedly slim novel's main narrative are framed by two chapters, entitled "Anonymity" and "Anonymity 2," in which an unnamed character watches and reflects on Douglas Gordon's *24 Hour Psycho* at the Museum of Modern Art. Gordon's installation consists of a soundless projection of Hitchcock's *Psycho*, slowed down so the movie now takes exactly 24 hours. If this double ekphrasis recalls *Falling Man*, the relation between the different moments in this process of remediation point to a rhythm that is very different from the compulsive repetitions of DeLillo's earlier novel. For one thing, Gordon's installation constitutes a revision of traditional models of subjectivity. It takes up a film that is often seen as a paradigmatic illustration of Freudian psychoanalysis, only to remove the model of subjectivity that underlies it. The strategy of slowing down the action breaks open the normal pacing of human action and perception in order to remove it from the realm of the eventual ("whatever was happening took forever to happen" [2011: 4]); and further, its decision to slow down the movie to exactly 24 hours synchronizes human life with the cosmic rhythms of night and day – a shift beyond human categories that the novel's main narrative, which takes place in a desert that refuses to be constrained by human names ("the Sonoran desert or maybe it was the Mojave desert or another desert altogether" [2011: 25]), will repeat. As Gordon's installation also removes the sound that is such a crucial part of the effectiveness of Hitchcock's climactic scenes, the spectacle becomes "all broken motion, without suspense or dread or urgent pulsing screech-owl sound" (2011: 11); the viewer is, in Philip Monk's description, "always out of sync with the time of the action, which sunders our experience" (2011: 60). If *Psycho* is famously a movie about psychosis, a pathological dissociation from reality, Gordon's installation actualizes that dissociation through formal means by evacuating the psychoanalytical (or any other) framework that may still try to account for this disturbance in psychological terms. DeLillo's elaborate ekphrasis of this installation signals his ambition to repeat this depsychologizing operation in the novel form, a form that is traditionally beholden to social and psychological realism. *Point Omega*'s evocation of Gordon's installation announces its intention to disturb customary accounts of human perception and thought, including those that the post-traumatic patterns of *Falling Man* failed to undo.

While it is easy enough to read the novel's engagement with *24 Hour Psycho* as a reflection on the ontology of art, or as another instance of DeLillo's long-standing fascination with slow motion (Marcus 2013: 175), we can't fail to note the extent to which the encounter with this artwork is described in temporal terms. The viewer's "watchfulness" corresponds to "[t]he film's merciless pacing" (2011: 6), which liberates the viewer from customary experiences of suspense and dread and gives access to "pure time," as "[t]he broad horror of the old gothic movie [i]s subsumed in time" (2011: 7). Crucially, this different mode of temporality is *not* described as an escape from human time into a timeless realm that successfully transcends it – instead it is an experience that locates a rupture *within* human life. The film offers an experience that is "*near to* elemental life, a thing receding into its drugged parts" (2011: 12, my italics); it consists of "film stills *on the border of* benumbed life" (2011: 15, my italics). As Laura Marcus has noted, the novel never allows the reader to surrender to the magic of cinema and to forget "film's photogrammic basis, the materiality of film stock" (2013: 175). Gordon's installation uses a VCR, a videocassette, a video projector and a suspended screen, and the novel emphasizes that "this wasn't truly film … It was videotape" (2011: 14). The first movie of Finley, the movie maker in the novel's central narrative, is entirely based on footage of Jerry Lewis, and relies on "kinescopes," offering an image of "some deviant technological lifeform struggling out of the irradiated dust of the atomic age" (2011: 32).

A temporality that interrupts the customary scale of human experience; a temporality, also, that is as finite and material as human life, and that is therefore less *an alternative to* than *a disjunction within* human experience: this is the very structure of the temporal provocation that cultural geology and the Anthropocene formulate for contemporary fiction. If the main narrative of *Point Omega* engages these issues on a thematic level, as we will see, their temporal implications are already negotiated in the frame around that narrative. The encounter with *24 Hour Psycho* provokes a recalibration of the scales of human experience, as it trains the viewer "to feel time passing, to be alive to what is happening in the smallest registers of motion" (2011: 7). Projecting only two frames a second, the installation foregrounds the interstices of time – what *Point Omega* calls "submicroscopic moments" (2011: 21) – that are neutralized in ordinary perception. These infinitesimal interstices have as much of a disruptive impact on the human scale as the appeals to cosmic vastness that we find in the novel's central narrative; as Mark McGurl notes, "the scale of the posthuman resides both on the small side of the human and on the large" (2012: 551). McGurl draws attention to "physical processes so fast, so brief in duration," that foregrounding them in the way *Point Omega* does intimates "*[o]ur utter undermining by the small*" (2012: 552). Slowing down narrative draws attention to the infinitesimal, and it is simultaneously "like watching the universe die over a period of about seven billion years" (DeLillo 2011: 59). McGurl associates these procedures with the "horrible minimalism" of the workshop story on the model of Raymond Carver's short fiction (2012: 552), which helps make sense of the remarkable slimness of DeLillo's novel. If *24 Hour Psycho* is a defamiliarized film narrative situated in the darkness of an exhibition room, *Point Omega* offers a pared-down narrative captured between two "Anonymities" – or chapters entitled "Anonymity," at least.

It is instructive to distinguish this set-up from one with which it unavoidably resonates – Vladimir Nabokov's dictum, in the first sentence of *Speak, Memory*, that "our existence is but a brief crack of light between two eternities of darkness" (1966: 19). While Nabokov's second sentence, which refers to man's "forty-five hundred heartbeats an hour," immediately opposes cosmic vastness to man's biological nullity, *Point Omega* locates the tension between different temporalities at the very heart of human life. The framing chapters do not promote an alternative artistic temporality that escapes narrative, but rigorously maintain the continuous interaction between art and the human. They also attach this interaction to the novel's minimal plot, as part of the anonymous narrator's experience in the exhibition room is the passage of two visitors who, the reader can infer, are the filmmaker and the aging academic whose relation takes up most of the middle chapters.

This disjunctive temporality is also encrypted in the way the novel reflects on its title – a title that DeLillo, as Mary Holland has established, had been entertaining for several of his novels since 1982 (2013: 10). Lifted from the work of the Jesuit thinker Pierre Teilhard de Chardin, "Point Omega" – or, more customarily, "Omega Point" – names a state of maximal consciousness and complexity to which the universe, according to Teilhard, is evolving (Marcus 2013: 176). Richard Elster, the aging academic turned defense consultant in the novel's central narrative, glosses this teleological notion as "[a] leap out of our biology" (2011: 67), as "a sublime transformation of mind and soul" (2011: 91). The novel's last mention of this notion gives the lie to this dream of transcendence, as we witness Elster grieving over the disappearance of his daughter. His loss reconnects her – and him – to a fleshy contingency that the novel does not allow human life to overcome: "The omega point has narrowed, here and now, to the point of a knife as it enters a body. All the man's grand themes funneled down to local grief, one body, out there somewhere, or not" (2011: 124). Against Elster's fantasy of transcendence, the novel's structure presents the disjunctions between narrative rhythm, biological change, and geological time as integral to human life. As I already remarked, this brings its peculiar temporality in dialogue with discourses of cultural geology and the Anthropocene. In a sense, this connects the novel to a *different* Teilhard who has recently been recovered in work on the Anthropocene: *not* the teleological thinker of the Omega Point, but the thinker who, together with the Russian geochemist and naturalist Vladimir Vernadsky, is credited as a precursor of the notion of the Anthropocene through their coinage in the 1920s of the term "noösphere," a notion that refers to "the anthropogenic transformation of the Earth system" (Steffen et al. 2011: 844). *Point Omega*'s experiments with temporality show how these transformations make it imperative to think disjunctively about human life, rather than to imagine its transcendence.

"This was desert": *Point Omega*'s vastness

The novel's central narrative fills in the temporal template its frame provides by staging a confrontation between human finitude and the geological time that is one of its constituents. It focuses on the encounter between Jim Finley, a young filmmaker who recalls DeLillo's earlier filmmakers in *The Names* and *The Body Artist*, and Richard Elster, a "defense intellectual" (2011: 35) who has retired to the desert after he had provided the Iraq campaign with "words and meaning" (2011: 37). This gesture of old age withdrawal not only recalls *Underworld*, but also the setting of DeLillo's play *Love-Lies-Bleeding* (Cowart 2012: 45). One way to read the novel is then as an attempt by DeLillo to recycle a number of his classical narrative devices for an exploration of a new temporality. Indeed, even if this withdrawal may seem to signal a choice for a melancholia that recalls *Falling Man* (De Marco 2012: 20) and an attempt to explore "the outer limits of the temporality of trauma" (Dunst 2012: 61), it is remarkable to what extent the narrative avoids the repetitions and instantaneity that mark the narrative grammar of trauma. Instead, the narrative reads like a sustained training session in protracted eventlessness: one character is living out the afterlife of his tangential involvement in a war in which he "was not one of the strategists" (2011: 35), while the other is preparing for a movie that will never be made.

The novel describes the desert as "the protoworld ... the seas and reefs of ten million years ago" (2011: 25). For Elster, the "Pleistocene desert" is located in "deep time, epochal time" (2011: 91). The novel associates the city Elster and Finley have fled with "the slinking time of watches, calendars, minutes left to live" (2011: 75); in the desert, urban devices like laptops and cell phones are "overwhelmed by landscape" (2011: 82), a landscape marked by "the force of geological time, out there somewhere, the string grids of excavators searching for weathered bone" (2011: 24). This last formulation makes clear that human life is implicated in this geological dimension; it portrays "the mutual penetration between people and the landscape characteristic of the anthropocene era" (Laist 2010: 90), a concern that Randy Laist has traced back through DeLillo's oeuvre to the famous sunset descriptions in *White Noise*. In *Point Omega*, Elster works hard to resist the sense of sublimity that the sunsets in *White Noise* still evoke: "To Elster sunset was human invention, our perceptual arrangement of light and space into elements of wonder" (2011: 22). For Elster, there is "nothing but distances, not vistas or sweeping sightlines but only distances" (2011: 22); "There's none of the usual terror ... time is enormous ... Time that precedes us and survives us" (2011: 56). While Elster believes geological time can offer a refuge from war, the novel presents both war and deep time as related domains that destabilize human life, even as they are decisively inflected by human activity.[3] The Anthropocene makes visible that particular human lives suffer the effects of

---

[3]For a reading of the novel that does present it as "a return to the natural world and to the rhythms inherent within it as an antidote to the poisons of technological overkill" see Butler (2011: 102–103). De Marco incorrectly reads Elster's turn to the desert as a disavowal of "extinction understood as death produced by the conflict in Iraq" (2012: 21). See also Dunst's related argument that "*Point Omega* is set in a traumatized present outside of history" (2012: 60), rather than, as I am arguing, engaging in a more radical reimagining of temporality.

environmental changes that are themselves the result of accumulated human activities that never intended those consequences; *Point Omega*'s articulation of geological time and war then shows that the U.S. foreign campaigns that serve as the novel's background have a comparable structure. Wars, like climate change, are what Timothy Morton calls man-made "hyperobjects," assemblages that are something more than objects in that "they're massively distributed and so are unavailable to immediate experience" (2010).[4] When Morton notes that "[w]e have created things that we can hardly understand, let alone control, let alone make sensible political decisions about" (2010), he is primarily thinking of global warming, but *Point Omega* also qualifies war as something we can only imagine if we change our customary modes of thinking and perception.

Finley's original film project still approaches war as a matter of individual responsibility. He wants to interview Elster in "[o]ne continuous take," "[j]ust a man and a wall," in which the man "relates the complete experience" (2011: 26–27). The minimalism of this endeavor inevitably invites comparison to the ambition of DeLillo's novel itself – a novel that works in a form that has historically excelled at both "depicting the interior life of a singular conscious-ness and casting a wide narrative gaze over a complex social universe" (Woloch 2003: 19). If Finley's proposed project represents the cinematographic counter-part of the former (psychological) option, he explicitly opposes it to the counter-part of the latter (social) option: "There's a Russian film, feature film, *Russian Ark*, Aleksandr Sokurov. A single extended shot, about a thousand actors and extras, three orchestras, history, fantasy, crowd scenes, ballroom scenes" (2011: 27). *Point Omega* refuses both these options – after all, as I showed in the previous section, it has already found the cinematographic counterpart that it needs in order to bring into relief the co-implication of human time and geolo-gical time, of human agency and natural force, that neither psychological nor social realism can capture.

Point Omega can be read as an attempt to overcome the reliance of the novel form on distinctive events and identifiable individual agents, which can be considered as limitations on the novel's ability to abandon conventional realisms and imagine the geological ramifications of culture. The anonymity of the obsessive observer in the novel's two "Anonymity" sections is one aspect of this exercise; the sustained eventlessness of the central narrative is another. There is exactly one plot twist in the novel, which takes the form of a missed event: Elster's daughter, who is visiting, suddenly goes missing while Elster and Finley

---

[4]Mary Favret usefully distinguishes between the concepts of "wartime" and "war" when she defines wartime as "the experience of those living through but not in war" (2009: 9). "Wartime" underlines how "war at a distance" becomes part of the barely registered substance of everyday life in countries that are at war abroad. While Favret's book draws on a romantic archive, one difference with the recent campaigns in Iraq and Afghanistan is that the latter take place in a globalized world where the relative distance of wartime can at each moment spill over into war at home – where, indeed, the threat of such a shift sustains the normalization of wartime as a general condition. For U.S. audiences, then, contemporary wartime has a structure that is comparable to that of the Anthropocene; wartime, like the Anthropocene, is an assemblage in which one is mini-mally implicated as an agent, and which can never be definitively outsourced. For an evocation of the resonances between the Iraq campaign and the Anthropocene, see Scranton (2013).

are away on an excursion.[5] The novel scrupulously resists developing this twist into a detective story. There are rumors of a stalker, and a knife is found, but the desire to individualize responsibility and to identify the events that led to the disappearance is consistently frustrated. The novel invites the reader to sustain that ignorance, and to entertain new ways to think of agency, action, and responsibility. When Finley faces up to the impossibility of identifying the suspected stalker,[6] he decides to drive Elster out of the desert and back to the city. On the way, he gets a phone call, but this potential clue is disabled as the display identifies the caller as "blocked caller" (2011: 125–126) – the same message that had earlier prevented the identification of the alleged stalker. The novel later reaffirms the futility of identification and the necessity of accepting anonymity when the anonymous viewer, in the novel's last section, is approached by a woman trying to make sense of the film and asking (about the murder on screen) whether she really "want[s] to know who's stabbing him": "He decided on the answer no" (2011: 133). When he tries to recall the name of Janet Leigh's character, he accepts defeat (2011: 137). Through its insistence on non-identification, *Point Omega* frustrates narrative expectations and points to the limits of all too human (and all too novelistic) concerns.

Near the end of the novel the relations between human life and geological time have been reversed (and this, more than anything, makes it impossible to read *Point Omega* as merely an extension of the trauma template). The indifference and the vastness of geological time are no longer incorporated into a psychological drama; this vast anonymity has overwhelmed the bare outlines of a human plot, and come to assert itself as a blockage on the human scale it encompasses. This blockage is a powerful reminder of the challenge to reconfigure human agency, a movement that is underlined when the novel takes the reader back to the room at the MoMA to observe an artwork that, like DeLillo's novel, refuses to offer the narrative and affective satisfactions of a thriller, and instead reconfigures narrative elements in a way that positions them "outside all categories, open to entry" (2011: 129), as elements that contemporary fiction is reconfiguring into new constellations of agency and worldliness. *Point Omega* breaks with the conventions of traumatic realism, not, as Gray and Rothberg recommend, in order to adopt a more transnational or cosmopolitan perspective, but in other to intimate ethical and political challenges that cannot be represented along the (all-too-human) spectrum between the domestic and the global. This also explains why the novel revisits crucial tropes from DeLillo's work – deserts,

---

[5]The novel subtly undercuts the irruptiveness of this event by already mourning Elster's daughter Jessie before she disappears. I am thinking especially of the elegiac tone in passages such as the following, in which the combination of the past tense, the suggestion of iterative narration, and the emphasis on Jessie's fleetingness already seems to present the cohabitation of Elster, Finley, and the daughter as complete, as decidedly a thing of the past: "We shared a bathroom, she and I, but she rarely seemed to be in there. A small airline kit, the only trace of her presence, was tucked into a corner of the windowsill. She kept soap and towels in her bedroom ... Her bed was never made. I opened the bedroom door and looked several times but did not enter" (2011: 62).
[6]Acceptance here also means facing up to the temporality of the desert, and refusing the pathetic fallacy that reads the landscape as a reflection of human concerns. If initially, "every passing minute [was] a function of our waiting" (2011: 110) and the desert seems "clairvoyant" (2011: 109), Finley comes to accept that it is indifferent to human concerns: "[i]t was too vast, it was not real... the indifference of it," as it refuses to yield an answer or a corpse (2011: 116).

sunsets, withdrawals: they are part of a strategy to reorganize novelistic material from the past into a form that is more responsive to the exigencies of an uncertain future. The novel ends with a return to the artwork that served as its model for posing that question – which is also to say that it has not yet managed to answer it.

Conclusion: The novel and the human

Through the device of a protagonist who worked as a defense intellectual, *Point Omega* ponders the question of cultural causation – of the impact that rarified cultural artifacts can have on worldly matters. Elster is the author of a controversial scholarly article on the word "rendition" – a word that, in the phrase "extraordinary rendition," had become one of the enabling euphemism of the war on terror. Elster's article, however, only obliquely alludes to the term's use "as an instrument of state security" (2011: 44), and is instead occupied with the word history of the term, "with references to Middle English, Old French, Vulgar Latin and other sources and origins" (2011: 42). The essay's refusal to pose questions of "crime and guilt" (2011: 44) is widely criticized as a disabling evasion of worldly responsibility. Yet the afterlife of the article does not stop there, as it earns Elster an invitation to "freshen the dialogue, broaden the viewpoint" (2011: 36) in strategic discussions over U.S. military campaigns. Elster and the strategists there coin new words in order "to create new realities overnight," "words that would yield pictures eventually and then become three-dimensional" (2011: 36).

Elster's job description comes close to the task I have ascribed to DeLillo's novel: that of moving beyond available imaginative templates and of devising new forms to reflect, map, and energize altered understandings of human life as it finds itself overwhelmed by forces it has itself helped generate. Yet Elster's mission does not model itself on the novel form, but rather on the haiku, a genre that, for Elster, has the power to alter people's relation to "transient things": it "[b]ares everything to plain sight," allows people to "[s]ee what's there and then be prepared to watch it disappear" (2011: 37). The novel chastises this destructive fantasy while proposing a sustained disjunction that learns to maintain both human agency and its geological ramifications. The difference between the novel form and the haiku, in the world of *Point Omega*, is conceived as the opposition between two kinds of temporality. *Point Omega* is not the only contemporary novel to which a reimagining of temporality is crucial. As Peter Boxall has remarked, "DeLillo's relationship with lateness, singular as it is, resonates with a group of late stylists who register a kind of untimeliness, and who produce forms with which to explore a disjunction between newly passing time and the expired narratives with which we have made time readable" (2013: 30). As *Point Omega* shows, the intrusion of the Anthropocene is one crucial aspect of the untimeliness of the present, and of the need for contemporary fiction to think beyond the continuum ranging from the local to the global.

The interface of literature and the Anthropocene is often referred to an environmental thematics: from Rob Nixon's study of aesthetic figurations of the environmentalism of the poor (2011), over Ursula Heise's eco-cosmopolitanism (2008), to the mobilization of Henry David Thoreau as a witness of climate change (Primack & Miller-Rushing 2012). My reading of *Point Omega* argues that the recalibration of human life that geological change initiates also generates a fundamental reorganization of ethical and political categories, and of the forms through which these categories are transmitted, inculcated, and imagined. Claire Colebrook has remarked that the Anthropocene calls for a rethinking of "the terms of our ethical vocabulary – justice, fairness, respect, forgiveness, hospitality or virtue" (2012: 185, 187–188). As DeLillo's formal and thematic meditations on scale suggest, this rethinking will affect the cultural forms that have traditionally consolidated the ethical and political terms that are now under erasure. At the same time, the turn to temporality in contemporary fiction suggests that it is easier to formulate the challenge to conceive of a new form of the human than to offer a determinate response to that challenge. Indeed, it is significant that *Point Omega* worries over the residual possibilities for cultural work to impact on the ways of the world – and even Elster's cynical recalibration of transience in times of war finally proves powerless in the face of "priorities, statistics, evaluations, rationalizations" (2011: 38). This raises the question whether the novel form will be able to respond to that imaginative challenge, or whether its undeniable limitations as a cultural force will limit its role to communicating the urgency of a new law of the earth it is no longer able to legislate.

REFERENCES

Banita, Georgiana. 2012. *Plotting justice: Narrative ethics and literary culture after 9/11*. Lincoln, NE: University of Nebraska Press.

Boxall, Peter. 2013. *Twenty-first-century fiction: An introduction*. Cambridge: Cambridge University Press.

Butler, Jonathan. 2011. Ecospirituality in the age of technological overkill: Domestic reclamation in the fiction of Alan Lightman and Don DeLillo. *Ecozona: European Journal of Literature, Culture and Environment* 2(2),100–119.

Chakrabarty, Dipesh. 2009. The climate of history: Four theses. *Critical Inquiry* 35 (2), 197–222.

Chakrabarty, Dipesh. 2012. Postcolonial studies and the challenge of climate change. *New Literary History* 43(2),1–18.

Colebrook, Claire. 2012. Not symbiosis, not now: Why anthropogenic change is not really human. *Oxford Literary Review* 34(2),185–210.

Cowart, David. 2012. The lady vanishes: Don DeLillo's *Point Omega*. *Contemporary Literature* 53(1), 31–50.

Crutzen, Paul & Will Steffen. 2003. How long have we been in the anthropocene era? *Climatic Change* 61(3), 251–257.

DeLillo, Don. 1986. *White noise*. New York, NY: Penguin.

DeLillo, Don. 1997. *Underworld*. New York, NY: Simon & Schuster.

DeLillo, Don. 2006. *Love – lies – bleeding: A Play*. London: Picador.

DeLillo, Don. 2008. *Falling man*. New York, NY: Scribner.

DeLillo, Don. 2011. *Point omega*. London: Picador.

De Marco, Alessandra. 2012. Late DeLillo, finance capital and mourning from *The Body Artist* to *Point Omega*. *49th Parallel: An Interdisciplinary Journal of North American Culture* 28, http://49thparalleljournal.org/2014/07/12/issue-28-spring-2012/ (last accessed on 5 May 2014).

Dunst, Alexander. 2012. After trauma: Time and affect in American culture beyond 9/11. *Parallax* 18(2), 56–71.

Favret, Mary. 2009. *War at a distance: Romanticism and the making of modern wartime*. Princeton, NJ: Princeton University Press.

Gourley, James. 2013. *Terrorism and temporality in the works of Thomas Pynchon and Don DeLillo*. London: Bloomsbury.

Gray, Richard. 2009. Open doors, closed minds: American prose writing at a time of crisis. *American Literary History* 21(1),128–148.

Gray, Richard. 2011. *After the fall: American literature since 9/11*. Chichester: Wiley-Blackwell.

Heise, Ursula. 2008. *Sense of place and sense of planet: The environmental imagination of the global*. Oxford: Oxford University Press.

Holland, Mary K. 2013. This is the point. *American Book Review* 34(4), 10.

Laist, Randy. 2010. *Technology and postmodern subjectivity in Don DeLillo's novels*. New York: Peter Lang.

Luckhurst, Roger. 2008. *The trauma question*. Abingdon: Routledge.

Luckhurst, Roger. 2012. In war times: Fictionalizing Iraq. *Contemporary Literature* 53(4),713–737.

Marcus, Laura. 2013. The death of cinema and the contemporary novel. *Affirmations: Of the Modern* 1(1),160–177.

McGurl, Mark. 2011. The new cultural geology. *Twentieth Century Literature* 57(3–4), 380–390.

McGurl, Mark. 2012. The posthuman comedy. *Critical Inquiry* 38(3), 533–553.

McGurl, Mark. 2013. Critical response ii: "Neither indeed could I forebear smiling at my self." A reply to Wai Chee Dimock. *Critical Inquiry* 39(3),632–638.

Monk, Philip. 2003. *Double-cross: The Hollywood films of Douglas Gordon.* Toronto: The Power Plant and Art Gallery of York University.

Morley, Catherine. 2011. "How do we write about this?" The domestic and the global in the post-9/11 novel. *Journal of American Studies* 45(4),717–731.

Morton, Timothy. 2010. Hyperobjects and the end of common sense. *The Contemporary Condition*, http://contemporarycondition.blogspot.se/2010/03/hyperobjects-and-end-of-common-sense.html (last accessed on 18 March 2014).

Nabokov, Vladimir. 1966. *Speak, memory: An autobiography revisited.* London: Weidenfeld & Nicolson.

Nixon, Rob. 2011. *Slow violence and the environmentalism of the poor.* Cambridge, MA: Harvard University Press.

Palumbo-Liu, David. 2012. *The deliverance of others: Reading literature in a global age.* Durham, NC: Duke University Press.

Primack, Richard & Abe Miller-Rushing. 2012. Uncovering, collecting and analyzing records to investigate the ecological impacts of climate change: A template from Thoreau's Concord. *BioScience* 62, 170–171.

Rothberg, Michael. 2009. A failure of the imagination: Diagnosing the post-9/11 novel. A response to Richard Gray. *American Literary History* 21(1),152–158.

Scranton, Roy. 2013. Learning how to die in the anthropocene. *New York Times*, http://opinionator.blogs. nytimes.com/2013/11/10/learning-how-to-die-in-the-anthropocene/ (last accessed on 10 November 2013).

Steffen et al. 2011. The anthropocene: Conceptual and historical perspectives. *Philosophical Transactions of the Royal Society* 369, 842–867.

Szerszynski, Bronislaw. 2012. The end of the end of nature: The anthropocene and the fate of the human. *Oxford Literary Review* 34(2),165–184.

Vermeulen, Pieter. 2012. The critique of trauma and the end of the novel in Tom McCarthy's *Remainder. Modern Fiction Studies* 58(3),549–568.

Versluys, Kristiaan. 2009. *Out of the blue: September 11 and the novel.* New York: Columbia University Press.

Woloch, Alex. 2003. *The one vs. the many: Minor characters and the space of the protagonist in the novel.* Princeton, NJ: Princeton University Press.

The Space of Genre in the New Green Novel

CAREN IRR

Since the late 1980s, a new variety of English-language political fiction has developed – the green novel. Organized around tropes of crisis and decay, the new green novel gives generic form to the pervasive sense of urgency attached to environmental problems in the late twentieth and early twenty-first centuries. It is easily distinguished from neighboring forms, such as the fiction of urban crisis, by its treatment of Romantic and dystopian elements. These predecessor styles appear in transposed form in the new green novel, and the genre coheres around a stable set of motifs that update central ideas from the predecessors. In its most common version, the green novel expresses a critique of liberal individualist approaches to planetary problems, but in a few key works this critical tendency deepens into a more collective and affirmative mapping project.

To identify the generic qualities of the new green novel we need to recognize the explanatory force of genre itself. This concept has, after all, been under attack since the heyday of poststructuralism when Jacques Derrida (1980) and Maurice Blanchot (1986) famously assaulted it. There is no pure genre and therefore no faithful subject of the law of genre, Derrida and Blanchot argued. To this well-known critique of genre as a *principle*, Tzvetan Todorov offers a useful rejoinder. Countering Blanchot in particular, in "The origin of genres," Todorov (1976) understands genre as the codification of human discourse – that is, as a more or less complex sequence of *processes* performed on a discursive germ or kernel. Todorov enumerates these operations and risks a claim about the initial speech act that serves as the kernel for particular genres. For Todorov's speech-act theory of genre, purity does not define genres, so generic hybridity does not disintegrate a genre. Todorov readily recognizes that "a new genre is always the transformation of one or several old genres," in addition to having variable social functions (1976: 161). From this perspective, the key to successful genre analysis lies in a combination of analytic rigor and speculative boldness. In Todorov's work, these result in a number of productive schemata; his analysis abounds with concrete and precise accounts of a range of operations – such as the assertion that a new genre will either invert, displace, or extend its predecessor as it elaborates on its founding speech act. In other words, Todorov's approach to genre invites consideration of the mutability of literary forms alongside speculation about their ideological effects for social subjects. The latter concern is crucial. "A society chooses and codifies the acts that correspond most closely to its ideology," Todorov writes; "this is why the existence of certain genres in a society and their absence in another reveal a central ideology, and enable us to establish it with considerable certainty" (1976: 164). By exposing the ideological commitments of a particular society, genre analysis provides insight into aesthetic and social history simultaneously.

The following effort to define the emerging genre of the green novel draws on Todorov's methods. A brief account of this new form's relationship to its generic predecessors precedes a detailed description of the core operations of a group of novels devoted to environmental problems. These genre-defining motifs derive from a speech act – the eco-lament – shared by a body of well-received novels that participate in several literary traditions. Selected from among the dozens of green works collected by authors such as Thomas J. Lyon (2001), Bonnie Roos and Alex Hunt (2010), these works articulate concerns expressed in the literature of several nations, and they address a diverse array of ecosystems. Since the goal is to identify the parameters of an infrequently recognized "heuristic genre," only positively reviewed fiction by established authors writing in English about explicitly ecological subjects has been included; works participating in clearly defined "institutional genres" (e.g., science fiction, thrillers, horror novels), as well as memoirs, essays, and tracts, have all been excluded (Wegner 2014). While a different selection of core texts might have slightly affected the emphasis given to individual genre elements, the patterns that emerge from this group are pervasive enough to suggest that the core argument does not rest on these instances alone. This pervasiveness is explained by Todorov's thesis about the ideological work of genre. The ideological consistency required by social structures regulates genre norms, lending them the feel of inevitability even very shortly after their origination. These repeated norms are not invented by individual authors but instead express social imperatives. Nonetheless, the ideological effects of these patterns do show some variability. As the concluding section demonstrates, individual works reveal tensions within the spatial consciousness of the new green novel, as some works shift the dominant tendency away from elegiac description and toward a collective project of future-oriented mapping.

Origins of the new green novel

This distinctive contemporary genre arises at the intersection of the Anglophone political novel and literary nature writing, adapting conventions from both forms. From the political novel, it borrows a preoccupation with collective actors and the limitations of public action. These features organize ecological writing in the utopian subgenre of the political novel in particular – especially works such as Ernest Callenbach's *Ecotopia* (1976). Outlining a detailed program for social renewal via recycling and "romantic collectivism" in the near future, Callenbach's work uses the classic utopian device of an unrepresented revolutionary rupture from everyday life in the reader's present (Bramwell 1994: 73). In the new green novel, by contrast, the collectivist concern survives, but deep anxiety about the likelihood of a rupture with the present displaces Callenbach's utopian enthusiasm.

Meanwhile, from Romantic nature writing, the new green novel derives a holistic spatial consciousness, a satirical eye, and a special treatment of the exploration narrative. These well-established features of nature writing characterize many essayistic memoirs inspired by Henry David Thoreau's *Walden* (1854) – from Edward Abbey's *Desert solitaire* (1968) and Annie Dillard's *Pilgrim at Tinker Creek* (1974) to Terry Tempest Williams' *Refuge* (2000). Typically devoted to intense first-person observation of a single site from which a critique of socially dominant practices is launched alongside a sense of personal release into a more cosmic dimension, Romantic nature writing perpetuates a devotional practice grounded in faith in the ecosystem's inherent ability to regenerate itself. In the post–climate change world described so devastatingly by Bill McKibben (2006) and others, this confidence has become difficult to sustain. Consequently, the new green novel pulls Romantic narrative conventions of the personal quest into a more dystopian universe, shifting the values they express from an essentially spiritual framework to a more wide-ranging materialist satire.

The primary processes of the green novel are familiar enough that critics of the form have already suggested directions in which it might develop. Dana Phillips (2003) made a case for a more postmodernist literature of nature, a style open to exploring the complex epistemological questions that bedevil scientific knowledge of nature. Ursula Heise (2008) has called for an environmental writing that still more radically transforms the American sense of place in particular into an epic sense of planet and resists conflation of natural and social history. Rob Nixon (2011) advocates a strain of green fiction that counters the rapid turnover of the news cycle with a more politically and structurally minded attention to "slow violence" in the environment. Rarely have any of these agendas been fully adopted, however. Instead, existing versions of the new green novel follow critics in reformulating the concerns of predecessors such as Callenbach (1977) and Thoreau, but they tend to do so by making the local scene more symbolic and satiric, rather than questioning the epistemological certainty of their narratives, expanding their scale, or slowing the pace.

These symbolic and satiric tendencies are abundantly evident in recent fiction by Graham Swift (1983), Lionel Shriver (2009), T.C. Boyle (2000; 2011; 2012), Suzanne Matson (2007), Susan Elderkin (2003), Karen Russell (2011), Helon Habila (2011), Indra Sinha (2007), Ian MacEwan (2010), Joy Williams (2000), Lydia Millet (2008) and others. The most central and frequently repeated features of this group of green fictions appear in Table 1.

Features of the new green novel

No single item on this table is entirely unprecedented in literary history or logically necessary to the genre. Genre, after all, does not consist of a set of rules or a checklist of traits. Instead, it is defined by a cluster of interdependent features that emerge through a set of narrative processes or operations. Independently examining each of the generic features that result from these processes allows us to demonstrate its relation to its predecessor and companion genres before we begin an analysis of its ideological function.

Table 1. Features of the new green novel.

Hero	Cranky, ill, thwarted
Plot	Intellectual exploration, travel into the archive
Setting	Toxic Eden and the underworld
Companions	Charismatic megafauna and sexy nurse
Antagonist	Scary nature goddess and masculine principles of industry
Climax	Horrific confrontation with coupling of nature and industry
Closure	Paradoxical defeat

1. Hero: *cranky, ill, failed activist*

Continuing the legacy of Thoreau, whose foundational writings on nature are thoroughly saturated by curmudgeonly satire, contemporary authors such as Shriver, Elderkin, MacEwan and Sinha (not to mention the prolific Boyle) have consistently developed heroes who live apart from their human peers largely by design. Although sometimes protagonists such as Sinha's Animal comment on the folly of their peers, rarely does this genre provide contemporary versions of Thoreau's pointed aphorisms on fashion, property, or spiritual life. More frequently, the target of the fractious hero's satirical wit is the paltriness of collective action designed to prevent damage. Sinha's hero Animal gripes at the pseudo-democratic process of middle-class idealists in the wake of Union Carbide's contamination of the city of Bhopal. Shriver dissects the logical consequences of positions taken by First World population experts, describing said experts' conspiratorial plans for drastic population reduction as well as the failure of that kind of fantasy. Meanwhile, Elderkin's more magical realist narrative casts a grim eye on economic development and eco-tourism in the Australian outback, describing both from the vantage point of crabby and lethargic aboriginal spirit-voices.

Rather than turning their animus outwards, these crotchety heroes begin from a position of compromised entanglement with the green positions that they satirize; they are always partially self-corrosive. A host of illnesses, both physical and mental, makes this complicity concrete. Habila's novel about the oil industry in Nigeria, for example, uses a heroic journalist's alcoholism as a figure for energy addiction; Boyle's Tyrone Tierwater has creaky joints that associate his advanced age with that of the social systems he decries; and Graham Swift's narrator explores his family's history of madness, retardation and alcoholism in the phlegmatic English fens. These maladies do not simply miniaturize environmental damage in the metaphorical fashion to which Susan Sontag objects in her important essay on the literature of cancer and AIDS. Instead, human illness becomes in the new green novel the signal that the hero is metonymically linked to an environment that is also in crisis. The heroes of the new green novel renounce the Romantics' temporary respite in nature, electing instead to permanently inhabit an environment that offers no avenues of retreat or hope of cure.

2. Plot: *quest to explore, know place more deeply*

In another maneuver reminiscent of Thoreau's *Walden*, the new green novel borrows liberally from quest and exploration narratives while also ironizing that form's exoticizing tendencies. Agreeing with Thoreau that the swiftest traveler goes afoot, its heroes adapt exploration motifs to intensive examination of the local scene. This almost reflexive localism ensures the quests organizing the new green novel are mainly intellectual adventures. MacEwan's *Solar* (2010), for example, ridicules the notion that a Scandinavian junket is necessary to deepen his scientific hero's knowledge of climate change, while some of Boyle's historical fiction probes the various land management conflicts occurring on a tiny island chain in the Santa Barbara Channel. Similarly, Swift's historian-hero in *Waterland* (1983) describes to his students the surprisingly scandalous backstory of the draining of the English fens and the rise of a distinctive brewery culture, while Russell (2011) undertakes a similarly archaeological excavation of the federal mismanagement of the Florida Keys. Each of these narratives describes the protagonist's intensive research into situations predating the novel's present; these archival plots make time travel the essence of exploration in a world of closed frontiers. Conflict and its resolution thus arise in moments when the flow of information is impeded or eased. The physical hardships of the hero and his primary companions recede behind the scenes the hero so attentively observes. Even Lydia Millet's *How the dead dream* (2008), which closes with a dangerous trek through a tropical forest, resolves in the hero's renunciation of his drive to know his environment; the calm radiated by a mysterious mammal companion supersedes the hero's mortal dread, even though both creatures are shadowed by the threat of extinction.

In neither crisis nor resolution, however, does the Thoreauvian model (or Callenbach's later variation on the plan) inspire the new green novel. While *Walden* climaxes in the ecstatic revelations of the sliding bank and the mystical experience of holistic identification with the scene this provides the narrator, these late twentieth- and early twenty-first-century fictions typically diminish the role of the narrating consciousness as the novel proceeds, so that physical place itself rises closer to the foreground in dramatic vistas of fire (Sinha), swamp grass (Russell), flood (Swift), or storms (Millet). Even a novel, such as Shriver's *Game control* (2009), that deviates most fully from the exploration plot (turning instead to the logic of conspiracy for its narrative principle) still incorporates arguably gratuitous travel elements – moving its protagonists around contemporary Kenya from deep-sea diving on the coast to mountainous colonial outposts, desert salt lakes, and various gated communities and slums of Nairobi. The narrative frame of exploration endures, even though the scale and dimension of travel change in the new green novel.

3. Setting: *Toxic Eden and exhilarating underworld*

In addition to displacing exploration to the archive and concretizing the hero's social critique in illness, authors of twenty-first-century green fiction typically employ a symbolic treatment of setting, favoring quasi-allegorical changes of scene over didactic explanation. Though usually beginning in decaying built environments (contaminated cities, impoverished ranches, obsolete villages, old-fashioned tourist attractions, and the like), their narratives send heroes on a quest for an imagined Eden that quickly reveals itself to be full of toxic horrors. Toxicity itself is a dominant concern (Buell 1998). Russell's alligator-wrestling protagonist in *Swamplandia!* (2011), for example, heads out into the magical Everglades in a boat in search of her missing sister, while Boyle's eco-activist and his wife spend a month in the wild entirely naked in an effort to publicize their anti-logging cause. Similarly, Habila's journalist renews himself in a coastal island commune subject to attack, and Sinha's Animal runs from the burning city to the green forest where he has hallucinatory visions of exotic flowers before recovering. These symbolic Edens are not origin points, nor do they provide safe refuge. In each case, Eden is a far more perilous, uncomfortable, and besieged middle point on the hero's uneasy journey.

Redrawn as a contaminated, hybrid space, Eden becomes a passage to the underworld. It is not the garden from which innocents are expelled; the time for innocence has long since elapsed in these post-Romantic fictions. This Eden is swallowed up into an increasingly gothic underworld, and this motif is not difficult to discern. Russell's alligator park, for example, faces stiff competition from a Disneyesque "World of Darkness" theme park in which whole families slide down the tongue of fiery demons. Sinha's Animal reflects innumerable times on the transformation of his city into a living hell, while his Christian mother-figure worries about the imminent "Apokalis" and a Muslim brother-figure carries him across burning coals during the festival of Muharram. Elderkin's Australian hero descends into mines and on his emergence completes a terrifyingly botched indigenous circumcision ritual. Leaving these underworld scenes of torture and humiliation does not restore the traditional balance of seasons or prompt wistful abandonment scenes. No persimmon ties beautiful Persephone to her husband in Hades in contemporary eco-fiction; instead, the underworld swells to absorb the living world, making Eden a parcel within its expanding, corrosive sprawl.

These underworlds turn out, after all, to be inhabitable, even companionable – although aesthetically suspect, crammed with microwaved pizza, excess phlegm, and painful scars. Accommodation to these inglorious underworlds requires the governing tone of these eco-fictions to be gothic-flavored satire rather than full-blown apocalyptic terror, as was more common in environmentally themed science fiction of the 1950s (such as Nevil Shute's post-nuclear bomb narrative, *On the beach*, 1957). The mission of contemporary green fiction is not to forestall an apocalyptic future but rather to probe ways of sustaining life in our already damaged scene. Here, these works most closely heed Rob Nixon's call to give greater attention to the everyday and "slow" horrors environmental contamination has already created. We are already post-apocalyptic, these narratives of quotidian crisis suggest, if only we look hard enough at where we are.

4. Companions: *Single charismatic megafauna, sexy nurse*

To render the scene as well as the pace of the post-apocalyptic underworld endurable, the green novel turns toward intense emotional relationships that promise renewal. In this sense, the green novel arguably partakes of the "new sincerity" more commonly associated with 1990s-era personal narratives of affective self-discovery (Kelly 2011). This effort to resolve material problems by emotional means is, of course, a convention of the modern post-chivalric romance – with its characteristic swerve from investigation of self in an abstract space to attachment to an object of desire who reflects an image of the achieved self back to the subject and launches a new genealogy (Bakhtin 1981). However, in the new green novel this romantic procedure does not so much resolve the narrative's central conflict as shift its register.

The hero's first source of romantic communion is typically a single endangered specimen of one of those species that conservationists call "charismatic megafauna." Like the panda or the grey wolf, charismatic megafauna are those adorable large mammals (preferably fuzzy) whose image enlists the sympathies of the public in projects designed to restore or manage an ecosystem as a whole (Leader-Williams & Dublin 2000). The use of charismatic megafauna, in other words, is a green advertising ploy, a self-conscious bit of sentimentalism in which one indulges for presumably noble purposes. Its mostly unsatirized presence in the new green novel, then, is not entirely surprising. Although Boyle takes the most skeptical look at this practice, switching out the predictable lion companion in *Friend of the earth* (2000) for the tougher case of the Norwegian rat in *When the killing's done* (2011), a novel that directly addresses the attempted elimination of invasive species, most of these green novels comfortably attach their heroes to a single large mammal species who functions simultaneously as a totem and as a canary in the coal mine, testing the air of the underworld for the inevitable toxins. Russell's heroine, for instance, has a uniquely mutated red alligator secreted about her person; Elderkin's boy-wonder is fascinated by kangaroos and mourns the accidental death of a single animal for decades. Swift's novel makes the eel its unlikely (but tasty) animal icon, and even Shriver's eccentric protagonist develops his theories about human population control largely on the basis of his emotional attachment to elephants. The most mega of the megafauna, the elephant is (like other animal companions in these not fully realist fictions) mute and yet intimately tied to the human protagonist's psyche. The animal companion functions almost too literally as a mirror, reflecting the human dilemma in a contaminated world without advancing toward a resolution. This tendency is succinctly summarized in Millet's *How the dead dream*, when the hero discovers himself co-sleeping with an unknown mammal – "not a jaguar, not an ocelot or a margay, nothing feline and sly – more likely a young tapir or a paca, large, stout, snouty and ground-dwelling" (2008: 240) – in the novel's final revelatory pages.

To achieve resolution, though, the cranky, ill heroes typically must redirect their energies away from the animal and accept the healing offered by the truly amazing abundance of sexy nurses in the green novel. Elderkin's novel introduces Cecily, a robustly erotic Aborigine who brings the protagonist back to health and aids his escape from the confines of an Alice Springs hospital in the frame narrative. The plot of Sinha's *Animal's people* (2003) turns on the arrival and activities of an American doctor clad in jeans so tight they remind the lascivious narrator of "blue skin." Shriver's *Game control* (2009) initially seems to be "healing" its female reproductive rights worker by giving her a stylish makeover and revealing her sexual side, but soon the direction of healing reverses, and Eleanor becomes the sexy nurse to the increasingly mad Calvin's patient. Habila's protagonist connects with a nurse serving the community on which he stumbles. Millet's hero is plagued by would-be Florence Nightingales before later gravitating toward an emotionally strong paraplegic in a wheelchair.

The figure of the female nurse/healer whose sexual availability restores the suffering male hero to full (or at least fuller) powers in a damaged world perhaps offers homage to Callenbach, whose *Ecotopia* (1977) includes erotic massage in its account of the holistic medicine of the future. But, more immediately, this figure results from a) the figuring of ecological crisis in the body of the protagonist and, b) the genre's habit of personalizing and individualizing problems relating to action. The green novel's swerve toward erotic love allows its readers to imagine a provisional and localized resolution to a collective, even planetary problem. To the extent that the green novel invests in eros as a solution to ecos, it embraces the sensibility of liberal globalism expressed in many geopolitical fictions (Irr 2013). That is, when the sexy nurse (a classic Proppian "donor," similar to the fairy godmother in Cinderella tales) heals all wounds and by extension renders the contaminated environment inhabitable again, then we recognize that the governing fantasy of the green novel is that the ethical actions of healthy individuals adequately compensate for environmental damage. To the extent that the sexy nurse and erotic healing more generally fail to resolve the narrative, we discover resistance to that model.

The sexy nurse wish-fulfillment scenario is so entrenched in the genre that it has already been ironized. Russell's *Swamplandia!* parodies this tendency to make the erotic relationship salvational in two subplots. Her young heroine has two siblings – the older of whom (a boy) is linked by the media to a young woman whom he rescues from drowning in a World of Darkness swimming pool. After a sexual encounter, this boy learns the would-be victim has orchestrated the whole event; his lifeguard ministrations then appear far less genuinely heroic than the less-publicized rescue of his own sister in a later scene. This middle child has herself been lured by fantasies of romantic union with a ghost to run off into the swamp. Ultimately suicidal in character, this ridiculous vision of erotic salvation finally cedes ground to the more affirmative restoration of the multi-generational oddball family. The resistance to the trope of sexual healing exemplified in Russell's *Swamplandia!* underlines the persistence of this figure as well as its limitations as a prospect for collective action in a damaged world.

5. Antagonist: *Distant masculine principle of industry*

The use of heterosexual healing as a figure for political commitment or conversion follows, presumably, from the quite conventional gendering of nature as female and industrial civilization as a masculine principle that typifies this emerging genre. From Swift's *Waterland* in 1983 to Russell's 2010 *Swamplandia!*, this pattern of gendering has remained consistent. Swift makes the male Atkinsons the engine of industrial development in the Fens, while on the periphery of masculine industry he locates Martha, a witchy abortionist whose pre-modern knowledge of the reproductive cycle aligns her not only with the mysterious genesis of eels but also with the watery disobedience of the fens themselves. Similarly, in Russell's novel, the hyper-capitalist World of Darkness theme park is managed by resentful male nerds, and the heroine's father and brother are the only family members who retain some hope for profiting from this scene; by contrast, the women of Russell's clan remain committed to the family's more traditional and nature-oriented life on the Keys. That environment also houses another swamp witch named Mama Weeds. "She looked like a woman," the teen narrator observes, "but I wouldn't be fooled. I saw my mother's dress hanging off her, and I knew this creature was a thief, a monster" (Russell 2011: 288). Mama Weed's quasi-feminine monstrosity derives from her scandalous annexation of the benevolent maternal role, and in this manner, in this novel as in so many others, an intense encounter with a horrifically mutated mother nature overpowers the emotional effects of the dismal masculine industries that actually initiate the horror. Throughout the genre, numerous sublime vortices (water holes, drowning, psychotic episodes and hallucinations) provide indirect figures for this horrific maternal/paternal inversion. These swirling abysses typically appear at the emotional climax of the green novel.

6. Closure: *Thwarted or paradoxical direct action*

The terrifying confrontation between maternal nature and paternal industry in the green novel invokes an adolescent aversion to directly envisioning the copulation of one's parents. As the sexy nurse motif reminds us, this aversion sits comfortably with an embrace of the adolescent's own, purportedly more appealing libido. This swerve to a forestalled sexual union in the future replaces the possibility of achieving closure through secure knowledge of the way masculine industry distorted a feminine nature in the past. However, the union rarely arrives on time, and its belatedness ensures that eco-fiction feels more satiric than romantic. Moments of the protagonist's possible erotic satisfaction are delayed, while the narrative closes with thwarted actions or paradoxical effects. Matson's *The tree-sitter* (2007) offers the clearest example of this trend. Its story concerns eco-anarchist anti-logging initiatives that backfire, killing allies and disrupting collective action. The same tendency appears when Boyle's noblest idealist, the teenage Sierra, falls to her death from her tree-sit, or Shriver's would-be mass assassin is duped by his own colleagues into spreading an inactive virus. The protagonists of the green novel rarely achieve any of their political goals, nor do they fully comprehend the toxic Edens they inhabit. After exposure to the brutal (often vaginal) horrors of nature's underworld, these novels tend to offer retreats to provisionally safer locations, rather than sweeping vistas or secure new homes, as they wind down.

The final pages of the new green novel shift toward meta-fiction and the appearance of a symbol signaling an on-going and unresolved process: ticking clocks, spinning potters wheels, foxes masquerading as dogs, a solitary man walking off into the desert, and so on. The narrator's relation to these ominous figures makes it clear that a more dramatic story than the one just provided remains to be told. "This world is painted on wild dark metal," Matthiessen's narrator concludes (2008: 892); "if she'd gone outside she would have seen the smoke twist out of the chimney, reaching as high as it could go till the wind flattened it and drove it out to sea," remarks Boyle's observer in *San Miguel* (2012: 367); while Matson's *Tree-Sitter* closes with the protagonist sleeping and "someone [rising] to inherit the day we left undone" (2007: 246). In their final images, these novels reflect on the incompleteness of the knowledge of the environment gained on the narrator's quest. They leave readers with an aftertaste of lament and anxious urgency, but on the whole the need to address the conditions creating these sensations remains felt rather than explained.

Most commonly, new green novels make the politics of representation their project – suggesting, in the usual circular manner of writers writing about writing, that more stories are necessary to raise consciousness of environmental problems. The genre rarely initiates reflection on the inadequacies to date of that approach as a political tactic or as a literary task. In this regard, the genre tends toward ideological fatalism, depicting an ill and emotionally stunted protagonist who is satirically incapable of facing the crisis of which he is also a result.

Nonetheless, a few competing tendencies do occasionally arise. Shifting attention away from the narrating human consciousness and toward the vibrating setting or scene (always a crucial element of environmental writing) reveals some important spatial motifs. These may not result in a coherent political program, but they do remind us that the genre, like any genre, perhaps, is animated by a social problem rather than a single overdetermined ideological solution. These spatial motifs, in other words, keep a more collective political vision in circulation precisely because it provides a necessary counterpoint and interlocutor to the often fatalist positions adopted in other versions of the green novel.

Boyle, Oates, and Ghosh

The spatial imaginary of eco-fiction sometimes allows proto-political attitudes at odds with liberal globalism to emerge. Formally, these appear in the narratives as alternatives to the conventional bird's-eye views of a static landscape and variations on the "voice of God" narratorial commentary that often accompanies them. In plots often dominated by other concerns, these features of the spatial imaginary of contemporary eco-fictions invoke a collective subject that engages in new forms of interactive, politicized, and collaborative mapping.

This pattern is most obvious in Boyle's lively satire, *Friend of the earth* (2000). In this novel, Boyle explores the hopelessly paradoxical and ineffectual efforts of an eco-activist group very similar to Earth First! The noble idealism of tree-sitters like Julia "Butterfly" Hill, as well as the top-secret sabotage undertaken by the main character (whose backstory is strongly reminiscent of the Earth

Liberation Front's Daniel McGowan), and the more official and public Greenpeace-like initiatives of spokespeople all fail in this novel to stave off major changes to Earth's weather patterns and the concomitant collapse of much of the food system. Alternating between passages set in the activist 1980s and the halfway-to-hell conditions of 2025, Boyle underscores the futility of all of these actions through apparently inevitable changes in the setting.

Initially, the narration of scene appears conventional. Opening passages reveal a narrator ensconced in his 2025 position as zookeeper to the eccentric, super-wealthy pop star Macvolio Pulchris (whose frequently mentioned "eel-whip" hairstyle recalls the 1980s-era coiffure of Michael Jackson). Although the novel begins on the ground and in the mud, Boyle's narrator is soon positioned via a quick zoom-out: "I occupy a two-room guesthouse on the far verge of the estate, just under the walls of Rancho Seco, the gated community to the east of us" (Boyle 2000: 6). Similar situating passages appear in Boyle's other California novels, some of which even include the traditional map as endpaper and suggest the stable point of view of spatial mastery associated with an exploration motif. At least one critic has commented on the conventional spatial associations Boyle has cultivated – northward movement, for instance, representing an escape from soiled multicultural urbanism and retreat to white-bread local purity (Schäfer-Wünsche 2005).

However, the apparently secure spatial meaning of such passages quickly erodes. Boyle seems fascinated by sites, such as Jackson/Pulchris's inaccessible ranch, that convey hyper-specificity alongside willfully confused anonymity throughout the novel. The sites of tree-sits described in the novel can also be mapped in a very general way onto EF! actions launched in the Siskiyou National Forest, but like the ranch the specific locations of preserved trees are – even within the novel – left intentionally obscure. The activists hike in only at night and cover their tracks by slipping "sweatsocks over their hiking boots" (134). Far from being solidly rooted to the ground, then the symbolic tree from which angelic Sierra (the narrator's daughter) falls to her death becomes Ent-like, traveling throughout the forest to nearly any potential location. Uprooted trees are also crucial to the discoveries the narrator and his ex-wife make when they return to another willfully obscured location, the African-themed safe house in the Oregon mountains where they had earlier hidden out during a period of legal insecurity. Returning to this cabin, they must chainsaw their way through toppled timber first in order to get to the door, because the climate-change-induced melting of permafrost has so destabilized the ground. These disputed trees are not secure landmarks; they are dangerously mobile, signaling the unsteadiness of the ground itself in the near future of the Anthropocene.

Boyle's interest in a morphing landscape is also installed in the design of the novel. His futuristic scenes take place at a halfway point where it rains far too often and his characters suffer from the mucosa, a highly unpleasant rhinovirus that gives them all a perpetual cold. The swirling shapes of rain clouds, together with the ceaseless circulation of phlegm, make Boyle's 2025 mobile and vis-cously unsettling. The hero attempts to stop the flow – e.g., by converting his suburban lawn into a wildlife refuge favored by migratory birds, bombing electricity towers, or preserving ultra-endangered mammals – but he is unsuc-cessful. Boyle allows no return to a primordial Eden; too many physically challenging processes of change are already underway. When nature itself is understood as anthropogenetic and dynamic, preservationist efforts simply slow the rate of change without altering its basic structure. Instead, one must engage in its processes and "go with the flow" rather than viewing it statically from above, as it were. Boyle's satiric sensibility thus drives him toward innumerable doorway scenes emphasizing spatial rupture – e.g., a lion bursting out of the dumbwaiter, a government agent intruding on domestic bliss, Sierra awakening on her tree-sit platform to fight off a menacing climber, and so on. These are not turning points in the plot, so much as they are repeated figurations at the social level of the mutability crisis occurring in the natural scene.

In her 2004 novel *The Falls*, by contrast, Joyce Carol Oates also develops figures of spatial transformation, although within the constraints of a realist historical novel. Oates' narrative begins in the nationally symbolic and exaggerated sublime setting of Niagara Falls when a newly married fossil hunter throws himself into the falls in hopes of quenching his sexual despair. The geologic layers in which the fossils reside provide the first of several maps of the deep structure of the site. The next day, the fossil-hunter's widow begins obsessively "retrace[ing] the route" he took, passing by the colorfully named sites to arrive finally at "the Devil Whirlpool... a gyre of Hell" (2004: 76). This contrast between the apparently fixed geologic substructure and the tormented surface of the water reiterates the social mapping undertaken by the novel. Initially it appears quite fixed and hierarchical; a family manor, for instance, is described authoritatively through conventional literary mapping of fixed social and geographic spaces. "The Burnaby house," Oates write, "on six acres of prime riverfront property, was a smaller replica of an English country estate in Surrey, built of dark-pink limestone on a knoll overlooking the Chippewa Channel (facing Ontario, Canada) of the Niagara River" (2004: 89). The abundance of place names and the proliferating details about the number and kind of materials as well as the spatial orientation of key sites continue to accumulate in the early portions of the novel, suggesting a readily mappable and fully known universe. In contrast, the psychic meaning of the river and the canal are much less secure. In one of many scenes establishing this pattern, the widow's second husband contemplates the doom-laden rapids in another dangerous area known simply as "*the Deadline*. Dirk drank scotch, and considered what this might mean" (2004: 95).

Oates' family group returns repeatedly to study the ominous falls, but the disruptive significance of this liquid environment only becomes fully evident when the social map is affected. In an omniscient interlude, Oates disrupts focalized reflections of "the fantastical mist-shrouded Gorge" (2004: 166) with a more discordant vision of industrial development. The family travels inland to discover "familiar sights ... becoming unrecognizable, torn up and jumbled like a Tinkertoy earthquake. ... raw earth was becoming cement. Trees were toppled, sawed into pieces and hauled away. Giant cranes and bulldozers were everywhere" (2004: 166). The wealthy family at the center of the novel had no prior vision of this "no-man's-land, claimed for factories, warehouses, employee parking lots" and initially sees in it only the shocking possibility of profiting from this disruptive building project. Ultimately, only the father, Dirk, fully connects this world to his own, developing a connection with an erotic healer consumed by the "pollution of a neighborhood, of earth, soil, water" at Love Canal. This interpersonal link prompts him to remap his environment. In his "big luxurious boat of a car," the father feels himself quite conventionally to be "like Charon's barge crossing the Styx" and "descending into the underworld" (2004: 219), but his hell is not the psychosexual torment of his wife's first husband; it is instead the social hell of realizing that he now inhabits two cities. The "gleaming tourist-city on the Niagara River" has a poisoned industrial twin: "The one was beauty and the terror of beauty; the other, mere expediency and man-made ugliness" (2004: 219). Only when Dirk can begin to map on the surface of the earth and in his social life the passageways linking these two cities – rather than letting the underworld consume the entire scene – can he or others fully inhabit this environment.

Within Oates' novel, the labor of data collection is performed by the twin cities' most vulnerable residents. They assemble a catalogue of illnesses (punctuated by "miscarriages … and miscarriages. And miscarriages") and pinpoint the locations of clusters of cancer and other ailments (2004: 232). Access to this map of horrors is restricted by the courts, willfully ignored by the widow as long as humanly possible, and melodramatically lost with the death of her second husband. The last third of the novel veers away from mapping, exploring Oates' signature themes of downward mobility and bereavement. Only the concluding scene (a long overdue funeral service) renews this theme with its suggestion of a community unified by the memorial project. Here, the turn toward geologic time introduced in the opening passages returns, and the sublimely spectacular tourist landscape is reclaimed through admission of its entanglement with industrial contamination.

To arrive at this sober resolution with all its traces of the green novel's fatalist lament, Oates had to manipulate the history and – more to the point – the scene of her novel. She is dealing with facts on record and told interviewers she aimed to be essentially faithful to the legal history of Love Canal (BookBrowse). However, having initially conceived of *The Falls* as a novel focused on the redemption of the father, she exaggerated the lawyer/patriarch's initiative in the court proceedings somewhat, embroiling him in a host of imagined ethical and erotic complications. Oates also modified distances; perhaps to keep locations of her characters intentionally hazy, she sets many reflective scenes drifting on a boat. The fatherly lawyer floats, anxious and volatile himself. His unanchored sensibility undercuts the authority of the realist assertion following shortly thereafter that Love Canal is a mere "twelve miles" from his family home (2004: 228). Socially mobile, too, he wishes to remain behind the scenes so he will not be perceived as a class traitor by other members of his old boy network, and this uneasy desire for mobility fights with his need for a new kind of fixity and certainty in his social mapping. The novel introduces this spatial conflict in its most clearly invented passages, retaining a kind of uneasiness in its own mournful hope that a new map of cross-class relations can be drawn. Oates then closes the novel by invoking the notion that a community of mourners will serve as the ideal mappers of geologic space in the future. In "Prospect Park, close by the Niagara Gorge, the air is fresh as if charged with electricity. You want to live: you want to live forever," the memorial attendees reflect (2004: 481). However, the intense social anxiety associated with this Romantic revival makes its realization uncertain.

Perhaps for this reason, Amitav Ghosh largely resists the transcendent reunion trope. Like *The Falls*, his *The Hungry Tide* (also 2004) tackles community knowledge and management of a natural environment endangered by human activity. Set in the Sundarbans, a massive tidal mangrove forest located in the delta shared by Bangladesh and Bengal, Ghosh's novel narrates the migration into the area by refugees (and their flight following a state massacre) as well as the fortunes of quasi-socialist utopian communities on the islands. Readers enter into this scene from the double points of view of a middle-aged, world-weary Bombay businessman and an American scientist with Bengali parents. These two cosmopolitan guides to the scene approach a local community they only partially understand. Ghosh introduces the possibility of erotic bonds smoothing entry into the local community, as Kanai (the businessman) reflects on the fascination for a local girl he developed during an extended visit to the islands during his adolescence. Similarly, Piya (the scientist) becomes acutely self-conscious of her physical proximity to Fokir, an island fisherman married to a kinswoman of the object of Kanai's youthful desire.

Despite the convenient death of the local woman, however, Ghosh's plot does not turn on the consummation of erotic bonds that fold the cosmopolitan wanderers into the island community. He resists the most conventional displacement of the green novel. Instead, at the novel's action climax, Fokir and Piya lash themselves tightly to a tree in order to ride out an unexpected cyclone, but the scene of protracted physical intimacy becomes a tragic sacrifice rather than an erotic union. "Their bodies were so close, so finely merged that [Piya] could feel the impact of everything hitting [Fokir]," Ghosh writes, "she could sense the blows raining down on his back. She could feel the bones of his cheeks as if they had been superimposed upon her own; it was as if the storm had given them what life had not; it had fused them together and made them one" (2004: 390). Fokir has of course died in this barrage, and Piya absorbs his life force and knowledge into her own project, returning to the islands in the coda to begin a scientific project designed to support the inhabitants.

In place of an erotic union, Ghosh provides a map. Fokir had been assisting Piya in her effort to track the migrations of a type of dolphin known to frequent the Indian Ocean. She wants to study their movements and uses a GPS tool to gather data for her study; Fokir becomes an invaluable guide, steering her directly to areas where the dolphins can be observed. Piya asks herself "how could he have known that they would run into a group of Orcaella, right then and right in that place?" (2004: 113) before later coming to appreciate the value of folklore (especially stories of Bon Bibi, another dangerous maternal goddess) as a guide to natural processes. Piya's dawning appreciation for indigenous knowledge of the environment culminates in a sense of bittersweet triumph when she realizes that Fokir's wisdom did not die with him in the cyclone but in fact had been preserved in the navigation device she used to record the movements of the dolphins. Although her written notes were lost as well, Fokir's sacrifice preserved "one map [that] represents decades of work and volumes of knowledge" (2004: 398).

As in Oates' model, then, Ghosh's synthetic map – joining the collection work of locals to the scientific synthesis provided by elite visitors – is conceived as a memorial. Piya's research project is to be named after Fokir. She, like Kanai, the businessman, comes to see herself as at home in the tidal zone, adding to the geological mythology dreamt up by Kanai's idealistic uncle decades before – a dream of a map revealing that the entire delta is fed by an underground extension of the Ganges. In a clearly politically charged vision, all the novel's protagonists rejoin a more cosmic, international mapping project in the novel's final pages, but the difference is that they do so without forging a single community. As numerous commentators on the novel have noted, Ghosh imagines a new relation of solidarity between techno-cosmopolitans and dispossessed refugees as the necessary complement to shifting from "a shift from a *perception* of a landscape as a *scene* or a setting to an *experience* of it as an *environment*" (Nayar 2010: 91).

The Hungry Tide's familiar turn toward memorializing should not lead us to confuse the project it advances with Oates' or Boyle's – or, beyond them, the most conventional green fiction's. Ghosh's novel differs significantly from Oates'. For Oates, portions of the human population are endangered while the deep structure of the earth is known and endures, but for Ghosh the map itself is at risk of being lost alongside the people. The possibility of losing the map and the fusion of indigenous knowledge and techno-savvy data collection that produced it lies at the heart of his novel. This loss is not presented as equal in weight to historical massacres and the associated scenes of social devastation, but it does approximate the quite active possibility of losing knowledge of and access to utopian ideals, such as those of the Scottish philanthropist who influenced the settlement of the region.

In Ghosh's novel, in other words, maps – especially those of underwater trenches, like those where the dolphins hide during storms – require collaborative data collection and updated tools for preservation, circulation, and use. His narrative suggests that the representational tools themselves need to be revolutionized, alongside the persons who contribute to them. Ghosh takes the changeable, crisis-ridden nature of Boyle's fictional universe and couples it with the attention to new social relations of information-gathering we observed in Oates' novel in order to create a narrative that generates for its imaginary resolution of this on-going problem an image of future collective map-making. His novel does not end on a note of Thoreauvian isolation – waiting out the Dark Ages in a cozy cabin, like Boyle's hero. Nor does he claim too easy a foothold in the heavily compromised tradition of the sublime, like Oates. Instead, Ghosh's novel turns toward an implied audience (whether that audience consists of non-resident Indians, internationally mobile trading clans, Anglophone greens, or migrants everywhere?) that is imagined as capable of action, if not exactly equipped for immediate rescue missions.

Of course, there is some irony involved in Ghosh's deployment of a conventional middle-class realism as a literary style in which to articulate content advocating new representational strategies, and the largely ethical appeal to solidarity is similarly an ideal rather than a practice. More generally, one certainly might question whether writing any sort of fiction, no matter what the story or style, makes a consequential intervention into climate change. Nonetheless, this essay has been less interested in evaluating the ideological work performed by Ghosh's or any other individual author's particular vision than in identifying the syntax of an emerging genre of the political novel and marking its commitments. With Ghosh, Oates, and Boyle, despite their differences in tone, style, subject, and political point of view, we find an important piece of the social dialogue around environmental issues expressed. In their shift toward problems of collective survival, memorialization, and mapping these authors deepen the genre of the green novel. They complement fatalistic visions of a toxic underworld with a subdued alternative – one that restores some forms of collective intellectual labor to the narrative and provides objects of affection that are not exclusively colored by despair, anxiety, or satiric horror. This dialogue within the genre of the green novel is crucial to recognize if we follow Todorov in understanding genre as a codification of socially necessary ideologies. If the green novel retains some space for alternate forms of resolution to environmental crisis, perhaps this signals a lingering social openness to initiatives that take collective responsibility for preventing a total environmental collapse.

REFERENCES

Abbey, Edward. 1968. *Desert solitaire: A season in the wilderness.* New York: Touchstone.
Bakhtin, Mikhail. 1981. Forms of time and of the chronotope in the novel. In Michael Holquist (ed.), *The dialogical imagination: Four essays*, trans. Caryl Emerson & Michael Holquist, 84–258. Austin: University of Texas Press.
Blanchot, Maurice. 1986. *Le livre a venir.* Paris: Gallimard.

BookBrowse. An interview with Joyce Carol Oates. http://www.bookbrowse.com/author_interviews/full/index.cfm/author_number/1054/joyce-carol-oates (last accessed on 20 May 2014).

Boyle, T. C. 2000. *Friend of the earth*. New York: Penguin.

Boyle, T. C. 2011. *When the killing's done*. New York: Penguin.

Boyle, T. C. 2012. *San Miguel*. New York: Viking.

Bramwell, Anna. 1994. *The fading of the greens: The decline of environmental politics in the West*. New Haven: Yale University Press.

Buell, Lawrence. 1998. Toxic Discourse. *Critical Inquiry* 24(3),639–665.

Callenbach, Ernest. 1977. *Ecotopia*. New York: Bantam.

Dean, Sharon L. 2006. History and representation in *The Falls*. *Studies in the Novel* 38(4),525–531.

Derrida, Jacques. 1980. The law of genre. *Critical Inquiry* 7(1),55–81.

Dillard, Annie. 1974. *A pilgrim at Tinker Creek*. New York: HarperCollins.

Elderkin, Susan. 2003. *The voices*. New York: Grove.

Ghosh, Amitav. 2004. *The hungry tide*. New York: Penguin.

Habila, Helon. 2011. *Oil on water*. New York: Norton.

Heise, Ursula. 2008. *The sense of place and the sense of planet: The environmental imagination of the global*. New York: Oxford University Press.

Irr, Caren. 2013. *Toward the geopolitical novel: U.S. fiction in the 21st century*. New York: Columbia University Press.

Kelly, Adam. 2011. Beginning with postmodernism. *Twentieth Century Literature* 57(3–4), 391–422.

Leader-Williams, Nigel & Holly T. Dublin. 2000. Charismatic megafauna as "flagship species." In Abigail Entwhistle & Nigel Dunstone (eds.), *Priorities for the conservation of mammalian diversity*, 53–81. Cambridge: Cambridge University Press.

Lyon, Thomas J. 2001. *This incomparable land: A guide to American nature writing*. Minneapolis: Milkweed.

MacEwan, Ian. 2010. *Solar*. New York: Random House.

Marcus, Sharon. 1999. *Apartment stories: City and home in nineteenth-century Paris and London*. Berkeley: University of California Press.

Matson, Suzanne. 2007. *The tree-sitter*. New York: Norton.

Matthiessen, Peter. 2008. *The shadow country*. New York: Modern Library.

McKibben, Bill. 2006. *The end of nature*. New York: Random House.

Millet, Lydia. 2008. *How the dead dream*. Berkeley: Counterpoint.

Nayar, Pramod. 2010. The postcolonial uncanny: The politics of dispossession in Amitav Ghosh's *The hungry tide*. *College Literature* 37(4),88–119.

Nixon, Rob. 2011. *Slow violence and the environmentalism of the poor*. Cambridge, MA: Harvard University Press.

Oates, Joyce Carol. 2004. *The falls*. New York: HarperCollins.

Phillips, Dana. 2003. *The truth of ecology: Nature, culture and literature in America*. Oxford: Oxford University Press.

Propp, Vladimir. 1968. *The morphology of the folk tale*. Bloomington: Indiana University Press.

Roos, Bonnie & Alex Hunt (eds.). 2010. *Postcolonial green: Environmental politics and world narratives*. Charlottesville: University of Virginia Press.

Russell, Karen. 2011. *Swamplandia!* New York: Vintage.

Schäfer-Wünsche, Elisabeth. 2005. Borders and catastrophes: T.C. Boyle's California trilogy. In Klaus Benesch & Kerstin Schmidt (eds.), *Architecture | Technology | Culture*, vol. 1: *Space in America: Theory - history – culture*, 401–417. Amsterdam: Rodopi.

Shriver, Lionel. 2009. *Game control*. New York: HarperCollins.

Shute, Nevil. 2010 [1957]. *On the beach*. New York: Vintage.

Sinha, Indra. 2007. *Animal's people*. New York: Simon & Schuster.

Sontag, Susan. 1979. *Illness as metaphor*. New York: Vintage.

Swift, Graham. 1983. *Waterland*. London: Penguin.

Thoreau, Henry David. 2008 [1854]. *Walden*. New York: Norton.

Todorov, Tzvetan. 1976. The origin of genres. *New Literary History* 8(1),159–170.

Wegner, Phillip E. 2014. *Shockwaves of possibility: Essays on science fiction, globalization, and utopia*. New York: Peter Lang.

Williams, Joy. 2000. *The quick and the dead*. New York: Vintage.

Williams, Terry Tempest. 1992. *Refuge: An unnatural history of family and place*. New York: Vintage.

A Sociological Imagination

SUSAN HEGEMAN

In the context of the apparent closure of neoliberalism, I can think of no more profoundly humanist statement than *"no mode of production and therefore no dominant social order and therefore no dominant culture ever in reality includes or exhausts all human practice, human energy, and human intention"* (Williams 1978: 125). Raymond Williams's comment, which he thought important enough to render in italics, is a powerful reminder to those of us who analyze culture that we must both attempt to interpret the present, with all the hazards that entails, and – even more precariously – anticipate the ways in which the future may yet answer back to it. This small essay is written in the spirit of that important goal. I will first give one narrative of the cultural dominant of intellectual life in the twentieth-century United States, and then offer some thoughts on alternatives that may yet emerge, especially in the wake of the financial disaster of 2008. Because I am interested in the cultural dominant, I will take examples not only from academic intellectuals, but also from popular literature, the arts, and ultimately, from experimental social movements. I will therefore necessarily be skimming over the surface of a great deal of complexity, but my hope is that my map will open up interesting places for others to explore. In particular, I am interested in tracing the fate of the "sociological imagination," which, as C. Wright Mills wrote a half century ago, "enables its possessor to understand the larger historical scene in terms of its meaning for the inner life and the external career of a variety of individuals" (1959: 5). It seems to me this sociological imagination was accessible in the early twentieth-century United States, and continues to be useful, if not crucial, in a moment like ours.

Like Mills, I'm uninterested in the classic disciplinary divisions between social scientific fields like anthropology and sociology. More important for me is the distinction between this mode of thought and a traditional humanism, in that the former understands humanity as always, already embedded in historically, spatially, and materially contingent social contexts. As such, this way of thinking represents something like a middle position between humanism and posthumanism, between the epistemological certitude of *man* on the one hand, and the "dissolution of the subject" on the other (Collins 2012: 47). It is also characterized by certain interpretive strategies and goals. For Mills, it was the project to "characterize societies as wholes" (1959: 17) that united literary travelers and historians like Tocqueville and Taine to the grand tradition of nineteenth-century social scientific thought, as represented by names like Comte, Durkheim, Weber, Marx, Mauss, and Veblen. But I would add that this mode of thought also includes the strategy of estranging received social common sense with the wealth of other possibilities enabled by experiences of cultural diversity. This is already present in the earliest example of anthropological writing, Montaigne's famous "Of Cannibals," in which native Brazilians, brought to the court of the French boy king Charles IX, are reported to wonder that the "injustice" of the monumental disparity of wealth that they see in France has not yet caused a violent insurrection (1958: 159).

I've argued at length elsewhere that this form of estrangement, honed in the early twentieth-century United States by the Boasian anthropologists, was part and parcel of a modernist aesthetic and intellectual project (see Hegeman 1999). But by and large, Americans have been relatively resistant to both the totalizing and estranging impulses of the sociological imagination. The years around World War II, in which the United States consolidated its position as a global power, represent in particular a moment of strong divergence from the sociological imagination. During the war, the exigencies of propaganda and morale made the accustomed social scientific practice of holding one's society open to examination through the strategy of cultural estrangement virtually politically untenable. That is, the very existence of Nazi Germany, and to a lesser extent Tojo's Japan and Stalin's Soviet Union, disallowed the conventional anthropological stance of cultural relativism, and thus strategies of intercultural comparison. But just as significantly, this ideological shift coincided with the dramatic growth and increased prestige of the social sciences in the United States. Mobilized into wartime bureaucracies, social scientists found new and expanding roles to play in such areas as cold war intelligence and the bureaucratic management of populations on the home front. Meanwhile, thanks to the GI Bill's educational benefits, the sheer numbers of social scientists increased, and academic programs proliferated – especially in the new fields of "area studies" (Patterson 2001: 103–134; Wallerstein 1997: 195–231). Social science's corresponding popular prestige at this time is reflected in the emergence of figures like Margaret Mead, Alfred Kinsey, John Kenneth Galbraith, E. Franklin Frazier, and many others as popular experts on everything from race relations to sexuality and child rearing. Increasingly, American social scientists were finding a popular role as definers and propagators of behavioral norms.

Mills' *Sociological Imagination* was largely a complaint against this instrumentalization of mid-twentieth-century social science and its newfound power and prestige, not as a capacious eye on society but a tool of hegemony: of marketing, governance, intelligence, and the social order. And yet Mills was no more optimistic about humanist intellectuals – who, in retrospect we now see, were also being incorporated into bureaucratic structures of their own, notably the university and the corporate media. Mills lamented,

> What fiction, what journalism, what artistic endeavor, can compete with the historical reality and political facts of our time? What dramatic vision of hell can compete with the events of twentieth century war? What moral denunciations can measure up to the moral insensibility of men in the agonies of primary accumulation? (Mills 1959: 16)

Literature, he worried, had become a "minor art," inadequate to the task of describing the complexity of contemporary social life.

We could object to Mills' sentiment by referencing an individual favorite midcentury work of art, or perhaps by identifying in Mills a Lukács-like nostalgia for the imaginative totalities of nineteenth-century realism. But I think the more interesting insight to be drawn from his comment is that the American late-modernist separation of art from society, often characterized as an ideological impulse of the cold war, was not simply a product of new critical desires to rescue art from a fallen world, but a more generalized sentiment from across the political spectrum that art was somehow inadequate to the task of the sociological imagination. This partially rescues for me the otherwise numbingly banal midcentury handwringing over how the Nazi commandant could possibly enjoy Beethoven (what the British artist Banksy has recently brilliantly glossed, in a brilliant détournement of a tacky landscape painting, as the "Banality of the Banality of

Evil" [Stuart 2013]). In other words, Mills helps us see that it was not simply that art was intractably separated from morality, politics, or social life; it was that it was perhaps fundamentally incapable of bridging the gap between individual subjectivities and the perceived unrepresentability of the postwar social order.

I contend that this basic view of the irreconcilability of art and the social has been the intellectual dominant in the United States throughout the American century. I recognize that this is a potentially controversial claim, especially given the significant art and culture that accompanied or was inspired by such social movements as civil rights and black power, second-wave feminism, Chicano-Latino movements, and queer activism, among others. But the position of these movements and forms, relative to the dominant social and cultural order, was avowedly minoritarian: explicitly poised against or in light of a presumptive social order. As such, most multiculturalism has been readily absorbed into the cultural dominant, in the form of inclusive codices to business as usual, while the most radical elements of these movements – the Black Panthers, AIM, La Raza, Redstockings – were actively criminalized, and discredited (see Glick 1999). Nowhere is this clearer than in the academic incorporation of these movements, which often began at the behest of student activists but then found their legitimation by incorporating the norms and structures of the academy as a whole. For example, Jane Gallop (1991) has shown at length how feminism achieved status in the literary academy largely via incorporating continental theory. While many good things can be said about this convergence, particularly how it forced a reconsideration of the subject, much of its critical edge was blunted. By the 1970s continental theory had been scrubbed of a good deal of its radicalism, and with it, a good deal of its own commitment to the sociological imagination (see Christofferson 2004). Theory, and postmodernism specifically, came to the United States possessing a characteristic "incredulity toward metanarratives" (Lyotard 1979), which the particularisms of multiculturalism ended up reinforcing. At least in regard to the broken dialectic of the subject and the social, postmodernism represents no break at all from American late modernism, but perhaps something more like another symptom of American global hegemonic reach during the longer cold war.

Which brings me (albeit hurriedly) to our neoliberal present, whose structures of feeling seem to revolve around temporal stasis and irresolvable historical inevitability. In addition to Margaret Thatcher's famous slogan "TINA: There is No Alternative," we find historical time expressed in terms of gerunds like "unwinding" and "dithering" (Packer 2013; Robinson 2012: 245), which suggest a prolonged, indeed barely perceptible sliding into some perpetual future.[1] Or, using a metaphorics of extended illness, we are in a mode of what Laurent Berlant calls "slow death," or what Eric Cazdyn denominates a "new chronic mode" of temporality, where resigned accommodation to a broken present seems less horrible than the annihilation represented by real historical rupture (Berlant 2011: 95–119; Cazdyn 2012: 5). Never as much as now have we seemed to need something like the sociological imagination, in order to confront this frustrating sense of historical closure.

One way to confront this closure is to uncover the repressed sociological imagination of neoliberalism itself. We may as well begin with another of Thatcher's famous neoliberal slogans: "There is no such thing as society." Of course,

---

[1] From the perspective of 2312, Robinson narrates, "How they despised the generations of the Dithering, who had heedlessly pushed the climate into a change with an unstoppable momentum to it, continuing not only into the present, but for centuries more to come" (Robinson 2012: 316).

what she meant was that there should be no such thing as a social welfare state. But what Thatcher also hinted at was something Michel Foucault had already identified in 1979 in regard to what he called "American neo-liberalism": its radical propensity to replace all forms of interpretation of human sociality and behavior with some extrapolation of economics, the logic of the marketplace (Foucault 2008: 243). Neoliberalism, in other words, represents the triumph of a very specific understanding of humanity: the *Homo economicus* of Adam Smith's invention, whose natural drive to "truck and barter" is tempered only by rational self-interest.

This allegiance to the conception of human beings as centrally and primarily rational, self-interested actors was integral to the financial disaster of 2008.[2] Blind faith in *Homo economicus* drove neoliberalism's architects and agents to see only the good in loosening the fetters on both capitalism's instruments of creative destruction and the economic choices of individuals, who were now encouraged as never before to enter the financial markets, and thereby gamble with their homes, their retirement savings, and their emergency funds. But all this changed when the credit markets froze, investment firms collapsed, and countless people saw their lives and communities upturned in the economic chaos. *Homo economicus* was not simply rattled, but unseated. A small space, I believe, has finally opened up for new ways to understand the relationship of the subject and society.

A number of developments have pointed in this direction for some time, including the fairly decisive end of incredulity toward metanarrative, a significant intellectual push to rethink the social, as well as a drive to rethink the subject. When Lyotard wrote of the postmodern incredulity toward metanarrative, he was writing from within a late cold war context in which metanarrative constructions of all kinds were implicitly tarred with the brush of totalitarianism. Totalization was, de facto, totalitarian. The end of the cold war has helped to end this particular intellectual ban. Thus, in 2006, the Retort collective, which includes the art historian T. J. Clark, decisively wrote,

> We take it the time is over when the mere mention of such categories [as "capitalism" and "primitive accumulation"] consigned one – in the hip academy, especially – irrevocably to the past. The past has become the present again: this is the mark of the moment we are trying to understand. (It is "the end of Grand Narratives" and "the trap of totalization" and "the radical irreducibility of the political" which now seem like period items.) (2006: 9)

Not surprisingly, then, many of the classic metanarratives have lately reemerged. For evidence of this, one need look no farther than the *New York Times* nonfiction bestseller list, which, in the spring of 2014, was topped by a book titled *Capital in the twenty-first century* (*New York Times* 2014).[3] Clearly, the pressing desire to register certain recent massive global changes – in, for example, the

---

[2] Following Cazdyn I am referring to the events of October 2008 as a financial "disaster," and not a "crisis," which is the common usage. Cazdyn points out that "crisis" is the common condition of capitalism, whereas "disaster" is when "the sustainable configuration of relations fail," and is thereby temporarily made visible (Cazdyn 2012: 53–55).

[3] In addition to exemplifying the return of metanarratives, Thomas Piketty's *Capital in the twenty-first century* also participates in the trend toward interrogating neoliberal economism. From within the field of economics, Piketty critiques his discipline's pretensions – especially in the United States – to scientific objectivity and its related blindness to social issues such as income inequality. He writes bluntly, "[t]he truth is that economics should never have sought to divorce itself from the other social sciences and can advance only in conjunction with them" (2014: 32).

climate, population flows, financial structures, and the global political system of sovereign nation-states – has encouraged metanarrative usages like "modernity," "globalization," and the "anthropocene." Correspondingly, popular social science continues apace in a virtual efflorescence of "big idea" thinking. One perhaps slightly under-discussed element of the current massive changes underway in intellectual life due to internet technologies – in the face of the decline of the traditional academic humanities, TV, and print journalism – is the creation of a new lucrative form of high-tech edutainment, in the TED talk and the corporate lecture circuit: a kind of monster hybrid of long-form journalism, highbrow chat show, self-help seminar, and academic lecture. The related crossover books, many by social scientists like Jared Diamond, or by social science interpreters like Malcolm Gladwell, are in this sense just the tip of the "big idea" iceberg. Big thinking is not only not banned these days, it's *hot.*

As far as reconsiderations of the subject are concerned, we could certainly point to new ideas of the "posthuman" that transcend the traditional species boundaries of subjectivity. More specifically regarding Adam Smith's *Homo economicus*, the relatively new field of economic behaviorism, which focuses on the *limits* of human rationality and enlightened self-interest, has simultaneously become an important subfield and internal critique of classical economic theory. Books on these issues by Nobel laureate Daniel Kahneman (*Thinking, fast and slow*, 2011), Dan Ariely (*Predicatably irrational*, 2008), and Nassim Nicholas Taleb (*Fooled by randomness*, 2001, and *The black swan*, 2007), among others, have garnered both academic respect and made it to the bestseller lists. Most significantly, it finally seems acceptable again in some political circles to propose that one function of government is to protect consumers and citizens from the irrational functioning of markets, bad actors, and their own potentially self-destructive economic behavior.

But what is a human, if not a rational, self-interested economic agent? This, of course, is a question that social scientists, humanists, and artists have all long entertained. Economic anthropologists and historians have pretty much demolished as a myth Adam Smith's famous economic origin story about how primitive barter systems led, on grounds of efficiency, to the abstraction of a money economy (Graeber 2011: loc. 600; see also Humphrey & Hugh-Jones 1992). But more broadly – beginning with Marcel Mauss' *The gift* (*Essai sur le don*, 1925) – a wide-ranging strain of thought has elaborated alternative theories and examples of human interaction, reciprocity, resource use, and social organization that radically estrange this long-held version of socio-economic common sense. Mauss himself was a political activist and a proponent of the cooperative movement. His interest in the Northwest Indian potlatch and Melanesian kula rings was therefore hardly a mere sojourn into exoticism; it was an investigation into how human economies extend beyond the ideological frameworks of rational choice and possessive individualism (Hart 2007). This is an urgent task of a renewed sociological imagination. But it is one that must somehow find common cause with artists, activists, and a larger society.

This is where the Occupy movement is interesting to me. Not because it represents a definitive political rupture of our time (far from it), but because it seems to contain the elements both for reconceptualizing humans in society, and for enacting it in both creative and political ways. At the heart of the Occupy movement there was at least one social scientist, the anarchist anthropologist David Graeber, whose book *Debt: The first 5000 years* became a surprise hit during the Occupy year of 2011. An organizer of the New York demonstrations, Graeber also provided Occupy with some foundational political-economic ground-clearing: his text framed debt not as an individual's obligation to repay on penalty of legal action, but as the basis of all kinds of social obligation and reciprocity in general. This struck a chord with the debt-burdened members of the "GWAF generation" ("graduates without a future"); that is, the ambitious and creative, but underemployed aspirants to the now largely decomposed professional-managerial stratum of the middle class (Ehrenreich 2013). Famously, they formed the backbone of the Occupy movement. This movement, in turn, and particularly its encampments, became experiments in creating alternatives not only for community governance – the hand signals and general assemblies that got all that media attention were just that – but for human community built on radically alternative bases of sharing, giving, and reciprocity. Moreover – and it is here that I return to my larger narrative of the long twentieth century – Occupy appears in retrospect to be an intensely fertile laboratory for connecting art back up to the social – and sociological – imagination. Occupy offered up an explosion of intellectual activity and aesthetic expression, ranging from graphic design and literature and cultural criticism, to theatrical performances and high concept art installations. Established figures in diverse media and genres, including Shepard Fairey, Eric Drooker, Philip Glass, Talib Kweli, Tom Morello, and Pete Seeger demonstrated a living connection to older and other forms of politicized art (Sekoff 2012). But for every star associated with Occupy, there were legions of inspired young fine artists and graphic designers, musicians, dancers, puppeteers, and performance artists who were still grappling with forms of expression that directly addressed their political goals. Also, in insisting, as many did, on connecting art with public space, Occupy artists expressed a common mission not only of engaging in explicit social commentary but of revising the traditional economic structure of the practice of art, literature, and criticism. Perhaps this took place out of necessity: they have in many respects been "freed," for better or worse, from the institutional fetters (and supports) of their elders. As Christopher Kulendran Thomas, a London-based visual artist put it: "I can't see what will emerge afterwards, any more than I can see what the world economy might look like after Western dominance, but Occupy art can be seen as foreshadowing what replaces Contemporary Art" (qtd. in Mason 2012). Whether or not, in years hence, we still think of something called Occupy art, or think of the Occupy movement as a central watershed moment, we should at least be cognizant of the fact that a whole generation of artists and intellectuals have cut their teeth in and around Occupy encampments and actions. It's with them especially that I envision the efflorescence of a renewed sociological imagination, and therefore the end to the stasis of our eternal present.

REFERENCES

Ariely, Dan. 2008. *Predictably irrational*. New York: HarperCollins.
Berlant, Lauren. 2011. *Cruel optimism*. Durham, NC: Duke University Press.
Cazdyn, Eric. 2012. *The already dead*. Durham, NC: Duke University Press.
Christofferson, Michael Scott. 2004. *French intellectuals against the left: The antitotalitarian moment of the 1970s*. New York: Berghahn Books.
Collins, Jacob. 2012. An anthropological turn? The unseen paradigm in modern French thought. *New Left Review* 78, 31–60.
Ehrenreich, Barbara & John Ehrenreich. 2013. Death of a yuppie dream: The rise and fall of the professional-managerial class. *Rosa Luxemburg stiftung*, http://www.rosalux-nyc.org/death-of-a-yuppie-dream (last accessed on 10 November 2013).
Foucault, Michel. 2008. *The birth of biopolitics: Lectures at the College de France, 1978–1979*, ed. Michel Senellart, trans. Graham Burchell. New York: Picador.
Gallop, Jane. 1991. *Around 1981: Academic feminist literary theory*. New York: Routledge.

Glick, Brian. 1999. *War at home: Covert action against US activists and what we can do about it.* Boston: South End Press.

Graeber, David. 2011. *Debt: The first 5000 years.* New York: Melville House.

Hart, Keith. 2007. Marcel Mauss: In pursuit of the whole. *Comparative Studies in Society and History* 49(2),473–485.

Hegeman, Susan. 1999. *Patterns for America: Modernism and the concept of culture.* Princeton, NJ: Princeton University Press.

Humphrey, Caroline & Stephen Hugh-Jones (eds.). 1992. *Barter, exchange and value: An anthropological approach.* New York: Cambridge University Press.

Kahneman, Daniel. 2011. *Thinking, fast and slow.* London: Macmillan.

Lyotard, Jean-François. 1979. *The postmodern condition,* trans. Geoff Bennington and Brian Massumi. Minneapolis: University of Minnesota Press.

Mason, Paul. 2012. Does Occupy signal the death of contemporary art? *BBC News,* http://www.bbc.co.uk/news/magazine-17872666 (last accessed on 10 November 2013).

Mills, C. Wright. 1959. *The sociological imagination.* New York: Oxford University Press.

Montaigne, Michel de. 1958. Of cannibals. In *The complete essays of Montaigne,* trans. Donald M. Frame. 150–158. Palo Alto, CA: Stanford University Press.

New York Times. 2014. Best sellers, hardcover nonfiction. http://www.nytimes.com/best-sellers-books/2014–05–18/hardcover-nonfiction/list.html (last accessed on 15 May 2014).

Packer, George. 2013. *The unwinding: An inner history of the new America.* New York: Farrar, Straus and Giroux.

Patterson, Thomas C. 2001. *A social history of Anthropology in the United States.* New York: Berg.

Piketty, Thomas. 2014. *Capital in the twenty-first century,* trans. Arthus Goldhammer. Cambridge, MA: Harvard-Belknap Press.

Retort [collective consisting of Iain Boal, T. J. Clark, Joseph Matthews & Michael Watts]. 2006. *Afflicted powers: Capital and spectacle in a new age of war.* New York: Verso.

Robinson, Kim Stanley. 2012. *2312.* New York: Orbit.

Ross, Dorothy. 1991. *The origins of American social science.* New York: Cambridge University Press.

Sekoff, Hallie. 2012. Occupy Wall Street and the arts, one year later. *Huffington Post,* http://www.huffingtonpost.com/2012/09/17/occupy-wall-street-and-th_n_1890789.html (last accessed on 15 May 2014).

Stuart, Theresa. 2013. Banksy's *The banality of the banality of evil* sells for $615,000. *Village Voice,* http://blogs.villagevoice.com/runninscared/2013/10/banksy_banality_of_evil.php (last accessed on 10 November 2013).

Taleb, Nassim Nicholas. 2004. *Fooled by randomness: The hidden role of chance in life and in the markets.* New York: Random House.

Taleb, Nassim Nicholas. 2010. *The black swan: The impact of the highly improbable.* New York: Random House.

Thatcher, Margaret. 1987. Interview for *Women's Own. Margaret Thatcher Foundation,* http://www.margaretthatcher.org/document/106689 (last accessed on 10 November 2013).

Wallerstein, Immanuel. 1997. The unintended consequences of cold war area studies. In Noam Chomsky, et al., *The cold war and the university,* 195–231. New York: The New Press.

Williams, Raymond. 1978. *Marxism and literature.* New York: Oxford University Press.

The Role of Place in the Post-Apocalypse:
Contrasting *The Road* and *World War Z*

PETTER SKULT

Introduction

Post-apocalyptic fiction, as I define it, is a narrative of a period of time from a pre-apocalyptic past through a cataclysmic event (or series of events) that culminates in an entirely new world order – the post-apocalypse. During this transition from pre- to post-apocalypse, the landscape and geography of the world change drastically: usually from a recognizable, urban "normality" to an uncanny wilderness. The majority of stories that belong to the post-apocalyptic canon are set in a post-catastrophic version of our own recognizable Earth, and thus comment on our own reality, and it is largely from this immediate connection that the genre derives its strength: through the imagined destruction of our world. From the earliest examples to the latest, through cataclysms of plague to nuclear war and zombie diseases, the genre describes the collapse of nations and cities and the ruins they leave, the recognizable places of our world. At the end of *The Planet of the Apes* (1968) we come across the Statue of Liberty, which in a flash turns the entire movie into a post-apocalyptic epic and a potent expression of Cold War fears: all through a recognizable, nameable place-marker. In this article I wish to discuss the role of place and space in a genre that, in recent years, has become increasingly prevalent. Place, I argue, is a necessary component for the creation of hope, meaning and a sense of the future, without which it becomes impossible or very difficult to reconstruct a lost world or construct an entirely new one. I will approach this by analyzing two recent, critically acclaimed post-apocalyptic novels, *The Road* (2006) by Cormac McCarthy, and *World War Z* (2006) by Max Brooks, using various theories of space and place, notably Gilles Deleuze and Felix Guattari's theories of striated and smooth space. These two works exemplify two extremes of the representation of place in the post-apocalypse: the almost complete effacing of place, and the utter dependence on place.

A Pulitzer-prize-winning work, *The Road* (2006) is a bleak post-apocalyptic tale of a father and son trekking south, away from the approaching winter, following an unknown apocalypse that seems to have ignited the entire world. The question is: "south" from where, to where? Despite its almost total lack of proper nouns (including place names), we the readers seem to know that the story takes place in the United States: "From what we can discern, this is post-apocalyptic Tennessee," Shelly L. Rambo (2008: 100) claims, a return to the south for McCarthy. Tim Blackmore calls it a slog "toward the Pacific Ocean" (2009: 22), which would place *The Road* somewhere around New Mexico, also familiar ground for McCarthy. On the other hand Graulund (2010: 58) points out that *The Road* is a departure, rather than a return, since, although it is set "in an unspecified region of America," it is also "the first of his novels to be detached entirely from history" and, most importantly, the first to break "with his famous attention to place" (2010: 58–59). Consider the very first proper spatial orientation marked within the opening pages of the story, after the boy and the man "woke in the woods in the dark" (McCarthy 2006: 1): "When it was light enough to use the binoculars he glassed the valley below. Everything paling away into the murk. The soft ash blowing in loose swirls over the blacktop. He studied what he could see. The segments of road down there among the dead trees" (2006: 3). In this short segment, we are given the basics of spatiality in *The Road*: the murk that envelops the world, the near-constant rain of ash, the dead trees and – of course – the road itself; but no indications of where we are.

By contrast, Max Brooks' *World War Z* (2006) is built entirely around specific places, and there is never any doubt as to where the events have taken place. The narrative, announced in the subtitle as an "oral history of the Zombie War," is framed as a series of interviews with various survivors and community leaders around the world following a global zombie apocalypse – the "human side" of a more formal UN report on the titular "World War Z." Each interview begins with a place-identifier, e.g. "Parnell Air National Guard Base, Tennessee" (Brooks 2006: 168), followed by a short, bracketed and bolded third-person narration of the context for the interview, absolutely rife with real-world referents. The author-insert narrator travels through the world, from China, Greece, Brazil, Barbados, Israel, Palestine, to various places in the United States, Finland, Antarctica, India, Russia, Greenland, South Africa, Ireland, Ukraine, Canada, Bohemia, Micronesia, South Korea, Japan, Cuba, Australia and Chile. The very first interview begins with a lesson in geography and history:

> The first outbreak I saw was in a remote village that officially had no name. The residents called it "New Dachang," but this was more out of nostalgia than anything else. Their former home, "Old Dachang," had stood since the period of the Three Kingdoms, with farms and houses and even trees said to be centuries old. When the Three Gorges Dam was completed, and reservoir waters began to rise, much of Dachang had been disassembled, brick by brick, then rebuilt on higher ground. (Brooks 2006: 4–5)

This short passage immediately places the world in context; even the officially unnamed village is given a name, a history, and a rough location. Often interviews take place in a widely different context than its content, such as the tale of an Iranian expat interviewed in Greenland, or a South African interviewed on Barbados, further accentuating the temporal and spatial connectedness of the narrative.

Place and Space

When speaking of place, it is important to note its sister concept of space. Like Bakhtin in *The Dialogic Imagination* (1981), I contend that it is impossible to write a narrative without considering space (and time), but spatiality is not the same as locality. The distinction between the two is generally made as one of levels of abstraction, the word *place* denoting an actual, real-world locality, often with a referent proper name, like the city of London or the San Joaquin Valley in California. When Westphal in *Geocriticism* (2011) speaks of "real and fictional spaces," he is mainly speaking about what I would call *places*: places that have real world referents. *Space*, on the other hand, tends to be approached in a metaphorical manner, often as a mathematical (length, breadth, width) or logical description of spatiality, time being its fourth dimension. Henri Lefebvre for instance makes a distinction between "the general (logical and mathematical)" and "the singular (i.e. 'places' considered as natural, in their merely physical or sensory reality)" (1991: 16), although he does not make a categorical, or rather lexicological, distinction between the words "place" and "space." The philosopher J.E. Malpas points out that these twin concepts are often confused and conflated in various ways, but that this lack of definition is a necessary expression of its complexity "and its necessary implication of concepts of both dimensionality and locale" (1999: 26). Cultural geographer Yi–Fu Tuan in his *Space and Place: The Perspective of Experience* (1977) distinguishes between the two on the level of human experience: according to Tuan "space becomes place as we get to know it better and endow it with value" (1977: 6). To be in space, according to Tuan, is to be in the open, to be "free" but also, on the flipside, to be "exposed and vulnerable." Place, by contrast, "is a calm center of established values" (1977: 54). Place can be considered something that exists within a wider space, while also allowing space a broader, more metaphorical interpretation. The broadest interpretation of space is also in a sense the scientific definition of it: the universe and everything that exists within it, including purely fictional worlds.

I would further argue that, especially for non-mimetic genres, place is a tool by which authors and readers can navigate what Alan Palmer (2004) has termed the "ontological gaps" (2004: 34) that permeate all fiction. An ontological gap (or blank) as defined by Palmer is a lack of knowledge about something within a fictional world. As Palmer points out, "[n]o discourse could ever be long enough to say in its story all that could be said about the whole storyworld" (2004: 34): we assume humans to have two arms and two legs and so forth also within fiction unless otherwise stated. Therefore, all fictional worlds are created largely through the cognitive supplementation (and deletion) of key aspects, one of those being recognizable places. Doležel puts it in simple terms: "the world is constructed by its author and the reader's role is to reconstruct it" (1998: 21). Since all fiction is ontologically incomplete and thus needs to be "filled in" by the author and reader in tandem, by mentioning known places – cities, countries, roads or states – the ontological gap is made less acute. This is particularly significant for a genre such as the post-apocalyptic one that straddles the mimetic and the fantastical, as among others David Ketterer (1974) has argued (he makes no distinction between apocalyptic and post-apocalyptic):

> Apocalyptic literature should be distinguished from mimetic literature on the one hand, and fantastic literature on the other. While mimetic literature addresses itself to reproductions of the "real" world, fantastic literature involves the creation of escapist worlds that, existing in an incredible relationship to the "real" world, do not impinge destructively on that world. *Apocalyptic literature is concerned with the creation of other worlds which exist, on the literal level, in a credible relationship (whether on the basis of rational extrapolation and analogy or religious belief) with the "real" world, thereby causing a metaphorical destruction of that "real" world in the reader's head.* (Ketterer 1974: 13; original emphasis)

It is not undifferentiated space that is destroyed in the apocalypse and described in the post-apocalypse: it is our world. But in that destruction all that is not viewed, named, placed, by the author, becomes a sort of ontological gap in the reader's mind. They might know it exists, but their knowledge of what it looks like is likely to be out of date. It is quite natural, then, that place – defined as a locality in our real world, a part of our actual world encyclopedia, a place we are or can be actual residents of – is of utmost importance for the genre. But, as the discussion below will show, its importance can be expressed as much in its absence as in its presence.

World War Z and the transformation of place

World War Z is a retrospective, set roughly a decade after the end of its titular war. It is not so surprising then that almost every interview looks back to the pre-apocalypse, and then quite often details the entire chronotopic progression until the interviewees reach the fictional present, attempting to fill in as many onto-logical gaps as possible. For example Cuba, which in the fiction of *World War Z* became a post-war economic powerhouse with a democratically elected govern-ment, is introduced with a retrospective – "just look at where we were twenty years ago as opposed to where we are now" (Brooks 2006: 228) – followed by a discussion of the US economic blockade and the tyranny of Castro. The purpose is transparent enough: by connecting our recognizable past with the fictional present, the transition from the one to the other becomes easier, more believable. More importantly it connects the *issues* of the "past" with the issues of the "present." Explaining the cognitive estrangement (Darko Suvin's term) brought on by the idea that Cuba is now a "thriving, capitalist economy" (Brooks 2006: 232) is the main connecting thread through the interview. Consider the phrase "armada of boat people" (2006: 229) used to refer to the Yankee refugees who escaped the Great Panic (i.e. the apocalyptic portion of the zombie war) from the mainland, which offers an ironic reversal of the image of Cuban or Haitian refugees, so-called boat people, who attempted to immigrate to the United States in the 1980s and 1990s. The Americans, unlike the unlucky Cuban and Haitian refugees, were *not* turned back, but rather integrated into Cuban society. In the fiction of *World War Z* this eventually led to a social and political revolution that ended Castro's rule, allowing Cuba to spearhead the eventual reclamation of the world from the undead.

This kind of socio-political commentary, however blunt (and occasionally escapist, conservative and jingoistic), is, one can argue, the bread and butter of the zombie subgenre within post-apocalyptic fiction. The origin of the zombie as we perceive it today (not the voodoo-inspired earlier zombies) comes from cinema, more precisely George Romero's *Night of the Living Dead* (1968), which "function[ed] largely as a metaphor for the atrocities of Vietnam and racism" (Bishop 2009: 18), and Romero has been known for his socially con-scious zombies ever since. The zombies (almost always in the plural) often function as "gory allegorists of apocalypse" (Ahmad 2011: 132) or simply as "the ultimate Other" (Baldwin 2007: 412), an empty referent that can fill any role as harbinger of the apocalypse: disease, war, famine, (un)death. Filling the empty referent is generally the role of the critic: Ahmad for instance sees the "post-industrial, late capitalist, globalized zombie horde" of *World War Z* as challen-ging "racism and class privilege" (2011: 131), with examples from how the zombies are equated with the apartheid regime in South Africa to how unregu-lated black-market dealing in organs causes the disease to spread (2011: 134–135). Similarly, class differences are turned on their heads, as the former work-ing-class subalterns "become the saviors of post-apocalyptic America" (Ahmad 2011: 136), their practical know-how being much more valuable than service-based economic skills. Perhaps thanks to the ease by which it can be interpreted, the zombie has, in recent years, become one of the most recognizable icons of the post-apocalyptic genre, featuring in everything from novels to films to TV series and video games, not to mention worldwide zombie walks. Bishop (2009) explains the resurgence of the genre in the twenty-first century as an amalgam of post 9/11 fears, from fear of terrorism, infection, natural disasters (e.g. Hurricane Katrina) to less transparent topics like euthanasia and xenophobia. I would argue a simpler interpretation: the zombie functions as a meme, a short-hand for contemporary apocalypse that can be "used" by content creators, rather than a legitimate fear in itself, especially considering that the concept of the walking dead, when studied in the cold light of day, is rather ludicrous.

For the purposes of this article, I wish to look at one specific aspect of the zombie: its ability to *transform space*. By this, I mean the zombies' ability to render the safe, recognizable, human referent into something unknown, fearsome, dangerous and undifferentiated: this is apparent in the very aspect of the zombie itself as a revived body devoid of identity, personality or soul, interested only in killing and consuming, most often part of a "horde" or "swarm." Much as the zombie can render the human uncanny, they can do the same with place. Through the early parts of *World War Z*, references are constantly made to the so-called Redeker Plan, which became the *de facto* strategy by which the various nations of the world were able to withstand the zombie plague. According to the plan, the governments of the world would retreat to a "special 'safe zone,'" leaving civilians behind as bait for the zombies while keeping them alive for as long as possible, until the reclamation of the world could begin again (Brooks 2006: 108–109), thus dividing the world into two parts: safe and unsafe. Consider the following description of a military map, with little colored circles denoting safe zones on a map otherwise a uniform gray, used to denote zombie ("Zack")-infested areas:

> Islands in the Sea of Zack. Green denotes active military facilities. [...] The Red Zones were labeled "Offensively Viable": factories, mines, power plants. [...] The Blue Zones were civilian areas where people had managed to make a stand, carve out a little piece of real estate, and figure out some way to live within its boundaries. (Brooks 2006: 170)

Cutting the world up into safe and unsafe, not to mention useful and useless, in this manner has been a pattern of the genre arguably since the very first literary zombie-styled narrative, Richard Matheson's *I Am Legend* (1954), which has commonly been cited as Romero's inspiration for *Night of the Living Dead* (1968). In *I Am Legend* the protagonist is spatially restricted to his own home somewhere in Compton during the night, protected by garlic and mirrors from a plague of vampirism that has turned everyone but the narrator into what appears to be a traditional, blood-sucking vampire. Protection against zombies generally takes a more traditional form through high walls or fences and deep ditches, fortresses and gated communities designed to keep the hordes out. Although a spatially restricted post-apocalypse is hardly unique to the zombie genre (for instance in Hugh Howey's *Wool* (2011) the survivors of an unknown apocalypse all huddle inside underground silos while the surface of the Earth appears scorched and toxic), the zombie subgenre offers a singular method for converting the unsafe back into the safe: the simple eradication of the zombie. This is not necessarily unproblematic, considering the empty referent might easily be read as (for instance) a parable on immigrants or working-class hordes: Fred Botting for one criticizes the unethical treatment of the zombie in *World War Z* as an apolitical "other," the slaughter of which becomes "a condition for human renewal: a monstrous, excessive, inhumane idea" (Botting 2012: 27). The fact remains, however, that this is essentially the story of *World War Z*: the reclamation of a zombie-infested world through the act of killing the occupying Other.

The process by which this transformation of place into space operates can be elucidated by utilizing the theories of space that Gilles Deleuze and Felix Guattari introduce in *A Thousand Plateaus* (1987). In it, they use the terms *striated* (or sedentary) and *smooth* space as oppositional, which fit the situation in a post-zombie-apocalypse world surprisingly well: "[S]edentary space is striated, by walls, enclosures, and roads between enclosures, while nomad space is smooth, marked only by 'traits' that are effaced and displaced with the trajectory" (Deleuze & Guattari 1987: 381). It is relatively simple to superimpose it on the world of *World War Z* – striated "safe zones" versus smooth, zombie-controlled space. Significantly, striated spaces (i.e. places) belong to the State, while smooth space is the territory of the nomad; in other words, the civilized versus the barbaric. The devolution into a new barbarism is a very typical theme of post-apocalyptic fiction, going as far back as Richard Jefferies' *After London* (1885), which celebrated the wilderness consuming all of industrialized England after an unspecified apocalypse. Westphal points out that smooth space is "constantly threatened by the striating that civilized, settled society imposes" (2011: 40), but in *World War Z,* like in most post-apocalyptic fiction, it is the reverse that is true: civilized, settled society is at constant risk of being wiped out by the encroaching (in this case zombie-filled) wilderness. The inhabitants of smooth space, Deleuze and Guattari argue, can oppose striation through the so-called *war machine* (originally modeled on the Mongol hordes): "each time there is an operation against the State – insubordination, rioting, guerrilla warfare, or revolution as act – it can be said that a war machine has revived" (Deleuze & Guattari 1987: 386). The war machine itself operates within "a physics of packs, turbulences, 'catastrophes,' and epidemics corresponding to a geometry of war, of the art of war and its machines" (Deleuze & Guattari 1987: 490), thus going beyond the directly human, taking on the aspect of a force of nature or, as it were, the apocalypse. Rowland Curtis (2008) for instance has made the argument that Hurricane Katrina could be read as a Deleuzoguattarian war machine that violently smoothed the striated space of New Orleans, smashing buildings and turning the debris into a vortex of natural weaponry. Equating the zombie with natural disaster in this way is relatively common: the American Center for Disease Control and Prevention (CDC) famously published a parody "Zombie Preparedness" blog in 2011, detailing the response of the CDC to a zombie outbreak. In it the author points out that "[i]f zombies did start roaming the streets, CDC would conduct an investigation much like any other disease outbreak" and that the proposed emergency plan for a zombie outbreak can equally well be used "if there is a flood, earthquake, or other emergency" (Khan 2011).

The apocalypse of *World War Z* is much like a natural disaster in that the areas smoothed by the zombie hordes are, of course, not robbed of their proper names, but it is only in the context of their reclamation, or defense, that they are again named, as they emerge out of the ontologically gray-spaced unknown. For instance during the reclamation of the United States, the initial battle against the zombies takes place in "Hope, New Mexico" (Brooks 2006: 276; a real place). The soldier being interviewed was aware the choice was not random: "They say the brass chose it because of the terrain, clear and open with the desert in front and the mountains in back. Perfect they said, for an opening engagement, and that the name had nothing to do with it. Right" (Brooks 2006: 276). After the (successful) battle, the soldier reminisces about the emotions they all felt the next morning: "It was a different vibe, one-eighty from two days ago. I couldn't really put a finger on what I was feeling, maybe it was what the president said about 'reclaiming our future'" (Brooks 2006: 282): the actual place named Hope, situated on the map and now turned from unsafe to safe, had allowed the Americans to hope. In another interview, a pilot crash-lands between two safe zones. At first, she seems entirely lost, but then, coaxed on by a friendly voice on the radio, she slowly maps out the surroundings: "I realized that I did know this area well, that I *had* flown over it at least twenty times in the last three months, and that I had to be somewhere in the Atchafalaya basin" (Brooks 2006: 176). That realization leads to another: "At first, all I could remember were the trees, the endless gray landscape with no distinguishable features, and then gradually, as my brain cleared, I remembered seeing both rivers and a road. I checked on the map and realized that directly north of me was the I-10 freeway" (Brooks 2006: 176). Once she has found herself, and only then, can she formulate a plan and escape the smooth and return to the striated.

This entire idea is strongly tied to the American concept of "my home is my castle," also known as the *castle doctrine*: the legal right to defend one's home with deadly force. Home becomes (as Tuan suggests) the ultimate "place" that has to be defended at all costs. In *World War Z*, all homes have to become fortresses or castles that function as a "regulator of movement," a "stumbling block and parry" against the encroaching war machine (Deleuze & Guattari 1987: 386). This is as true of the military as of the civilian areas; consider for instance the town of Troy, Montana, which is described as a "New Community" for the "New America," a town built on stilts above ground, surrounded by a twenty-foot-high concrete wall, with wells, solar panels and lookout towers (Brooks 2006: 63–64). Brooks takes the castle doctrine, quite literally, outside of America as well. One such example is Windsor, featuring the Queen Mother herself, who stayed behind despite having the option to relocate somewhere safer. One interviewee, who helped defend Windsor (and the Queen Mother) against the zombie hordes, makes this comparison clear: the British Royal Family "were viewed very much like castles, I suppose: as crumbling, obsolete relics, with no real modern function [...] But when the skies darkened and the nation called, both reawoke to the meaning of their existence. One shielded our bodies, the other, our souls" (Brooks 2006: 194). Just as having safe zones, named places, fortresses, homes, is a necessary protection against the approaching war machine, so is having a Royal Family or other similar recognizable Heads of State necessary to build the nascent State around. It is notable that the Queen Mother is never identified by name but Windsor is, suggesting that the metonymic connection of place is more important than the actual personages of the Royal Family.

The alienated road of *The Road*

In *The Road*, using place to bridge the gap between past and present is much more difficult. Although the man and the boy follow a map, they never mention *what* road it is they are walking down: it is only ever "the road." At one point early on the father points out which roads are "our roads" on their "tattered oilcompany [*sic*] roadmap": "the black lines on the map. The state roads" (McCarthy 2006: 43). As the man accurately points out, although the state roads used to belong to the states, there are no longer any states. Even with the map they keep getting lost on the way, and unlike most other objects they need for their survival (shoes, food, water, cart, clothes, blankets, oil) the potential loss of the map is never brought up as something catastrophic. Graulund (2010) considers the most important characteristic of *The Road* to be space (as opposed to place), represented in the image of the desert, in its original etymological meaning of "absence": "a world where everywhere is nowhere, a world in which there is no difference between frontier and civilisation, no difference between being on the road or off the road," which leads to a world where there can be no significance beyond desertion, beyond "the fact that it has been forsaken" (Graulund 2010: 67). What becomes apparent is that in *The Road*, there are no longer places of permanent safety: if read like the military map in *World War Z*, everything on the map would be blanketed with gray; the zombies replaced by their fellow man, most often members of cannibalistic gangs. The man and the boy, described as "each the other's world entire" (McCarthy 2006: 4) pass through space that has been rendered entirely smooth by some unknown apocalypse, except that unlike the silo-dwellers of Howey's *Wool* or the crafty survivors of *World War Z* hiding behind their walls, there are no underground places of safety or tall barricades that can protect the pair from the unrelenting cruelty of the land. The idea of communes (people who have made a permanent home) and refugees (people with impermanent homes) can only be referred to obliquely in *The Road*, and even when thus referred to they rarely manifest themselves. Lacking nearly all references to place, the reading becomes spatial. It is a world entirely defined by movement through space, a world of migrants. Deleuze and Guattari (1987: 380) differentiate between *migrants* and *nomads* in that "the migrant goes principally from one point to another, even if the second point is uncertain, unforeseen, or not well localized" whereas "the nomad goes from point to point only as a consequence and as a factual necessity"; they inhabit the "intermezzo," the "in-between" (Deleuze & Guattari 1987: 380). Yet the boy and the man, and all the others they meet on the way, can in no way be considered nomads, inhabitants of the radically smoothened space of the post-apocalypse. Unlike the randomly wandering zombie, or even the traditional highway bandit of the post-apocalyptic narrative, the man and the boy cannot truly live in the "intermezzo" of the world, because *the entire world* is now an "in-between." Deleuze and Guattari's "points" no longer exist. The impetus to move in the novel, to become a migrant, is purely a matter of survival: "They were moving south. There'd be no surviving another winter here" (McCarthy 2006: 2).

There is a very limited set of proper place names found in the novel: Rock City, Tenerife, London, Cadiz, Bristol and, somewhat surprisingly, Mars. Rock City most probably refers to a tourist attraction, the Rock City Gardens, found in Tennessee, whose slogan is "See Rock City." The man notices it on a "log barn in a field with an advertisement in faded ten-foot letters across the roofslope [*sic*]. See Rock City" (McCarthy 2006: 20). Advertisements on billboards "advertising motels" (6) or "goods which no longer existed" (135), or "the logo of some vanished enterprise" (65) found on a bandit's cap are all spoken of in the context of something lost, vanished or non-existent; in this case Rock City, albeit a place in the real world, is no more actual than the unnamed motels, enterprises or generic goods advertised elsewhere. Tenerife is the home port of a stranded ship, *Pájaro de Esperanza* (the Bird of Hope), the hows and whys of it being washed up on the southern coast of the United States a mystery, like the fate of its crew. On board, the man finds a surprisingly well-preserved, beautiful, antique brass sextant: "It was the first thing he'd seen in a long time that stirred him" (McCarthy 2006: 243). On its base, a plate: "Hezzaninth, London." Despite its beauty, the man places it back into its box and only takes the food and medicine. The treatment of place here is telling: the sight of the place name as much as the thing itself is stirring, a hint of a time when there was opportunity to own beautiful but useless objects like the sextant, manufactured far away and long ago. The connotation of the sextant being a tool for navigation cannot be ignored either, but as is apparent throughout the novel, the stars that would be necessary for it to be used for that purpose cannot be seen; although there "were days when the ashen overcast thinned" (McCarthy 2006: 107), for the most part looking up at the "starless dark" (31) proves a fruitless exercise. Cadiz and Bristol are mentioned in connection with "the weathered timbers of an ancient ship," whose "pitted iron hardware deep lilac in color, smeltered in some bloomery in Cadiz or Bristol [...] good to last three hundred years against the sea" (290). Much like the state roads that the man says "should be okay for a while" (44), the relative permanence of man-made yet inanimate things only serves to emphasize the vulnerability of life. Cadiz, Bristol, London and Tenerife all point out the global reach of the apocalypse, and although choosing these particular places was presumably not random, they promise no more than the faded advertisement to "See Rock City." To put it in the context of *World War Z*, there will be no military march into Tenerife, Cadiz, Bristol or the Rock City Gardens to liberate them from their undifferentiated, dangerous placelessness: they will remain unreachable and empty forever.

The final named place, Mars, is what brings that point home with finality. Not unsurprisingly, the context of the mention is a query of place: the boy asks, "Do you know where we are Papa?" (McCarthy 2006: 166), to which the man answers: "Sort of." The conversation turns to an idiom, "as the crow flies," which turns to the question of birds, who "can go wherever they want" because they "dont have to follow roads" – a brief glimpse of utopia. The boy, perhaps gripped by the idea of not having to follow the road, asks: "Could they fly to Mars or someplace?" Naturally, they can't, and "[a]nyway they wouldnt know where Mars was" (McCarthy 2006: 167). "Do we know where Mars is?" the boy asks, and again the man answers "Sort of," as if their spatial coordinates on Earth are as uncertain as the location of Mars in the sky. The boy wonders if they could go there. "Well. If you had a really good spaceship and you had people to help you I suppose you could go there." The follow-up question is telling: "Would there be food and stuff when you got there?" The answer is "No. There's nothing there." They return to this conversation slightly later:

> There could be people alive someplace else.
>
> Whereplace else?
>
> I dont know. Anywhere.
>
> You mean besides on earth?
>
> Yes.
>
> I dont think so. They couldnt live anyplace else.
>
> Not even if they could get there?
>
> No. (McCarthy 2006: 260–261)

Ketterer claims that science fiction literature passes through "four relatively distinct phases" (Ketterer 1974: 123): from dystopian fiction, to apocalyptic fiction, to post-apocalyptic fiction, all of which "concern the planet Earth." The fourth phase by contrast "may be isolated in so far as the center of interest shifts to the cosmic voyage and worlds beyond Earth" (Ketterer 1974: 123). It is only this fourth phase that allows an exploration of the utopian motif, according to Ketterer, although equally often one will find the cycle of "decadence, destruction and regeneration" continue in the "increasingly widening setting" of the universe, but it is only in these fourth-stage narratives where the potential to discuss "the new Heaven and the new Earth" (Ketterer 1974: 124) is found. In *The Road*, this eventual "utopian excursus" (to misappropriate Westphal's term) is quite evidently impossible, a point which is reinforced time and again whenever the narration is, briefly, moved from the immediately visible and local to the coldness and vastness of space: "By day the banished sun circles the earth like a grieving mother with a lamp" (McCarthy 2006: 32). In reference to long-lost migratory birds: "Their half muted crankings miles above where they circled the earth as senselessly as insects trooping the rim of a bowl" (55). In another, we can see the true nihilism of this distanced view:

> [A]nd he saw for a brief moment the absolute truth of the world. The cold relentless circling of the intestate earth. Darkness implacable. The blind dogs of the sun in their running. The crushing black vacuum of the universe. And somewhere two hunted animals trembling like groundfoxes in their cover. Borrowed time and borrowed world and borrowed eyes with which to sorrow it. (McCarthy 2006: 138)

Slightly later, an image of the people in the millions dying: "Out on the roads the pilgrims sank down and fell over and died and the bleak and shrouded earth went trundling past the sun and returned again as trackless and as unremarked as the path of any nameless sisterworld in the ancient dark beyond" (McCarthy 2006: 193). The recurring image here of the earth (and other planets) circling the sun like "blind dogs" serves to undermine the normally comic (as opposed to tragic) idea of cycles, where at the end there is potential for regeneration, the story starting anew – in the cosmic perspective of *The Road* even this perennial symbol of renewal has been rendered impotent. Instead, what we will be left with is merely a rock circling the sun, not unlike the airless, lifeless "sisterworld" of Mars.

If we return for a moment to the possibility of transforming dangerous and undifferentiated space into recognizable and safe place, there is one scene in the novel that briefly offers that opportunity. At one point they providentially stumble upon an old fallout shelter, left unused by its maker and undiscovered by subsequent looters. The pair settles in, and for a short time live a life that could almost be compared to the pre-apocalypse: heating, clean clothes, warmed-up food, shelter from the weather, baths, cigarettes, alcohol. Perhaps in another kind of narrative, the pair would give the shelter a name and make it their home. Not so in *The Road*. The final decision to leave comes after the man has an unsettling dream about alien creatures skulking by his bedside in the dark:

> He'd been visited in a dream by creatures of a kind he'd never seen before. They did not speak. He thought they'd been crouching by the side of his cot as he slept and then had skulked away on his awakening. He turned and looked at the boy. Maybe he understood for the first time that to the boy he was himself an alien. A being from a planet that no longer existed. The tales of which were suspect. He could not construct for the child's pleasure the world he'd lost without constructing the loss as well and he thought perhaps the child had known this better than he. (McCarthy 2006: 163)

The use of "he was himself" an alien suggests that the creatures may well be related to the kinds of creatures told of in alien abduction stories (modern day succubae, brought on by sleep paralysis, perhaps). Except that in this context it is "he himself" that is a being from another planet, a planet now fast becoming as dead and desolate as Mars. Unlike the creatures in his dream he still speaks, but he is becoming aware that it is of little use: when speaking of the past to the boy, he sometimes makes things up, but "those things were not true either and the telling made him feel bad" (McCarthy 2006: 55). Place is what would be used to construct the "world he'd lost": in *World War Z* every story re-constructs the world, re-creates what was lost, and thus bridges the ontological gap between the pre-apocalyptic reality of the reader and the post-apocalyptic reality of the narrated world. The man in *The Road* understands this has become impossible without "constructing the loss as well." There are no stable referents left; the old world is truly gone, and a temporary safe place like the fallout shelter is at best a simulacrum. When they finally come to the sea, their ultimate destination and as much of a possible place as anything, it is described as "gray" and "leaden," and, again, the now-alien nature of the Earth is revealed: "Like the desolation of some alien sea breaking on the shores of a world unheard of" (McCarthy 2006: 230).

Conclusion

There are many variations in how post-apocalyptic novels treat smooth and striated space, or as it were, space and place: some, like Jefferies' *After London*, celebrate the disappearance of industrialized society and the walls that enclosed it. Others, like Matheson's *I Am Legend*, retreat into their safe place and attempt to survive even when it is no longer the best option: after all, the reason Neville is caught and killed at the end of the novel is because he refuses to uproot himself and hide someplace else. In general, most novels offer some kind of compromise between the two: the freedom of the open road and its opportunities versus the relative safety and insulation of communities. *World War Z* and *The Road* are, as I noted in the introduction, extremes: in *World War Z* there is no freedom in the zombie-infested space outside the fortress walls, but on the other hand there is the hope of survival and victory if one is lucky enough to have escaped to safety, turning uncontrolled space into recognizable, familiar place with every killed zombie. At the end, as the frame narrative of the novel proves, victory has been had, and the zombie has been vanquished, albeit at a cost. In *The Road*, conversely, it has become structurally impossible to establish place, turning the freedom of the open road into nothing but a vagrant, fearful flight from one event to the next, which is the very definition of *The Road*'s narrative arc. From the point of view of narrative, however, *The Road* probably comes out the stronger. Tuan (1977: 54) points out that open space "has no fixed pattern of established human meaning; it is like a blank sheet on which meaning may be imposed," this being the great strength of *The Road*'s spatiality. As Graulund says in the conclusion of his article, "*The Road* expresses a passionate hope that *hope itself* matters" (Graulund 2010: 76; his emphasis), which is some-thing McCarthy can achieve even without convoluted scenes built around small villages named Hope in the middle of the desert. For *World War Z*, one might be slightly more skeptical about the potential range of meaning within its carefully constructed framework of safety versus danger, the State versus the smooth. The majority of actual narrative, throughout the novel, is after all constricted to attempts to escape, evade or defeat the smooth: the striated offers no such potential. Even so, at the end of *World War Z* there is a sense of hope and potential, of the world being there for the taking, the gray zones ripe for recapture. *The Road*, however, warns of what happens when there is no *place* else to go, when even world itself – the only world we know of – becomes entirely alien.

REFERENCES

Ahmad, Aalya. 2011. Gray is the new black: Race, class, and zombies. In Stephanie Boluk & Wylie Lenz (eds.), *Generation zombie: Essays on the living dead in modern culture*, 130–146. Jefferson: McFarland.

Bakhtin, Mikhail Mikhailovich. 1981. *The dialogic imagination*. Austin: University of Texas Press.

Baldwin, Gayle R. 2007. *World War Z* and the end of religion as we know it. *Cross Currents* 57 (3),412–425.

Bishop, Kyle. 2009. Dead man still walking: Explaining the zombie renaissance. *Journal of Popular Film & Television* 37(1),16–25.

Blackmore, Tim. 2009. Life of war, death of the rest: The shining path of Cormac McCarthy's thermonuclear America. *Bulletin of Science Technology & Society* 29(1),18–36.

Botting, Fred. 2012. Love your zombie: Horror, ethics, excess. In Justin Edwards & Agnieszka Soltysik Monnet (eds.), *The gothic in contemporary literature and popular culture: Pop goth*, 19–36. New York: Routledge.

Brooks, Max. 2004. *The zombie survival guide*. London: Duckworth.

Brooks, Max. 2006. *World war Z*. London: Duckworth.

Curtis, Rowland. 2008. Katrina and the waves: Bad organization, natural evil or the State. *Culture & Organization* 14(2),113–133.

Deleuze, Gilles & Felix Guattari. 1987. *A thousand plateaus: Capitalism and schizophrenia*. Minneapolis: University of Minnesota Press.

Doležel, Lubomír. 1998. *Heterocosmica: Fiction and possible worlds*. Baltimore: Johns Hopkins University Press.

Graulund, Rune. 2010. Fulcrums and borderlands: A desert reading of Cormac McCarthy's *The Road*. *Orbis Litterarum* 65(1),57–78.

Ketterer, David. 1974. *New worlds for old*. New York: Anchor Books.

Khan, Ali S. 2011. Preparedness 101: Zombie apocalypse. *Center for Disease Control and Prevention*. http://blogs.cdc.gov/publichealthmatters/2011/05/preparedness–101–zombie-apoca-lypse/ (last accessed on 3 March 2014).

Lefebvre, Henri. 1991 [1974]. *The production of space*. Maiden: Blackwell Publishing.

Malpas, J.E. 1999. *Place and experience: A philosophical topography*. Port Chester: Cambridge University Press.

McCarthy, Cormac. 2006. *The Road*. London: Picador.

Palmer, Alan. 2004. *Fictional minds*. Lincoln & London: University of Nebraska Press.

Rambo, Shelly L. 2008. Beyond redemption? Reading *The Road* after the end. *Studies in the literary imagination* 41(2),99–120.

Suvin, Darko. 1972. On the poetics of the science fiction genre. *College English* 34(3),372–382.

Tuan, Yi–Fu. 1977. *Space and place: The perspective of experience*. Minneapolis & London: University of Minnesota Press.

Westphal, Bertrand. 2011 [2007]. *Geocriticism: Real and fictional spaces*. New York: Palgrave Macmillan.

Walking as a Metaphor for Narrativity

MARINA LUDWIGS

The title of *The Unnamed*, the 2010 novel by Joshua Ferris, refers, in all probability, to the unnamed affliction that affects its protagonist. Tim Farnsworth is a partner in a prestigious law firm in New York. He is a hard-working, talented, and successful trial attorney, who is devoted to his family, wife Jane and daughter Becka. However, Tim's successful career and happy family life are sabotaged and eventually destroyed by the baffling, hitherto unknown disorder that he suffers: his uncontrolled bouts of walking. When his walking episodes start, Tim must walk where his feet take him; he cannot be stopped nor stop himself. When the urge comes, he feels compelled to drop everything he is doing at the moment, whether he is in the middle of a trial or an important work meeting, and start walking in an unforeseeable direction until he collapses from physical exhaustion: his sore legs usually give out from underneath him, and he ends up in the coma-like narcoleptic state. In the beginning of the novel, his wife picks him after he awakens and calls her. But as the novel progresses, he starts wandering further and further from his home until he is no longer able to return. As his condition deteriorates, it takes over his life by destroying his career, his marriage, and his health, until it eventually kills him.

Thematically and conceptually, the novel is quite complex. Most reviewers and critics responded to the story of Tim's downward mobility, describing the novel as a narrative of an escape from the American Dream by a man who has everything. They noted that while Tim's rational, conscious mind experiences his compulsion to walk as something imposed on him from without, his disease, in fact, gives voice to his unconscious desires. Peter Ferry, for example, argues that the protagonist's disease is an unconscious expression of his rebellion against the pressures, expectations, and narrow confines of "hegemonic masculinity" (Ferry 2011: 57). Other critics focused on the theme of love between Tim and Jane, which endures almost unbearable trials, hardships, and losses, characterizing *The Unnamed* as a portrait of a marriage. Several reviewers, in addition, commented on the philosophical conceit of the book, which they saw as a literary take on the mind-body problem, explored in the novel through the lens of the struggle between Tim's uncontrollable legs and his resisting mind. Some critics felt that this topic was treated in an overwrought and pseudo-intellectualizing manner. But as cliché and overused as the allusion to the mind-body problem is, it deserves closer attention, because it taps into the heart of narrativity. Using the metaphor of compulsive walking, the text's metanarrative emphasis throws light on the captivating and irresistible nature of narrative desire, which sometimes appears to blur the boundaries between the reader's own agency, his or her choice to continue reading, and some outside force which holds the reader in its thrall.

In my analysis, I will postulate walking to be a figure for narrativity and consider connections between "narrative pull" and bodily locomotion or the act of crossing a terrain and narrative structure. To do this, I will briefly review and compare several theories of narrative motion and narrative desire. I will also demonstrate how the metanarrative structure of *The Unnamed* lays bare some of the mechanisms that are crucial to narrativity.

But before I proceed to discuss theories of narrativity, as mentioned above, I will mention Michel de Certeau's theorization of walking in the city, which he develops in *The Practice of Everyday Life* (1984). According to de Certeau, the city, with its landmarks (or, in fact, any mapped terrain with its "immense texturology" (1984: 9), is both readable and writable. Walking, he writes, is "an elementary form of [the] experience of the city," with the walker's body "follow[ing] the thicks and thins of an urban 'text'" (1984: 93). Charting a walking trajectory through the discreet, semiotic space of a city or other textualized grid is akin to writing a story of/with footsteps. Such a story takes the shape of a "pedestrian speech act" (1984: 97) insofar as it performs an act of "appropriation of the topographical system on the part of the pedestrian" (1984: 97). It can be seen as "a spatial acting-out of the place" (1984: 98). The experience of walking, whether as aimless meandering or a purposeful journey toward a destination, constructs a travel story. De Certeau asserts that the travel story is the model for all stories: "Every story is a travel story – a spatial practice" (1984: 115).

Ferris's novel too explores similarities between walking and narrativity, making the experience of walking and reading/writing a narrative dovetail quite explicitly toward the end of the novel. Tim Farnsworth's wandering through New York and its boroughs, and later through the American wilderness, becomes a metaphoric journey through the wilderness of his psyche toward a kind of self-knowledge or reconciliation with his condition. When the protagonist says that "The path itself was one of peaks and valleys, hot and cold in equal measure" (Ferris 2010: 247), he employs images that can be read as figures of narrative peripeteia that encode the plot dynamics of gains and reversals.

There are two dovetailing theories of movement emerging from the domains of phenomenology and cognitive psychology. Both of these theories suggest that our kinesthetic sense of movement, on the one hand, and capacity to think ahead, to represent the idea of the future to ourselves, on the other, are closely interconnected: our representational thinking is movement-based, making possible our capacity for what cognitive science calls "detached cognition." According to Maxine Sheets-Johnstone, a phenomenologist studying movement, "we have a bodily felt sense of the direction of our movement ... Our bodily feelings of movement have a certain qualitative character" (1999: 56). Even though self-movement, according to Sheets-Johnstone, is not, strictly speaking, a phenomenon in the phenomenological sense, an object of or for consciousness, it is a kind of "ground zero" that brings to our awareness "a felt unfolding dynamic and in virtue of this dynamic, a felt overall kinetic quality" (1999: 152), serving as the background of our sense of free agency. "Agents," she writes, those having the power to act – "necessarily have a kinesthetic sense of their own movement" (Sheets-Johnstone 1999: 58). Furthermore, the notion of agency is related to the body's learned kinetic competence that Sheets-Johnstone describes as a "species-specific range of movement possibilities, a repertoire of what might be termed 'I cans'" (1999: 70). One of the examples without which language would not be possible is an adaptation for the ballistic movement. As a capacity for this movement (namely, being able to take aim and hurl a projectile with precision) has evolved, it has transformed human perception of reality and range of possibilities. Having changed the way human beings conceptualize the world around themselves, ballistic movement is conducive to "a certain spatial resonance with the experience of acting at a distance" (Sheets-Johnstone 1999: 36), which allows for detached cognition.

For Peter Gärdenfors, an evolutionary biologist, detached cognition is one of the necessary preconditions for the emergence of symbolic thinking, language, and representation. Anticipatory planning, advanced visualization of future consequences, conceptualization of possibilities and choice – all derive from the emergence of detached cognition or detached representation, according to him. Like Sheets-Johnstone, Gärdenfors speculates that language is predicated on the ability to aim and throw, and that chimpanzees' inability to aim seems to be related to the fact that they have not developed symbolic thinking and representation. In people, on the other hand, "a kind of *simulator* has been created in the brain that quickly estimates what the *anticipated* results of the signals to the muscles will be" (Gärdenfors 2003: 29). Because it involves representation, anticipation, and purposiveness, human thinking can be described as being outside itself and often future-oriented. One could perhaps say that what detached cognition allows to emerge is a kind of gap between representation and the real, a transcendent sense of reaching "beyond the contingent," as it were. This gap signals a sense of incompleteness that comes from imagining something that is not there, engendering a desire to bridge it, which has something decidedly narrative about it, insofar as we can visualize a narrative trajectory moving towards a point of attraction, which can be represented as a point of narrative closure.

The connections between our embodied kinesthetic sense and imaginary detachment made by phenomenology and cognitive science are thus highly relevant to a conversation about narrative desire. If language and representation are made possible by or are, at least, coterminous (because an exact causal connection is not of principal importance here) with movement and projection, it stands to reason that narrative movement and narrative about movement have mutual resonance. However, describing narrative in ballistic terms, as a flight of a projectile from the point of the inciting incident to that of resolution, is not enough. Even though this model has some explanatory validity, it is, paradoxically, too static to explain how narratives are propelled forward, the trajectory metaphor being implicit in all discussion of plot typology. To leave the static terms of trajectories behind and find a better-fitting, more dynamic description of the compelling nature of narrative movement, I would like to turn to three other models: anthropological, energist, and reader-response. Each of these approaches engages with the dynamic nature of narratives.

The first perspective I want to introduce is that of Eric Gans and his concept of the "scenicity" of representation (Gans 2008). Gans's theory of Generative Anthropology is a linguistic and literary elaboration of René Girard's theory of mimetic desire. To say that representation is "scenic" implies that language operates on a scene that is differentiated between the center and periphery. According to Gans, language organizes itself around the sacred center. It is misleading to talk about representational space. Representation for him is not a space or a homogeneous field, a blank canvas on which we draw an imaginary picture of a horse that corresponds to the word "horse" and has a real-life referent. Discourse takes place on an imaginary scene, which is to say in a space, different parts of which have different characteristics, the center being more "magnetic" in that it exercises a pull on the periphery. In fact, the idea of scenic representation is already implicitly present in René Girard's mimetic triangle. The main tenet of Girard's theory is that desire is never original: we borrow our desires from others – the "disciple" imitating the desire of the

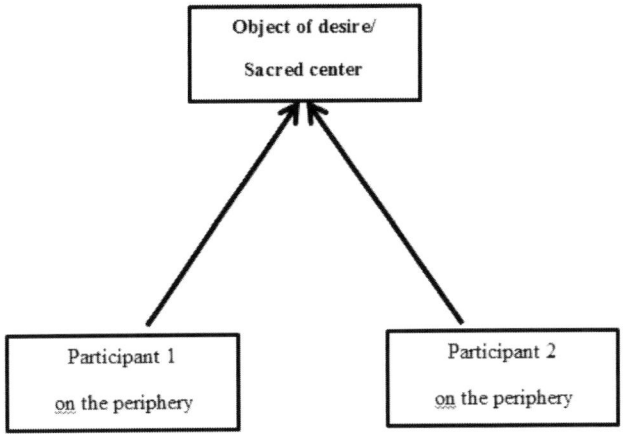

Figure 1. René Girard's mimetic triangle.

"model" for an object – and thus two directions of desire converge at the center, forming a mimetic triangle. The apex of the triangle is the desired object, and two points at the base represent the mimetic rivals (Figure 1).

Gans's model is essentially similar, except it puts more emphasis on the structural unattainability of the central object, which is the placeholder for the sacred. That is to say, in Gans's Generative Anthropology, the center emerges as a privileged position occupied by the appetitive object from which the rivals must abstain in order not to incite passions and to defer the threat of violence. It thus arrogates to itself the status of the sacred – something that must be left alone. In mimetic theory, the sacred is the structural center of representation, its "anchor". The subjects on the scene of representation abort the appropriative gesture, which becomes converted into a gesture of designation, the originary ostensive, while the object of contention is placed in the imaginary center, a special position to which no one has a right. We could theorize it as a transcendental signifier or a superego, a parent, teacher, or another figure of authority, or a political or ideological "sacred cow." We could also visualize it as a legitimate imaginary location for an officiant of a religious ceremony or an orchestra conductor.

But the center could also be occupied by a specific person, a participant on the imaginary scene of representation. In Girard, the center is occupied by a victim of mimetic violence, who is designated as a scapegoat. The position of the scapegoat becomes the site of the sacred after a period of peace and reconciliation follows on the heels of the scapegoat's murder. The victim is either very bad, occupying the center scandalously, or very good – a divinity, in fact. Gans's view is somewhat different. A person first comes on the center as someone who distributes the central object of significance. This could be a priest in the Christian Church, who symbolically distributes the body of Christ, or the Big Man of societies at an early stage of economic differentiation, who presides over the distribution of surplus food. In both models, however, the center is a desirable (albeit occasionally dangerous) place to be. This model of differentiation postulates the center to be the site of a gravitational force that exerts a pull on the periphery or a point lower in the gradient which acts as an attractor. It is the scenicity and eventfulness of representation (thinking through the implications of which amounts, for Gans (2011), to a "new way of thinking" that make this gravitational pull possible – the fact that there is only one center, which houses an object of significance. The latter serves as a focus of joint attention for many participants on the periphery, with each desiring it because others desire it. Gans's model connects desire and representation, providing a potential explanation of the engine of narrative desire as the desire for the center, which structures individual narratives. In the originary narrative, "The sign 'tells the story' of its own emergence" (Gans 1997a), which is the story of appropriating the appetitive object of desire. In more fully developed novelistic narratives, the movement from the periphery to the center often takes the shape of the trajectory of attainment of self-knowledge, mastery, or reconciliation. The center promises the attainment of significance, recognition, knowledge, fullness, wholeness – things that the protagonist on the periphery is lacking and to which he or she is therefore attracted. In the case of *The Unnamed*, the center of gravity represents, among other things, the home, to which Tim Farnsworth is trying to return. (As both Gans and Girard emphasize, the center–periphery configuration is unstable and fluctuating: the center, which is under a threat to be reconverted to an appetitive object, pushes back because it does not want to be consumed; it is also liable to inversion, corruption, or illegitimate arrogation by a false agency).

Another perspective is Peter Brooks's "narrative desire" (1984). Brooks's contention is that we cannot fully understand narrative without taking cognizance of the engine of desire that drives it. Even though the reader desires satisfaction when in the mood of suspense, the phenomenon of desire cannot be reduced to expectation and resolution. Brooks connects desire to the notion of energy, borrowing from Freud's psychoanalysis and writing that "since psychoanalysis presents a dynamic model of psychic processes, it offers the hope of a model pertinent to the dynamics of texts" (1984: 36). What drives narratives forward? They are driven forward and onward by the force of narrative desire, with this desire behaving and affecting us similarly to the way the fundamental psychic drives behave and affect us. "Desire as Eros," writes Brooks, "appears … central to our experience of reading narrative" (1984: 37). "Desire is always there at the start of a narrative, often in the state of initial arousal, often having reached a state of intensity such that movement must be created, action undertaken, change begun," he continues (1984: 38). What completes the thermodynamic analogy is Freud's economy of drives. Drives may either exist in the balance of homeostasis but, more commonly, in the state of dissipation. The homeostatic model is a perpetual motion machine describing the circulation of energy according to the principle of declining from equilibrium and then recharging and returning to the zero point. In limited contexts, it is possible to conceptualize narrative desire in terms of the homeostatic model, for example as the Freytag pyramid of dramatic structure (Figure 2), where the swell of rising action to the point of the climax has to be counteracted by the subsiding effect of the falling action. Once the energy has been restored, the process can start anew.

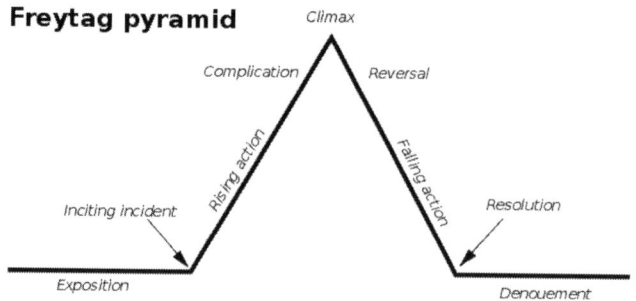

Figure 2. Freytag pyramid.

But as both Freud and Brooks suggest, there can be no recuperation of expended energy: something is inevitably lost. What in Freud is the death drive (originally, the nirvana principle), which is an urge on the part of organic life to return to the inorganic state (that is to say, the state of complete relaxation and release, of zero tension), is interpreted by Brooks within the domain of narrativity through the ideas of consummation and consumption, which defines the paradox of the narrative plot. On the one hand, we, the readers, according to Brooks, want the narrated events to restore their balance and the storyline reach its conclusion (consummation). But on the other hand, we do not want the narrative to reach its end, because when it comes to the end, we will have consumed the narrative we are reading, thus extinguishing our reading existence, metaphorically speaking. Brooks's example is that of Scheherazade and the sultan: the sultan wants to hear the end of the story, while Scheherazade wants to prolong the story-telling moment because she knows that when the story comes to the end, so will her life. In other words, narrative desire tugs us in two directions, insofar as we both desire and resist the ending.

What Brooks's analysis suggests is that there are two perspectives, two points of consciousness, that are incorporated into the very structure of narrativity, the future-oriented one, desirous of resolution, and the retrospective one that knows that stories have endings. Narrative possesses a certain intrinsic doubleness, the doubleness of perspective, and it unfolds dialogically between the text and the reader. Reading and writing, story-telling and story-listening are built into narrative, and not necessarily in a harmonious way, according to the communicative model of language (i.e. "You will tell me a cautionary tale, and I will adjust my behavior in response to it"), but sometimes at cross-purposes, as in the sultan-Scheherazade example. Narrative possesses double-consciousness; it is a canny, not a naïve genre. Much of the effect of a story's plot depends on our familiarity with the typology of possible plots. Roland Barthes names this phenomenon "deja-lu," *already-read* (1974: 19), meaning that the very possibility of recognizable cultural codes in the context of intertextuality implies doubleness. (Gans's model also recognizes narrative doubleness insofar as it conceptualizes the dynamics between the center and periphery as oscillation, as mentioned above: the periphery wants to move to and consume the center, but the center resists and repels the movement of assimilation as Scheherazade would).

A lucid and comprehensive analysis of narrative doubleness is proposed by Meir Sternberg in his investigation of the temporality of reading. Sternberg also points to "two rival teleo-logics":

> the one lifelike (e.g. the advance from the hero's character as cause to his misfortune or surprise as effect); the other born of art and going in reverse (the work's need for tragic misfortune or surprise effect to "cause" the hero's character, i.e. leading the tragedian to invest him with such features as will generate the needed action or reaction in the guise of human probability). (Sternberg 1992: 508)

But the two directions are not equal – there is an "epistemological dissymmetry" between them – which is reflected in the reader's future- and past-oriented narrative interests, which are different in nature: the forward or proleptic movement of suspense and the backward or retrospective movement of curiosity.

> Suspense derives from a lack of desired information concerning the outcome of a conflict that is to take place in the narrative future, a lack that involves a clash of hope and fear, whereas curiosity is produced by a lack of information that relates to the narrative past, a time when

struggles have already been resolved, and as such, it often involves an interest in the information for its own sake. (Sternberg 1978: 65)

Both curiosity and suspense are active states of mind. Sternberg points out that "suspense arises from rival scenarios about the future: from the discrepancy between what the telling lets us readers know about the happening (e.g., a conflict) at any moment and what still lies ahead" (2001: 117) and thus involves projecting ahead various plot possibilities and gradually ruling them out. Curiosity also involves the revision of various possibilities, "knowing that we do not know, we go forward with our mind on the gapped antecedents, trying to infer (bridge, compose) them in retrospect" (Sternberg 2001: 117). Often, the past-oriented inference of gapped antecedents would answer questions such as "What is this character's secret?" or "What was his motivation in doing what he did?" Even though Sternberg explicitly relates these narrative interests to the act of reading, it is implied that the reader, in her retrospective attitude of curiosity, mentally inhabits the writerly perspective of "the art of crooked disclosure" (1992: 514), thus reflecting the same dynamics as noted by Brooks.

The double perspective or double orientation of narrative is strongly in evidence in Joshua Ferris's *The Unnamed*, the novel which explores and exploits this double consciousness, drawing metanarrative parallels between walking and narrative movement. What is interesting about it is that it not only subverts traditional plot and the expectation of narrative closure in a way that has become familiar in contemporary novels, but that it subverts narrative closure on the "next level," as it were, not only by playing with it or doubting it but by playing with the very possibility of a collaborative interplay between the two perspectives on which narrativity is predicated. What I mean by this is that Ferris's novel is no longer a postmodern, but a post-postmodern text of a kind that Raoul Eshelman calls performatist. A performatist work of art is self-conscious about its double framing (the outer frame is usually that of the author-audience interaction and the inner frame is the work itself). Translating his model into Gansean terms, Eshelman explains his inner frame as the frame of the originary scene, "consisting of an intuitively perceived unity of sign and thing" (Eshelman 2008: 5). This frame is the focus of joint attention of the participants on the scene of representation (the sign-emitters) who find themselves on the periphery of the outer frame. The double frame model is infinitely generative: the originary, minimal double frame can become the inner frame of a larger configuration, and so on. According to Eshelman, performatism affords "a new, radical empowerment of the frame using a blend of aesthetic and archaic, forcible devices" (Eshelman 2008: 2). By various means, the viewer or reader is made aware of the artificiality of framing and is forced to accept an imposed "lock" between the two frames: "the outer frame imposes some sort of unequivocal resolution to the problems raised in the work on the reader or viewer" using "dogmatic, ritual, or some other coercive means" (Eshelman 2008: 2–3). A similar awareness of double framing is in evidence in the rhetorical approach to narrative, as practiced by James Phelan and Peter Rabinowitz, who write that "[n]arrative is somebody telling somebody else, on some occasion, and for some purposes, that something happened to someone or something" (Phelan & Rabinowitz 2012: 3). Their insistence that narrative is an "event" of "purposive communication" (Phelan & Rabinowitz 2012: 3) creates a new focus on the dynamics of the author-audience interaction, what Eshelman would call the outer frame, and brings to our attention to the fact that "we are interested not simply in the meaning of narrative but also in the experience of it" (Phelan & Rabinowitz 2012: 3). The awareness of the double consciousness of narrative belongs, as I would like to suggest, to the level of the outer frame or the interaction between the reading and writing perspectives, which is built into the narrative experience. The novel brings the outer frame into view by enacting the breakdown of harmony between the two perspectives and then imposing a closure by fiat, as it were.

Tim's official diagnosis is one of "benign idiopathic perambulation." Not sure what it means, he has to look up "*idiopathic* in the dictionary. 'Adj. – of unknown causes, as a disease.'... He took exception to the word *benign*. Strictly medically speaking, perhaps, but if his perambulation kept up, his life was ruined. How benign was that?" (Ferris 2010: 41). And this is eventually what happens: the disease takes complete control of him, depriving him incrementally of agency and convincing first his wife and then his daughter that "what afflicted him was not all in his head. His body was not his own if it continued to labor without his conscious input" (Ferris 2010: 127). Consequently, the onset of the protagonist's walking episodes escapes his awareness. These moments are either elided in the text or described as external to his consciousness, such as "Then he was made to stand and walk" (Ferris 2010: 221).

In the beginning, they try to restrain him by attaching his wrists to the bed's headboard with handcuffs. But this solution does not work in the long term, especially as the attacks become more frequent and long-lasting. "He was in one long nightmare of walking now: walk, sleep, wake up, wait for the next walk. His feet convulsed rhythmically against the restraints" (Ferris 2010: 127). They must also inject him with a sedative to be able to turn him over periodically in order to prevent bedsores. But when they give up and let him go, his health problems become more acute. The strain of walking, the chafing of his body against the clothes, and the exposure to extreme temperatures all cause blistering, swelling, frostbite, and, eventually, gangrene and organ failure. His toes and fingers have to be amputated.

This strand of the narrative, which describes the struggle between Tim Farnsworth's mind and his body, resonates not only thematically but in the particulars of the plot with Robert Louis Stevenson's *Strange Case of Dr. Jekyll and Mr. Hyde* (2002). In Stevenson's tale, Mr. Hyde, who is the alter ego of Dr. Jekyll, becomes unstoppable in his pursuit of evil, a condition hypostatized by trampling a little girl who gets in his way. In the opening scene, a witness reports seeing

> two figures: one a little man who was stumping along eastward at a good walk, and the other a girl of maybe eight or ten who was running as hard as she was able down a cross street... The two ran into one another naturally enough at the corner; and then came the horrible part of the thing; for the man trampled calmly over the child's body and left her screaming on the ground. (Stevenson 2002: 7)

In a similar scene, Tim, according to a witness, the doorman Frank, collides with a little girl:

> Neither of them saw the little girl. She broke away from her mother and went sidewise straight into Tim. The impact of his leg threw her to the ground ... Tim kept walking. "You looked at me terrified," Frank told him. "And I looked at you wondering why you weren't stopping. I mean, you'd told me you couldn't stop. I just didn't understand until then that what you meant was, you really couldn't stop." (Ferris 2010: 82)

Tim explains that he has no memory of the event. What is stressed here, as in Stephenson's novel, is that the main character is in a hypnotic, almost unconscious state when he cedes control to his moving body.

The link between the two narratives brings into focus the key idea of the split in consciousness that is the cause of this out-of-control behavior. As Dr. Jekyll writes in his letter:

> I learned to recognize the thorough and primitive duality of man; I saw that, of the two natures that contended in the field of my consciousness, even if I could rightly be said to be either, it was only because I was radically both. (Stevenson 2002: 56)

Similarly, Tim Farnsworth experiences an internal division between himself and some foreign agency: "He was one thing, his body a different thing altogether" (Ferris 2010: 221). He calls it "the Other" and sees it as a malevolent force that has "rob[bed him] of [his] will" and "troll[ed him] through the streets like meat on a hook" (Ferris 2010: 214–215). Just as Mr. Hyde, who is originally a small size (because he represents a smaller, less significant aspect of Dr. Jekyll) begins to grow in size as he takes over his host, so does Tim Farnsworth's Other become more dominant as the story progresses. When Tim yells at his Other in frustration: "You can't be smart ... Only I can be smart," he gets the answer, "I am evolving" (Ferris 2010: 217). Predictably, "the Other" represents the body, and the self stands for the mind.

The body not only insists on walking, but it also demands food and shelter. The only solution Tim can devise to release himself from the thrall of "the Other" is not to give in to its demands and thus kill himself by hunger, exposure, or exhaustion. He can exercise some modicum of power and control insofar as he can deny his physical needs and make his body suffer:

> He could have drowned himself in a body of water or thrown himself in front of a car ... but he failed every time to resist the call of sleep ... [when] the body released him, ... he walked ... to some dubious sanctuary, where they collapsed in a harmony of purpose ... In oblivion, they were at peace. (Ferris 2010: 215)

But most of the time, it is not clear who is dragging whom, Thanatos-like, towards the tensionless sleep of inorganic oblivion. Tim acknowledges his loss of agency when he asks "the Other": "What is your purpose, your aim, but to hurl us both into suffering and darkness? ...You have laid plain all my limitations and my total illusion of freedom" (Ferris 2010: 215).

In drawing attention to the parallels between *The Unnamed* and Stevenson's novella as well as using the language of strife between the two halves of the self, I want to suggest that the novel's allusion to the Freudian typology of the ego and the id is unmistakable. But this model of split consciousness extends further, in the direction of narratological analysis. It is not coincidental that when Tim ends up in a hospital at one point during his journey and is examined by a psychiatrist, who asks him whether he hears voices in his head, he explains that what he hears is not voices but a voice. In fact, "it's not really a voice. It's a point of view" (Ferris 2010: 227). I would like to claim that the idea of the voice of "the Other" voice as a point of view demonstrates the structure of the split narrative perspective. Indeed, Brooks's gloss of Freud's death drive through the model of competing perspectives belonging to the sultan and Scheherazade receives another interpretation here. The main character's desire to kill his body is yet another reading of the narrative engine's death drive enacted as a conflict between the two ends of the narrative consciousness: the retrospective, self-conscious position of Scheherazade that resists consumption and the prospective, unself-conscious position of the sultan that longs for consummation.

What the plot of the novel also demonstrates is that narrative suspense is formed by the tension between two perspectives, one that is naïve, expectant, predatory, and future-oriented and the other, the canny, impotent, backward-looking, between prospection and retrospection. A simple, goal-oriented action, like popping into a neighborhood store for a carton of milk, is not suspenseful, or not very much, because we can project its trajectory from inception to fulfillment in a straightforward, unopposed way. In following a narrative, on the other hand, we inhabit a passive role, as we keep in mind that the events in the story have already occurred. But as Meir Sternberg demonstrates, the attitude of suspense is active in its passivity. It is not a blind, content-free awaiting of what is about to take place. On the contrary, it is constituted by an act of continual revising, as additional circumstances accrue. The reader will ask him- or herself: "What kind of story is it? Oh, is it this kind of story? No, it must be another kind of story." The revision of expectation continues until the plot is resolved. While the story is unfolding, the backward-looking perspective sustains narrative tension by ambushing the future-projecting perspective with surprise developments. From the readerly perspective, the future is the site of the event horizon of inexhaustible strategies aimed at overturning the reader's expectations, which is the writerly perspective of Scheherazade, weaving her tale of "crooked disclosure" with a hidden and resistant motive of infinite deferral. There is a power shift at the point of resolution, however, when the narrative will have consumed itself.

An additional observation in the comparative analysis of the two literary texts is that there is a structural similarity between sinning, walking, and suspense, acts that put us vis-à-vis the Other, who cannot stop, whom we cannot stop. The novels help us appreciate the aptness of the sin metaphor for trying to get to the heart of narrative experience. Not only *Dr. Jekyll and Mr. Hyde*, but, especially, *The Unnamed* does more than merely point out that a sinner's experience resembles a battle between the constitutive yet fragmented parts of his or her psyche. A preacher, whom the protagonist meets in a roadside church, suggests that Tim's condition is as ancient as the world, and it is futile to always insist on rational explanations: sometimes, they are not furnished. What becomes apparent, in addition, is that the sinner cannot stop sinning – the problematic that is narrative in origin. The sinner is impelled by an irresistible force along a narrative path he or she can neither arrest nor reverse. Sinning is a kind of unstoppable movement, lent momentum by the sinner's unquenchable appetites. This unstoppability is highlighted not only by the episode of Tim's mowing down the girl on the street but also by Jane's struggle with alcoholism and daughter Becka's inability control her diet and lose weight. While Becka is initially critical and suspicious of her father's purported inability to control his behavior, she is blind to the irony of how similar their respective situations are: he cannot stop walking, while she cannot stop eating.

The resistance of "the Other" is performed with the help of the device of *peripeteia*. It is in the use of reversals, detours, interludes, and obstacles that a close linkage between the topos of walking and the operation of narrative suspense becomes explicit. It is Tim Farnsworth's inability to direct his movement that becomes the source of delays and suspensions. Another explicit intertextual reference that plays an important part here is that to Homer's *Odyssey*. In the second half of the book, the plot takes the recognizable voyage-and-return shape as the hero, who has involuntarily wandered off too far from home, all the way to the Pacific coast, is trying to return to his wife, first to the house in the suburbs, where they live as a family with teenage Becka, then to the townhouse in New York, which they buy after Becka moves out, and finally to the hospital where Jane is dying of cancer. Even though Tim manages to make it back each time (until he cannot in the end), his return journey is becoming successively more laborious and circuitous. The fact that he cannot control the direction of his movement and aim at a precise spot presents a true challenge. He contrives a strategy to walk during the night, when the sleep-deprived body is at its weakest, and then chooses an oblique, circular movement, hoping that its centripetal force will rope him in and draw him into the needed orbit. This works well when he plans to catch Becka's performance on stage. "I've been circling the city since you posted the tour dates. I turn around and walk back," he tells her (Ferris 2010: 260). But on the way to Jane, he is delayed or forced to sidetrack or retrace his steps several times.

In Ferris's novel, "the Other" functions neither solely on the level of characterization, nor simply as an allegory. Unlike *Dr. Jekyll and Mr. Hyde* and similar tales, *The Unnamed* is not just a story about the complexity and fragmentariness of consciousness but also a story about story-making, which performs on a metanarrative level the impossibility of narrative closure. This impossibility manifests itself as an unresolved conflict between the two narrative perspectives, represented by the self and the body, the conflict that makes it impossible for the narrative to follow a straight and intelligible path to a destination. The failure to reconcile the two perspectives is made conspicuous by the novel's repeated strategy of offering and withdrawing different closure scenarios, a feature, which, at some point, begins to feel deliberate and excessive. The unfolding story teases and disappoints the reader with its deceptive resolutions, deferrals, reversals, misdirections, and repetitions. The lack of "tidy endings for the characters in this book" (Manning 2009: 36) has been noted by a couple of reviewers and addressed by Joshua Ferris in interviews. To Stuart Evers of *New Statesman*, who comments that Ferris is "not afraid to leave plotlines unresolved," he answers that it is for the reader to resolve them, but that "narrative strands stop and start in the same way as … Tim's disease stops and starts" (Evers 2010: 45), thus lending support to my claim that the novel establishes an analogy between walking and narrativity.

One such inconclusive moment of closure is that of the main character's death. At one point, he almost dies of exposure, feeling "euphoric with the certainty of physical death" (Ferris 2010: 221). But the story does not stop there because he is taken to the hospital and subsequently – unexpectedly – recovers. Later, however, he does die. Neither of the two moments is justified by the narrative logic of the story; neither resolves or explains anything. Another subplot, which initially suggests that the novel is going to be a detective story, is abandoned and not adequately resolved. In this subplot, the claim of Tim's defendant, who is on trial for murder but claims his innocence, seems to be corroborated by the appearance of a man who shows Tim, who is walking at the time and cannot stop, a bloody knife and claims that he is the actual killer. At first, Tim is hopeful about the prospect of catching the real culprit and saving an innocent man, but after a while, it starts to appear as if Tim's encounters with the suspicious man are just figments of his imagination, and the built-up of narrative tension is defused. However, towards the end of the story, it is suggested that the man really does exist, a surprising development that is not explored further, however, and is eventually dropped.

Similarly, the trajectory of Tim's developing relationship with his wife is described as a series of loss-and-redemption episodes, such as Tim's increasingly challenging battle with his affliction and Jane's struggle with alcoholism, her affair with another man, and her health crises, which all promise poignant moments of resolution ahead, but produce instead anticlimactic misfirings. The strongest and most striking of these is Tim's return from the West Coast to his wife, who is dying of cancer on the East Coast. She is just barely hanging on to life in order to say goodbye to him. She is still alive when he eventually makes it to the hospital, and she has a chance to say goodbye to him in a very moving scene. This moment of closure, however, is deceptive and ironic in more than one way. For example, even though Jane says goodbye, she does not die: in spite of doctors' predictions, she begins a miraculous recovery. Tim, in turn, also seems to be gradually recovering from his disorder. But instead of remaining with Jane now, when they are happy and making future plans, he succumbs to another walking episode and is unable to come back. Moreover, Jane has a relapse, and this time she really does die. But the most interesting plot development in this part of the novel is Tim's learning to walk in a different way. When his body is taken over by his disease, he cannot look to the either side during his walks but only straight ahead and is thus incapable of taking in the sights and sounds of his surroundings. They remain outside the scope of his awareness, unnamed. To make his unstoppable body slow down and notice things, he buys a book on birds: "Name a bird and master the world" (Ferris 2010: 212). Naming or issuing an ostensive sign, as Gans's originary analysis suggests, is a way of grasping an object and is therefore indeed a gesture of mastery. But Tim has to wait a while longer before he can notice and name objects. This happens as he begins to take short walks around the hospital where Jane is recovering. Suddenly, he is capable of paying attention to things around him: "when he returned to her, he had observations of the outside world to share" (Ferris 2010: 287). As he sits by her bed, he rattles off a long list of things he has just seen, heard, and smelled: a woman smoking, the sound of running feet, the aroma of chocolate. It is as if by naming these things, he can for the first time harmonize the "two rival teleo-logics" of suspense and curiosity and create a narrative of his adventure. Tim's journey from being a single-minded, self-alienated careerist in the throes of an unrelenting locomotive instinct to becoming someone who can re-gather his fragmented consciousness into a narrative would make an emotionally powerful (if expected and somewhat clichéd) plot ending. Alas, this strong promise of a meaningful denouement, which comes late in the story, is also withdrawn. In the end, Tim Farnsworth's condition returns. He walks away and, finally, dies, having frozen to death somewhere in winter wilderness. His last moments are those of inner deliberation:

> Five minutes gave way to ten, and ten to twenty. There was no question now that he was starting to push his luck ... There were many things that awaited his command ... He languished another twenty minutes. Then he absolutely insisted that he rise that instant and take care of business ... But just then he realized that, at some point during his sumptuous idling, he had stopped hearing the wind. (Ferris 2010: 309–310)

It is not clear whose is that last summoning voice that spurs him to continue: the self or "the Other." This final moment is an inconclusive closure without a resolution. It cannot be determined which wins, the mind or the body. Perhaps both of them enter the mutual oblivion of peace, with the narrative simply running out of steam or petering out into the indifference of the vanishing point where the two perspectives meet. I read the final moment as an example of a performatist ending, insofar as it does not flow naturally, as it were, out of the emotional logic of the narrative but feels externally imposed after the internal rationale of working out a resolution is exhausted. We are asked to identify with the narrative voice of a character who has just died, and, in accepting this impossible position, we endorse what Eshelman calls "the artificially framed unity ... confirming the outer frame's coercive logic" (Eshelman 2008: 3). *The Unnamed* "performs" its closure by authorial decree after an inner-frame solution has proven impossible.

REFERENCES

Barthes, Roland. 1974. *S/Z: An essay.* (Tr. Richard Miller). New York: Hill and Wang.

Brooks, Peter. 1984. *Reading for the plot: Design and intention in narrative.* Cambridge, MA, and London: Harvard University Press, 1984.

Certeau, Michel de. 1984. *The practice of everyday life.* Trans. Steven Rendall. Berkeley, Los Angeles, London: University of California Press.

Eshelman, Raoul. 2008. *Performatism and the end of postmodernism.* Aurora, CO: Davis Books Publishers.

Evers, Stuart. 2010. Joshua Ferris: The books interview. *New Statesman* 139(4990), 45.

Ferris, Joshua. 2010. *The unnamed.* New York, Boston, London: A Reagan Arthur Book/Back Bay Books/ Little, Brown and Company.

Ferry, Peter. 2011. Reading Manhattan, reading American masculinity: Reintroducing the flâneur with E.B. White's *Here Is New York* and Joshua Ferris' *The Unnamed. Culture, Society & Masculinities* 3(1),49–61.

Gans, Eric. 1985. *The end of culture: Toward a generative anthropology.* Berkeley, Los Angeles, London: University of California Press.

Gans, Eric. 1993. *Originary thinking: Elements of generative anthropology.* Palo Alto, CA: Stanford University Press.

Gans, Eric. 1997a. Originary narrative. *Anthropoetics* 3(2), http://www.anthropoetics.ucla.edu/ ap0302/narrative.htm. (last accessed on July 16, 2014).

Gans, Eric. 1997b. *Signs of paradox: Irony, resentment, and other mimetic structures.* Palo Alto, CA: Stanford University Press.

Gans, Eric. 2008. *The scenic imagination: Originary thinking from Hobbes to the present day.* Palo Alto, CA: Stanford University Press.

Gans, Eric. 2011. *A new way of thinking.* Aurora, CO: Davies Group.

Gärdenfors, Peter. 2003. *How homo became sapiens: On the evolution of thinking.* Oxford: Oxford University Press.

Girard, René. 1965. *Deceit, desire, and the novel.* Trans. Yvonne Freccero. Baltimore: John Hopkins University Press.

Girard, René. 1977. *Violence and the sacred.* Trans. Patrick Gregory. Baltimore: Johns Hopkins University Press.

Girard, René. 1978. *Things hidden since the foundation of the world.* Trans. Stephen Bann & Michael Metter. Palo Alto, CA: Stanford University Press.

Girard, René. 2001. *I see Satan fall like lightning.* Trans. James G. Williams. Maryknoll, NY: Orbis Books.

Manning, Shaun. 2009. PW talks with Joshua Ferris: Grasping at hope. *Publishers Weekly* 256(46), 36.

Phelan, James & Peter J. Rabinowitz. 2012. Narrative as rhetoric. In David Herman, James Phelan, Peter J. Rabinowitz, Brian Richardson & Robyn Warhol (eds.), *Narrative theory: Core concepts and critical debates*, 14–19. Columbus: Ohio State University Press.

Sheets-Johnstone, Maxine. 1999. *The primacy of movement.* Philadelphia: John Benjamins Publishing Company.

Sternberg, Meir. 1978. *Expositional modes and temporal ordering in fiction.* Baltimore and London: Johns Hopkins University Press.

Sternberg, Meir. 1992. Telling in time (II): Chronology, teleology, narrativity. *Poetics Today* 3(3), 463–541.

Sternberg, Meir. 2001. How narrativity makes a difference. *Narrative* 9(2),115–122.

Stevenson, Robert Louis. 2002. [1886] *The strange case of Dr Jekyll and Mr Hyde.* London: Penguin Books.

Index

INDEX